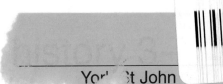

York St John
matic

a guide for teachers

Hilary Cooper

David Fulton Publishers Ltd
2 Park Square, Milton Park, Abingdon, Oxon OX14 4RN

www.fultonpublishers.co.uk

First published in Great Britain in 2006 by David Fulton Publishers

10 9 8 7 6 5 4 3 2 1

David Fulton Publishers is an imprint of the Taylor & Francis Group, an informa business

British Library Cataloguing in Publication Data
A catalogue record for this book is available from the British Library.

ISBN 10: 1-84312-459-9
ISBN-13: 978-1-84312-459-7

Typeset by RefineCatch Limited, Bungay, Suffolk
Printed and bound in Great Britain

Contents

Acknowledgements

History 3–11 draws on examples of practical, school-based research into the teaching and learning of history, case studies applying research to practice, and case studies illustrating innovative and creative approaches. I should like therefore to express my appreciation to recent research undertaken by history teacher educators from the United Kingdom and around the world who have explored primary school children's thinking. Their studies are discussed in Part 1. They include: Keith Barton, University of Cincinnati; Alan Cully, University of Ulster; Hilary Claire, London Metropolitan University; Dursun Dilek and Gulcin Yapici, University of Marmara; Penelope Harnett, University of the West of England; Pat Hoodless, Leeds Metropolitan University; Alan Hodkinson, University College Chester, Manchester Metropolitan University; Peter Lee and Rosalyn Ashby, London University Institute of Education; Peter Vass, Oxford Brooks University; Gail Weldon, Western Cape Education Department, Capetown; Yosanne Vella, University of Malta and Jayne Woodhouse, history education consultant.

I am grateful to the teachers whose case studies, described in educational papers and journals, demonstrate that energetic and lively new approaches to primary history can still be found, despite the constraints. These include teachers in Keyworth School in Kennington; Stephenson Way Primary School After School Club, County Durham; Southbank International School, Hampstead; St Illytd's School in Swansea; Pat Lewis in Blaenavon; the Lancaster City Museums Project; Wendy Scott from Fortune Park Day Centre, Islington and Alison Hocking, Goetre Infants' School. I am grateful to those who have published examples of their work in ICT and history and given recommendations of useful sites: Elaine Dawe, David Mason, Hugh Moore, Steve Mynard, Jo Peat, Stuart Roper and Ben Walsh.

I thank the students at St Martin's College who worked with me on some of the illustrative examples, Elizabeth Hart and Sarah Spink, for their Foundation Stage plans in Chapter 5 and colleagues at St Martin's, Sam Twiselton and Kath Langley Hamel on history and literacy, the late Robin Foster on history and mathematics, and Pete Saunders who commented on the section on history and ICT.

Thanks are due to the children and teachers who have worked with me on case study examples, including: Greenvale Primary School, Croydon; Stramongate School, Kendal and Eaglesfield Paddle School, Cumbria.

Finally I remember those who have encouraged and supported my interest in the teaching of history in primary schools over the years: Joan Blyth, author of *History in Primary Schools* (1982) (now over eighty and still interested), Roy Hughes, University of Leeds and until lately chair of the Historical Association Primary Committee, Jon Nichol (between us we created and manage the History Educators' International Research Network) and many more.

Introduction

New lamps for old?

The first edition of *The Teaching of History* was published in 1992, the year after the National Curriculum for History was introduced. Looking back at the series editor's foreword, Peter Robinson wrote:

> Hilary Cooper certainly breathes life into the dead land, as her text conveys the exciting prospects for history in the National Curriculum. She sets down a persuasive rationale for the study of history in primary schools that includes a concern to develop as well as inform the intellect . . . She justifies rather than assumes the value of historical studies.

And history at Key Stages 1 and 2 did indeed flourish during the next few years. I find that I wrote in the Introduction to the 1995 edition, published in response to the 1995 revision of the National Curriculum (DfEE 1995):

> In history the sea-change in four years has been amazing. In schools all over the country we find school museums, displays of 'old things', presentations of local and family history investigations, pictures and models recording visits to museums, galleries and Living History Reconstructions. These are often projects which teachers, particularly at Key Stage 1, embarked upon reluctantly but discovered how enjoyable and appropriate they could be. There has been massive support from publishers; books, posters, slides, replica sources, audio and video tapes have been designed. Organisations such as the National Trust, English Heritage and museum education departments have developed a wealth of materials.

The 1997 reprint recorded that 'history is now an established component of the primary curriculum'. The 1995/6 Report of Her Majesty's Chief Inspector of Schools recorded that 'in history improvements identified last year have continued and attainment is good in a high proportion of schools'. Yet there were ominous rumblings in the background. I wrote in 1997: 'We must not underestimate the progress we have made in teaching primary history, forged as it has been in a climate of increasing hysteria about uniform primary provision for teaching literacy and numeracy.' In September 1998 legal requirements to teach all of the Key Stage 1 and 2

programmes of study for history were 'relaxed', and guidance given for 'prioritising, combining and reducing the history curriculum' (QCA 1998: 10–11), as teachers
struggled to familiarise themselves with the *National Literacy Strategy* (DfEE/QCA
1998) and the *National Numeracy Strategy* (DfEE/QCA 1999). These were accompanied by target setting, testing and league tables. So the 2000 edition attempted to
investigate how history might be linked to the Literacy and Numeracy Strategies
and to ICT, in order to free up more time for history and to make the curriculum
more coherent and balanced. It was no longer necessary to teach history within
Initial Teacher Education Courses. Many students never have the opportunity to
teach history during their school placements, so limited is the time allocated for
history. They are supposed to learn from 'experienced teachers in schools' (TDA
2005). But there has been virtually no Continuing Professional Development in
history either.

Now we come to *History 3–11*. This follows on from *The Teaching of History* and
responds to the most recent documentation, the history dimension within the
Curriculum Guidance for the Foundation Stage (QCA 2000) and *Excellence and Enjoyment* (QCA 2003). For the curriculum creators have stumbled on some amazing
and potentially liberating factors. It is now seen to be desirable, if teaching is to be
excellent and learning enjoyable, that teachers are given the initiative in managing
time and are responsible for the curriculum, developing cross-curricular approaches
and creative and innovative activities in response to pupils' interests. The *Excellence
and Enjoyment* document omits to actually mention history, so preoccupied is it
with continuing to raise standards in literacy and numeracy, but it does make the
amazing observation that quality of achievement in literacy has been seen to occur
when it is applied in meaningful contexts across the curriculum.

So *History 3–11* attempts to rise to the challenge with a considerable amount of
new material. Part 1, What is history?, analyses each of the strands of historical
enquiry, making inferences about historical sources, understanding the reasons
for and evaluating different accounts or interpretations, and developing historical
concepts. Each strand is explored through recent action research, showing ways in
which children of different ages can engage with each strand of thinking.

Part 2, Planning and assessment, considers ways in which we can look at planning
in history with fresh eyes and in innovative and creative ways. It is supported by a
rich variety of case studies.

Part 3, Examples from practice, focuses on planning and teaching at each age
phase. Chapter 7 raises awareness of ways in which early years practitioners help
children to be aware of time and change. Chapter 8 contains two Key Stage 1 case
studies, one starting with children's personal histories and another considering
how a visit to a 'great house' can be planned and followed up in cross-curricular
ways, over a block of time. The Key Stage 2 case study in Chapter 9, on the Tudors,
is transferred from previous editions of *The Teaching of History* but has, in addition, a

section on Interpretations of Queen Elizabeth I, a case study with a Year 3/4 class, who particularly enjoyed seeing the Queen in *Blackadder* (all the rude bits having been removed), and who made some astute suggestions as to why she was differently portrayed in Benjamin Britten's *Gloriana* – 'the musical', – and in a BBC version of the Elizabeth and Essex love story.

Part 4, Principles, theory and practice, returns to the theory–practice links illustrated in Part 1. Chapter 10 describes children's deductions, inferences and questions about a variety of Saxon sources. This is included as an example of an interesting approach to the Invaders and Settlers unit of the National Curriculum. The chapter goes on to discuss manageable ways in which teachers can reflect on, systematically analyse and develop aspects of their teaching in history. The final chapter describes a larger empirical study of theory-based classroom practice.

I have tried to organise the book in a logical, linear way but, of course, the sections and chapters cannot be discrete. Many themes, for example spiritual, moral and cultural dimensions, citizenship, research, gender and inclusion issues, run horizontally through the book. These can be identified through the index.

References

DfEE (1995) *Key Stages 1 and 2 of the National Curriculum*. London: HMSO.

DfEE (1999) *The National Curriculum for England*. London: DfEE.

DfEE/QCA (1998) *The National Literacy Strategy*. London: DfEE.

DfEE/QCA (1999) *The National Numeracy Strategy*. London: DfEE.

QCA (1998) *Maintaining Balance and Breadth at Key Stages 1 and 2*. London: QCA.

QCA (2000) *Curriculum Guidance for the Foundation Stage*. London: QCA.

QCA (2003) *Excellence and Enjoyment: A Strategy for Primary Schools*. London: QCA.

Training and Development Agency for Schools (2005) *Standards for the Award of Qualified Teacher Status*. London: TDA.

What is history?

1

Changes in the teaching and learning of history

> ### *Drake's Drum*
>
> *Drake he was a Devon man an' ruled the Devon seas,*
>
> *(Capten, art tha sleepin there below?)*
>
> *Rovin' tho his death fell, he went wi' heart at ease,*
>
> *An' dreamin arl the time o' Plymouth Hoe.*
>
> *'Take my drum to England, hang et by the shore,*
>
> *Strike it when your powder's runnin' low;*
>
> *If the Dons sight Devon, I'll quit the port o' Heaven,*
>
> *An drum them up the Channel as we drumm'd them long ago.*
>
> (Sir Henry Newbolt 1897)

YOU REALLY NEED TO listen to the music to thoroughly appreciate this! It represents the view of the past as generally taught in elementary schools from about 1865 until about 1965: nationalistic, moralising, rousing. An example of this approach is H.E. Marshall's *Our Island Story* (1905), widely used in schools in the first half of the last century, recently republished by readers of the *Daily Telegraph* and enthusiastically reviewed by Debo, Duchess of Devonshire, in the *Spectator* (Devonshire 2005: 45). The text accompanying the illustration of our hero on page 321 must be the original 'cool Britannia': '"There is time to finish the game and beat the Spaniards too," said Drake.' The text continues: 'Day by day the wind grew fiercer . . . [the Spaniards] were shattered on unfriendly rocks . . . At last, ruined by shot and shell . . . about fifty maimed and broken wrecks reached Spain . . . Elizabeth ordered a medal to be made saying, "God blew with his breath, and they were scattered".' I have no problem with national pride but *Our Island Story* simply does not square with what is known. In the section on 'Good Queen Bess' it goes on to quote William Collins (1788–9).

> *There were so few rogues that would plunder and rob sir,*
>
> *That the hangman was starved for want of a job sir.*
>
> *Good neighbourhood too. There was plenty of beef,*
>
> *And the poor from the rich never wanted relief*
>
> *For the sovereign and subject one interest supported,*
>
> *And our powerful alliance was by all nations courted,*
>
> *Oh, the golden days of good Queen Bess.*

So what about the land taken over by wealthy sheep farmers, deplored in a contemporary work, *Utopia*, by Sir Thomas More, the resulting, homeless, 'sturdy beggars' passed on from village to village, what about the anti-Catholic laws, the Catholic plots, the fear of Spain?

This experience of history lessons was brilliantly satirised in 1930 by Sellar and Yeatman. The section on 'The Great Armadillo' recounts that,

> The Spaniards complained that Captain F. Drake had singed the King of Spain's beard, or Spanish mane as it was called . . . Drake replied that he was in his hammock at the time and a thousand miles away. The King of Spain however insisted that the beard had been spoilt and sent the Great Armadillo to ravish the shores of England.
>
> (Sellar and Yeatman 1930: 66)

If you do not think that is very funny – good. You did not experience this kind of history teaching! We have come a long way, as illustrated by the multi-perspectival Armada press releases written by Year 6 children on pages 165, 167–68. But perhaps you experienced no history at all. History was optional in primary schools until 1989. After the Plowden Report (1967), the emphasis was on direct experience through the senses; history was generally considered unsuitable for young children, being seen as concerned with the affairs of adults and abstract ideas which could not be meaningful to young children.

> History, it is said, again and again, is an adult subject. How can it be studied by children without being so simplified it is falsified? There is first the problem that it is not until the later years of primary school that some children develop a sense of time . . . Yet we visited an Infant school where one exceptional child had memorized the dates of the Kings and Queens of England, 'except for all the muddling Anglo Saxons.'
>
> (Plowden 1967, paragraph 620)

Only since the 1980s have we identified what exactly is involved in finding out about the past at any level and explored ways in which young children can actively engage with this process, in ways which develop critical and discursive thinking, rather than brainwashing, and justifying the reasons why they should do so. I read history at university, but found teaching young children, in the Plowden tradition, much more interesting than teaching history in the sort of High School for Girls which I had attended. After some time I was seconded to take an advanced diploma in child development, at the Institute of Education in London. There I realised that no one had ever systematically tried to apply theories of constructivist learning to the processes of historical enquiry, so I made this the subject of my dissertation. When I returned to school I used my work as a Year 4 class teacher to collect empirical data which informed my PhD on 'Young Children's Thinking in History' (Cooper 1991). Colleagues abroad, ranging from previously communist countries of Eastern Europe to previously fascist countries of Western Europe and South America, have also begun their own researches into the teaching of history to young children in their own contexts, which engage children in active enquiry rather than giving them a simple 'story of the past', which can be politically manipulated.

For, of course, young children are aware of times before their own, although their understanding may be incomplete and even stereotypical, if not mediated through education. From their earliest years children have some awareness of 'the past', through illustrations of traditional stories and rhymes, family photographs, old buildings, then later through film, television, heritage sites. But to begin to understand the past children must learn, from the very beginning, the questions to ask and how to answer them. Historical enquiry involves making deductions and inferences from sources, the traces of the past which remain, then selecting and combining sources in order to construct accounts of the past, tracing changes over time. This chapter explores the ways in which the interaction between the content of history and the process of historical enquiry have evolved. Chapter 2 goes on to consider the first strand of historical enquiry, making inferences from sources. Chapter 3 considers how accounts or interpretations of the past are created by making inferences and deductions about sources. Chapter 4 discusses the special language of history: key historical concepts. Each chapter, therefore, considers a strand of historical enquiry, how this relates to theories of how children learn, and recent research exploring children's ability to engage with historical enquiry in increasingly complex ways.

The content of history

Originally the story of a society's past was handed down orally, and in some societies it still is. In others it was written down: by the Greeks as epic poetry, in *The Odyssey*; by medieval monks as chronicles, lists of events, of battles lost and won; in Shakespeare's histories as the story of a nation's kings. The story was always told for a particular audience and a particular reason.

Over the past hundred and fifty years history has become recognised as an academic discipline and its scope has broadened. Frederick Maitland (1850–1906) justified history as the study of the law, in any society. Marc Bloch (1886–1944) drew on new disciplines to study human settlement: place name study, technology and social sciences. Lewis Namier (1888–1960) analysed political life and Mortimer Wheeler, archaeology. Fernand Braudel (1902–1985) linked geography and history, making connections over time and space and exploring the role of large-scale, socio-economic factors in finding out about the past.

A history, then, may be broad or in-depth. It may be about an individual, about social groups, economic or political movements, local, national or global. Historians have their own interests: women's history, Black history, the history of childhood, the history of a particular class, left-wing or right-wing perspectives. And since history is an umbrella subject which includes all aspects of life there are histories of music, art, science, religion, geographical histories, sports history.

But history is not just a story or a list of events. Whatever content an account of the past may focus on, it must be investigated through the process of historical enquiry.

The process of historical enquiry

The process of enquiry, too, has evolved gradually. Leopold von Ranke (1795–1886) studied records. How did this document come into existence? How has it come down to us? How do the answers to these questions influence its trustworthiness? How do they explain the differences between two accounts? For Marc Bloch, clarity of analysis and asking the right question were consistent criteria. What do we know? What can we know? How do we know? How can we communicate that knowledge? Herbert Butterfield (1900–1979) employed imaginative sympathy in describing characters and events.

R.G. Collingwood clarified the process of historical enquiry in his autobiography (1939). He saw historical enquiry as beginning with a complex of ordered, specific questions in the tradition of the great philosophers, Plato, Bacon, Descartes, Kant. He said that, just as philosophy had found it necessary to accommodate a revolution in thinking about the natural world, based on empirical observation and deduction in the seventeenth century, it must encompass a similar revolution in the way it studied man in constantly changing societies.

Collingwood worked out this philosophy of history through constant practical application in archaeology. He proceeded from specific questions about sources, the significance and purpose of objects, whether they were buttons, dwellings or settlements, to the people who made and used them. The sequence proceeded from what can be known about an object, then what can be 'guessed', then, finally, what he would like to know, in order to support, extend or contradict his guesses. For instance, he knew from concrete evidence that a Roman wall from the Tyne to the

Solway existed. He guessed that its purpose was to form a sentry walk with parapets as protection against snipers. He wanted to know if there were towers as a defence against vessels trying to land between Bowness and St Bees, in order to support his guess. A resulting search revealed that towers had been found but their existence forgotten, because their purpose was not questioned. History, then, involves inter-action between the known content and the process of enquiry, in order to try to make sense of it. First, then, we need to find out how historians use sources and how we can use them with children.

When I was invited to write *History 3–11*, it was recognised that many primary school teachers feel that their own subject knowledge is weak. It was suggested that the book should therefore be accompanied by a CD containing an outline of key knowledge. But how could this be selected? Inevitably there would be bias in the selection. When the National Curriculum was mooted there were fierce political dis-cussions about what was essential information. The Historical Association caused an outcry with its paper 'History in the Core Curriculum' (Historical Association 1987), recommending sixty chronological topics for pupils from five to sixteen. However, there are many websites where teachers can find key information about a topic they are teaching. Some are listed below:

www.learningcurve.gov.uk

www.bbc.co.uk/history

www.schoolhistory.co.uk

www.centres.ex.ac.uk/historyresource

www.woodlands-junior.kent.sch.uk/teacher/index.html

www.historymole.com (time-lines)

www.Ask.co.uk (search for 'primary history content' – lots of primary sources)

www.primaryhistory.org

www.gtce.org.uk/networks/articles (Black and Asian studies)

www.worldhistorycompass.com (information on world perspectives)

www.library.byu.edu (for sources including pictures, maps, facsimile documents with translations)

www.bbc.co.uk/history/forkids (good for content information)

References

Collingwood, R.G. (1939) *An Autobiography*. Oxford: Oxford University Press.

Cooper, H. (1991) 'Young Children's Thinking in History', unpub. PhD thesis, University of London.

Devonshire, D. (2005) Review of *Our Island Story*, *Spectator*, 19 November.

Historical Association (1987) 'History in the Core Curriculum'. London: The Historical Association.

Marshall, H.E. (1905) [2005] *Our Island Story*. Cranbrook: Galore Park.

More, T. (1997) *Utopia*. Dover: Thrift.

Newbolt, H. (1897) 'Drake's Drum', in *Admirals All and Other Verses*, set to music by Charles Villiers Stanford: The Very Best of English Song, CD2 EMI Classics.

Plowden (1967) *Children and Their Primary Schools* (the Plowden Report). London: HMSO.

Sellar, W.C. and Yeatman, R.J. (1930) *1066 and All That*. Harmondsworth: Penguin.

2

Historical sources

HISTORICAL SOURCES ARE ANY traces of the past which remain. They may be written sources: documents, newspapers, laws, literature, advertisements, diaries, place names. They may be visual sources – paintings, cartoons, film, video, maps, field patterns, plans – oral sources or music. They may be artefacts, sites, buildings.

Questions to ask about sources

The questions we ask about sources are valid if they lead somewhere. Collingwood (1939) identifies key questions. How was it made? Why? How was it used? By whom? Were there others? What did it mean to the person who made and used it? For example, a superior example a Roman shoe found at Vindolanda, the equivalent of one made by Gucci or Lobbe today, may tell us something about the social or economic structure of the fort. A letter from a first generation 'Dutch' Roman at the fort, asking for underpants and socks from Rome, may tell us about the economic and transport systems of the empire and the attitudes of the Dutch tribes to cold, clothes, culture. It is the graffiti on the door from Newgate Prison or the Robert Burns song scratched into the glass of a casement window that quickens the pulse – tangible links with other people who lived in other worlds.

Problems with sources

What makes sources intriguing is that they do not yield their secrets easily. We usually have to 'guess' what they may be telling us, based on what else we may know. There may be more than one possible inference to make about a source. Children particularly enjoy 'guessing' about a source, justifying it, arguing with other interpretations, when no single 'correct' answer may be known. Even if their hypotheses seem unlikely they are learning to engage with the process of historical enquiry; with maturity and greater knowledge children's 'guesses' become more valid, in that they conform to what is known about the period, what is likely and whether there is contradictory evidence. With experience and maturity they become more aware of the factors to take into account in asking questions about sources.

Asking questions about sources

- Sources may be of varying status, because they were created for different purposes: a diary, a newspaper account, an advertisement; portraits of, for example, Elizabeth I are masterpieces of propaganda, often conveyed through the symbolism of power and ambition (see page 170).

- Sometimes new evidence comes to light. Harlow (1996) describes the discovery of the site near St Paul's Cathedral of a 'forgotten' battle between Normans and Saxons which took place three months after the Battle of Hastings and was actually the point when the Normans conquered England. Norman propagandists wanted to portray William as a military genius capable of overwhelming the Anglo Saxons with one overwhelming blow at Hastings so they forgot about this final bloody confrontation. But other contemporary sources, such as William Jumieges, a French monk, dedicate as much space to this battle as to the Battle of Hastings and Guy de Amiens describes how Duke William of Normandy took the battle so seriously that he constructed siege engines and battering rams.

- Sources may be reinterpreted as society changes. In Monte Alban, the great abandoned city of pre-conquest Mexico, in tomb seven, the focus of the five hundred precious grave goods was said to be a priest associated with the god Xollotl. However, this was because, in archaeology, figures associated with wealth and power are generally assumed to be male. Dr Sharisse McCafferty has not come up with any new evidence but applied a modern feminist perspective to the grave goods. The weaving battens are a badge of femininity which boys were prevented from touching. There is also spinning equipment. What were originally thought to be false fingernails are, in the new interpretation, thought to be thimbles (Burne 1995). The skeleton, she argues, is therefore female.

- Sources may be cult or ceremonial objects which we do not understand. The Iron Age 'Waterloo Helmet' in the British Museum or the Uffington chalk horse in Berkshire may represent ideas or social practices about which we can only surmise. The recorded discussion of my Year 4 class about the meaning of the Uffington horse involved geology and the social organisation needed to make it and its practical and symbolic significance. They follow through and weigh each other's points of view, form imaginative ideas into logical arguments and use abstract concepts: co-operate, community, ceremonies, beliefs, customs. Here is a short extract.

> It looks like a bird.
>
> It's a horse.
>
> They could draw horses.
>
> So they had horses.
>
> They were hard workers . . . skilful . . . artistic . . .
>
> There must be a lot of chalk under the surface.
>
> So there won't be trees like oak trees – not many trees.
>
> They could live on the chalk; it's well-drained – the water would run away.
>
> The soil would be thin – it's easy to plough.
>
> Whatever tools they used it must have taken a long time. They must have co-operated. They lived in a community. It's not an ordinary horse. It's much more different from the ones we see.
>
> It must be a special one or they wouldn't go to all that trouble.
>
> It's probably a symbol for something – a clue.
>
> To bring a good harvest?
>
> A symbol of strength?
>
> To an enemy? Perhaps the horse brought bad luck so they stayed away.
>
> Perhaps if someone was ill they prayed to it. It gave them power when they were ill.
>
> Or perhaps they just had fun.
>
> Maybe they danced around it – or put fires on it and burnt something, maybe for the chief's birthday.
>
> I don't think they had birthdays.
>
> But they had beliefs and ceremonies . . .

■ We have to accept that sometimes we cannot know. A recently unearthed pot of Roman face cream has been described as showing the 'finger marks of the woman who used it' – but is this merely a stereotypical assumption? What had happened to the fifty-six, taller-than-average Romans, all prime-of-life males, whose cleanly beheaded skeletons were found in York in 2004? Were they legionaries killed in battle, the result of a pagan ritual, victims of each other as gladiators, punished as a unit found guilty of cowardice, loyalists of the Emperor Caracalla's brother? The opinions of experts vary. What is certain is that they died horrible deaths, were a mix of nationalities, that they were of high social status.

What is probable is that they were the elite victims of military persecution. What is possible is that they were killed for disloyalty or cowardice. The rest we can probably never know (Girling 2006).

■ Traces of the past may tell us something of people's actions, but we can never know the thoughts and feelings which underpin those actions. We cannot even know what a contemporary may be thinking and feeling. Sarah Wheeler, writing about historical biography, asks,

What is motivation? It is a deep sea fish swimming around in the fecund depths of the sub-conscious. Which of us can say that we understand the tangled skeins of fears and desires that control our own behaviour, let alone those of our husband or wife, letting even more alone that of a long dead stranger.

(Wheeler 2006)

Collingwood (1939) attempted to clarify the relationship between interpreting evidence and the thoughts and feelings of people. Historical evidence, whether it is an artefact, a building, a picture or writing, is the result of an action. An action is the result of rational thinking. Rational thought has its roots in feeling and imagination. Feelings and thinking only continue to exist to the extent that they are represented in the action, in the evidence. Collingwood says, for example, that we know that Julius Caesar invaded Britain in successive years, we can suppose that his thoughts may have been on trade or grain supply or a range of other possibilities and his underlying feelings may have included ambition or career advancement. Collingwood points out that an historian can share the thoughts of someone in the past because he has experienced similar feelings and thoughts within his own contexts through shared humanity but that, never-theless, they are different thoughts because the person was thinking them in response to a particular, ongoing situation at the time.

■ It is necessary to understand societies in the past from the standpoint of a person living at the time, in a society which may have had different attitudes, values and beliefs from our own. Collingwood (1946) says that man does not live in a world of hard facts, to which thoughts make no difference, but in a society with moral, economic and political structures and rules; as the structure changes, man's thoughts and behaviour change too. People may have had different values and beliefs from our own, because they had different knowledge bases. We need to try to see the world from the standpoint of other times to try to understand why the Saxons relied on ducking or burning to determine guilt or innocence; why sixteenth-century people thought the plague was a punishment from God; why Victorian children worked in factories or were sent to the workhouse.

■ New evidence may be discovered. For example, the Mildenhall Treasure in the British Museum, a hoard of Roman silver plate dug up fifty years ago in East

Anglia, is now thought to have been illegally imported from Italy or Africa by American troops immediately after the Second World War. This has forced historians to reassess their ideas about the quality of silverware used in Eastern Britain at the time (*The Sunday Times* 5 January 1997).

- Evidence is often incomplete. Historians need to use imagination in order to do what Elton (1970) calls 'filling in the gaps' in a narrative, when evidence is incomplete. Ryle (1979) sees this as cashing in on the facts and using them: ammunition shortage and heavy rain before a battle cause the historian to wonder about the hungry rifleman and delayed mule trains. But historical imagination is not free floating. It needs to be based on the most likely explanations of what is known.

For all these reasons several hypotheses about a source may be different but equally valid. Making inferences from sources involves giving reasons for your argument, listening to the views of others and being prepared to change your mind, or to accept that often there is no single, correct answer. We have to make reasonable hypotheses about what we can infer. Such 'guesses' are valid if there is no contradictory evidence, if they are reasonable and if they fit in with whatever else is known about the period.

Impact of learning theories on children's use of sources

Inferences, probability, argument, progression

The key constructivist theorists are Piaget, Bruner and Vygotsky. Their work has been both modified and developed over the years by many others but essentially their contributions to our understanding of learning remain central.

Inferences about sources

Piaget offers some insights into the progression in children's ability to make inferences from sources. His work suggests a sequence in development in which, at first, children's thinking is dominated by intuitive trial and error, by the child's own experiences and feelings. Wood and Holden (1997) found, in discussing old domestic objects with Key Stage 1 children, that the younger children drew *randomly* on their experience, including factual and fictional knowledge, although they were able to use this knowledge to make informed suggestions about how the artefacts were used; one child drew on his knowledge of Mrs Tiggy-Winkle. The older children's knowledge was more organised and they were increasingly able to draw on relevant information from their home and school experience.

At the next stage of concrete operations Piaget found that a child can take in information from the tangible and visible world, fit it into existing mental patterns, adjusting these when necessary to accommodate new information, and so store it, in order to use it selectively to solve problems. A child at this stage is therefore able to form a reasoned premise and support it with a logical argument. In Chapter 11, children retain vocabulary they have learned in one context and transfer it to new contexts. They interpret evidence in a previously unseen map by drawing on a field visit to a similar area, on previous class discussion and also on their own ideas. They transfer the thinking skills they have learned in whole-class lessons to group discussion when no adult is present.

At a third stage of formal operations, it is possible to think in terms of abstract and negative propositions (if . . . then; either . . . or; when . . . is not, both . . . and) and to weigh all the possible variants in an argument. The Year 6 newspaper accounts of the Armada (page 165, 167–68) show children just embarking on this stage.

Argument

Piaget's work on language (1926; 1928) suggests that a young child is able to communicate a valid statement of fact or description. This is followed by a stage of 'primitive argument', in which the statement is followed by a deduction going beyond the information given but the explanation is implicit. At the next stage a child attempts to justify and demonstrate an assertion using a conjunction (since, because, therefore), but does not succeed in expressing a truly logical relationship. The child eventually arrives at 'genuine argument' through frequent attempts to justify an opinion; is able to use 'because' correctly. An example of this is found in the archaeologist's report sheet on page 195. However, in history this sequence depends on the complexity of the evidence and the questions asked. Donaldson (1978) recognised that children's ability to reason depends on what the question is, how it is relevant to a child's concerns, the child's expectations of the questioner, the extent to which they concentrate on language and that language is related to non-verbal cues. She concludes that young children must develop their ability to reason and make inferences as early as possible by receiving the right kind of support.

Rules

Piaget (1932) suggested that children at first see no reason for rules. At the next stage they think that rules must be rigidly obeyed, then later they recognise that there are circumstances in which they should be challenged or changed. In an historical context, initially people's behaviour is idiosyncratic. Then people are seen as good or bad, heroes or villains, friends or enemies. At a later stage children can begin to understand and discuss the reasons for people's behaviour, the values of a society different from their own, why perspectives differ. This is illustrated by the four perspectives of the Armada (pages 167–68) and especially in the cartoon 'I thought God was on our side'.

Probability

Piaget's work on probability (Piaget and Inhelder 1951) also shows that at first children cannot differentiate between chance and non-chance but at a concrete level they have an increasing understanding of what we can know and what we can guess. Eventually they can differentiate between what is certain and what is probable. (See examples in Chapter 11.)

Teaching approaches and progression

Bruner (1963) introduced the notion of a 'spiral curriculum'. He set out the processes whereby a discipline may be structured so that the thinking processes which lie at the heart of a discipline can be tackled from the very beginning in their simplest form, then in increasingly complex ways. He said that this involved translating a subject into appropriate forms of representation which place emphasis on 'doing', on appropriate imagery, and a set of rules for making deductions and inferences. Problems, he said, must involve the right degree of uncertainty in order to be interesting, and learning should be organised in units, each building on the foundations of the previous one. He also said that we should define the skills children need in order to extrapolate from particular examples, from a memorable specific instance, to the general, in order to transfer the thinking processes learned to other similar problems; this gives confidence and avoids 'mental overload' of facts. Children learn, in whole-class lessons, how to ask and answer questions about sources, then are able to transfer this process to new sources (Chapter 11). They need opportunities to answer questions about tactile, visual and symbolic sources. This approach is also employed in the case study in Chapter 11. Each period is explored through site and museum visits, artefacts, pictures, diagrams, plans and written sources. Observations were recorded in a variety of ways using kinetic, iconic and symbolic approaches: through art techniques (painting, embroidery, lino cuts and silk screen prints, pottery), through science experiments (dyeing, firing clay, cooking food), through technology (building a model Roman kiln, an Iron Age hut), through writing in different genres (notes, poems, fiction, reports) and tape-recorded discussions. Bruner described the role of the teacher as 'scaffolding' children's learning, for example by questioning, cueing, providing resources. This was part of the whole-class lessons and is also exemplified in the structure of the archaeologist's report (page 195), which aimed to structure thinking by developing causal thinking, differentiating between what is known and what can be 'guessed' and what cannot be known, and by encouraging the use of abstract concepts to reach conclusions – 'hard words'.

Discussion

Vygotsky made two contributions to our understanding of children's ability to make deductions and inferences about sources. Firstly, he demonstrated the importance of social interaction and trial and error through discussion, forming a point of view, listening to others, modifying the original viewpoint (1962). Secondly, his work on the 'zone of proximal development' (1978) showed how, by working with an adult or more competent peer, children's thinking can be taken forward. Both aspects of Vygotsky's work, discussion and concept development, are illustrated in Chapter 11 and in Cooper (1993).

Recent research into children's use of sources

Understanding different attitudes and values

Bage (2000: 26) says that leading learners willingly into worlds different from the societies in which they exist is a moral and creative act of the highest order. Barton (1996) found that children often seem to feel impelled to respond to the challenge of explaining attitudes and values in the past. For example, younger children (Ashby and Lee 2001) suggested that the Romans executed slaves 'because they did not know about God and Jesus'; Saxons resorted to deciding guilt by oath-taking because 'They did not know about police courts – or medicines – or about floating and sinking', or 'because it was their religion'. Older pupils tried to unpack the values and beliefs behind the institutions, referring to culture and norms. However, it is important to notice that some Year 2 children responded in ways characteristic of fourteen-year-olds. They behaved as if they believed that even puzzling institutions could be made intelligible by understanding how people saw their world, not by reference to our world.

Distinguishing between validity and truth

Ashby (2004) investigated the development of the ability of pupils in Year 3, Year 6, Year 7 and Year 9 to grasp the difference between a true and a valid statement. She asked them how they could decide if the claim by the Welsh monk Nennius, that 'Arthur killed 960 Saxons at Mount Badon', was true. Their answers illustrated progression. The younger children wanted to find out from an authority, an adult or a book. They did consider the credibility of the author; 'monks would write the truth' (hem!). By Year 7 pupils recognised that books may differ, in which case they would see what most books say. Most Year 9 pupils questioned the author's claim on the basis of his ability to know. They recognised that inferences could be made from sources and considered whether these were likely. This study does explore progression in historical thinking but the methodology was based on a secondary school approach rather than starting from holistic primary practice so do not be pessimistic about the levels achieved here by some younger pupils.

Developing historical imagination

Vass (2004) described a way of developing historical imagination through story. He based his approach on the view that the outcome of the historian's labours is 'any patterned account, intended to be true, of any past happenings involving human intention or doing or suffering' (Hexter 1971: 3). He gave pupils artefacts from the Second World War (e.g. blackout curtain, ration book, gas mask) and invited them to 'fill in the gaps' to make their own stories, set in London in the Blitz. They used event framing. This enabled the stories to take place within a given chronological framework. One child, evaluating the stories, concluded that, 'I think Jodie's story is more like it was than mine. There is more evidence.' She was, Vass reflects, 'discovering that historical evidence is not as tangible or obvious as imagined'. Children decided on a 'key factor' which determined the origin of the stories (e.g. the ration book was lost in the dark). This gave rise to interesting discussions about 'unique events' – 'No two stories are ever the same, even in history books . . . It depends on who is writing the story' – and to discussion about chance: 'Most things happen by chance . . . this, therefore that . . . There was a good chance of an air raid during the war but you never know do you, if that was how the ration book was lost?' Secondly, Vass drew on the work of Ferguson (1997) who argues for a 'chaotic' model of historical forces, where the actuality of the past is seen as only one of many possible outcomes; he claims that this helps historians to understand better what actually happened and why. The children constructed 'counterfactual histories', beginning with a Bethnal Green air raid in 1943 and ending, via six event frames, with the commemoration of the victims thirty years later. One child's perceptive conclusion was that, 'It was the rockets that did it [caused panic in which people were crushed to death]. The sirens worried people but it was the rockets going off that caused the panic. They were new. People had never heard that sound before. It was the rockets that did it.'

Moving from abstract to concrete

Dilek and Yapici (2004) at the University of Marmara, in Istanbul, have challenged the notion that learning develops from concrete to abstract and, drawing on the research of Egan (1988) and others, suggested how a concept they call 'abstract thinking specific to childhood' might be developed through stories about the past. Gulcin Yapici read a story about 'Grandfather Seljuk' to a class, giving them opportunities for questioning and explanation during the story. The story was written to include descriptions of artefacts based on photographs in museum catalogues (Aydin *et al.* 1994; Altun 2001). When the story ended children were asked to draw certain artefacts described in the story. Similarities with and differences from the original artefacts were analysed.

Three levels of abstract thinking in the children's responses to the story were identified. The story described servants pouring rose sherbets into glasses from a ceramic flask 'round like a globe with peacock decoration and two handles next to the rim'. Pupils' drawings correctly reflected this description. Dilek and Yapici called this 'static imagination' because it simply recorded what had been described.

FIGURE 2.1 Example of 'static imagination'. Drawing of water flask described in the story as 'shaped like a globe, with two handles near the rim and decorated with a peacock'. (Information is recorded but no detail added.)

They identified the next level of response as 'transition' from 'static' to 'dynamic imagination'. Pupils were asked to draw a coin depicting Suleiman Shah on his horse, carrying weapons with three prongs. There were six pointed stars on each of his shoulders and down his legs. Around the edge of the coin was written 'Destroyer Prince'. In general pupils' coins looked very like the original but some had added details: headgear, saddle, boots not described in the story. They were 'filling in the gaps' in the information given, in valid ways. Similarly, one pupil added musical notes to a tray depicting wedding food.

At a third level Dilek and Yapici identified what they called 'dynamic imagination'. Some pupils devised historically acceptable symbols representing abstract concepts. For example, a coin, described in the story simply as a 'symbol of sovereignty', was

FIGURE 2.2 Example of 'transition from static imagination to dynamic imagination'. Drawing of a bronze tray described in the story as decorated with women in long dresses, some holding glasses. The pupil has added musical notes to reflect the musical instruments mentioned in the story.

depicted by a pupil as having a two-headed eagle, a symbol of the Anatolia Seljuks, on one side and Kabadabad Palace, symbol of the state, on the reverse. So the identified sequence was: description without addition; inclusion of valid details not given in the story; translating undisclosed symbols into images representing abstract concepts.

Distinguishing between what is known and what can be guessed

A group of eight-year-olds (Cooper 1991) who had been learning about the Saxons through class lessons which involved making deductions and inferences (good guesses) about a variety of sources were given previously unseen sources to discuss. One of these was a slide of a replica of the Sutton Hoo Sceptre. They interpreted this within the framework of the knowledge acquired through their sequence of lessons.

1   Where did the Saxons come from, where did they settle, when and why? This lesson was based on Saxon artefacts (wrist clasps, brooches, etc.) linked to maps showing where the artefacts had been found, written evidence of the Roman withdrawal and Saxon records of where they settled (Gildas, Bede, *Anglo Saxon Chronicle*).

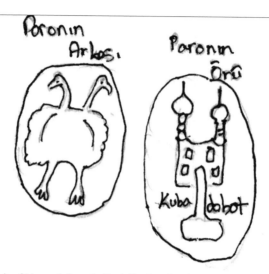

FIGURE 2.3 Example of 'dynamic imagination'. The two-headed eagle on the front of the coin is the symbol of the Seljuk Turks and Kabadabad Palace on the back represents the economic and political power of the state. Information in the story is shown symbolically.

2 Inferences about Saxon life based on extracts from *Beowulf* (Heaney 1999).

3 Map of the Seven kingdoms in AD 700, information about kingship from Bede (1990) and the *Anglo Saxon Chronicle* (Swanton 2000), and some seventh-century Anglo Saxon laws in Kent and Wessex.

4 Evidence of the spread of the Roman church and the Celtic church from Bede, linked to a map.

5 A local visit (Coulsdon) to trace evidence of Saxon settlements from spring line, place names and hedge dating.

Here are some of the children's (written) responses to the questions: what do you know, what can you guess and what can't you know about the Sutton Hoo sceptre?

- *I know: They had kings. Therefore they must have had to be obedient, they must have had to be loyal. They had a sceptre with an animal on it (deer). Therefore it must have been a symbol. It was precious. It took a long time to make. Therefore it must be unique.*

- *I can guess: The gold sculpture deer may be saying 'save our lives or where we live'. Therefore the sceptre may mean 'Kill us and be warned; you'll die'. That might be why the ruler carries it; to show he is the ruler for God on earth.*

- *I'd like to know: Why it's made out of stone because it must be heavy and why there is no picture of himself on it because it could tell us what sort of a king he was.*

These eight-year-olds are discussing an artefact and applying information and thinking processes previously learned to a new source (Bruner 1963). They are distinguishing between what they know, what they can guess and what they would like to know (Piaget and Inhelder 1951). They are using 'because' and 'therefore' to justify their statements about how it may have been made and used (Piaget 1926) and what it may have meant to the people who made and used it (Collingwood 1939). There are also attempts to consider the possible thoughts and feelings of these people (Collingwood 1946) and understanding that they probably had different values and beliefs as represented by the 'symbol'. Children were using their imagination, based on what they knew, and learning to make suppositions. The more they make, with maturity, the more valid these will become.

In an interesting study with seven-year-olds in Malta, Yvonne Vella (2004) describes a series of activities which were designed to help pupils to make inferences from pictures. At first the children were shown a painting and asked to 'say anything you wish about this painting'. The discussion was video-recorded. Activities followed which were intended to accelerate the children's ability to interpret visual sources.

- An early-twentieth-century photograph of a milk seller with goats. Children were asked what they thought was going on. Then the photograph was divided into four using two strips of paper and the children were asked to look at specific areas of the picture and were asked much more specific questions.

- The children were given a magnifying glass to look at a small eighteenth-century picture of a toddler in a baby walker made of cane. This picture was part of a larger painting, which was later uncovered. The children could see whether they had been correct in their first analysis.

- A nineteenth-century painting of sailors looking out from a boat. The children were asked to play a game in which the paper was lifted for a brief moment. Each time they were asked to say what they had spotted.

- Children were shown a nineteenth-century picture of a Maltese lady and were asked, 'Do you think this lady really looked like this?'

Then the children returned to the original picture. Again their discussion was recorded. They focused much more on the detail in the picture and the points they made were more complex.

Student teachers investigate children's inferences about sources

Paula Andrews wondered what sorts of questions her Key Stage 1 class should be encouraged to ask and what was the teacher's role. Is there progression from Year 1 to Year 2? What artefacts stimulate the most questions and why? She found that the youngest children made observations but needed help in turning these into questions. As they got older they were able to formulate their own questions and increasingly asked open questions which led to discussions: how things were made, how they were used and why. The artefacts which stimulated the most interest and discussion were things which worked and could be explored through manipulation.

Beverley Wright used a literacy session on adjectives to ask her Year 3/4 class to make inferences about the people depicted in Tudor portraits. She, like Claire (1996), found that children attributed strengths and weaknesses to male and female portraits respectively. Beverley used the plenary session to discuss this with them and challenge their assumptions.

Some ideas for practical activities using sources to engage you in reflection on your own practice

Writing, maps, pictures, artefacts

- Portraits. Put a portrait in the middle of a sheet of paper and invite children to make a spider graph of what they can infer from the portrait. Can they divide their ideas into categories; what categories? Do children get better at this activity with experience? In what ways? What was your role?

- For each group place the source in the centre of a large piece of paper with the heading, 'What does this source tell me?' This piece of paper stands on three pieces of paper of increasing size so that they overlap each other with the headings: 'What guesses can I make about it?' 'What does the source not tell me?' 'What other questions do I need to ask?' The children write their ideas on the appropriate piece of paper around the source. Are there more responses to one of the questions? Do some sources inspire more responses? Why? From everyone or some children?

- Site visits. Visiting a site is not mere information collecting. Children need a genuine historical puzzle within which to root their activity. The puzzle, or enquiry, must be historically worthwhile and personally motivating and negotiated with the children. Pupils need to work on their own line of questioning. They must be prepared before the visit, so that they arrive focused and ready to go and they need to know what they have learned about historical enquiry. (Examples are described on pages 75–80, 83, 145 and 147–57.) How many of the pre-visit questions came from the children? How many were answered? How many of the follow-up activities were their ideas? How much of their learning were they aware of; was it process plus content? Why did they enjoy this project?

References

Altun, A. (2001) *Aladdin's Lamp and the Art of the Anatolian Seljuks*: 45, YapiKredi Kultur Sanat Yayincilic.

Ashby, R. (2004) 'Developing a concept of historical evidence: students' ideas about testing singular factual claims', History Educators' International Research Network Conference, St Martin's College, Ambleside, England (www.heirnet.org).

Ashby, R. and Lee, P. (2001) 'Empathy, perspective taking and rational understanding', in O.L. Davis, S. Foster and E. Yaeger (eds) *Historical Empathy and Perspective Taking in Social Studies*. Maryland and Colorado: Rowman and Littlefield.

Aydin, S., Rifat, S. and Paksoy, I. (1994) *A Rainbow Linking East and West: coins of the Seljuks*: 26, 27, Yapi Kredi Kultur Merkezi.

Bage, G. (2000) *Thinking History 4–14, Teaching, Learning, Curricula and Communities, New Directions*. Oxford: Blackwell.

Barton, K. (1996) 'Narrative simplifications in elementary students' historical thinking', in J. Brophy (ed.) *Advances in Research on Teaching, Vol. 6: Teaching and Learning History*: 51–83. Greenwich: JAI Press.

Bede (1990) *Ecclesiastical History of the English People*. London: Penguin Classics.

Bruner, J.S. (1963) *The Process of Education*. New York: Vintage Books.

Burne, J. (1995) 'Sex change for skeleton after feminist enquiry', *Sunday Telegraph*, 15 January.

Claire, H. (1996) *Reclaiming the Past: Equality and Diversity*. London: Trentham Books.

Collingwood, R.G. (1939) *An Autobiography*. Oxford: Oxford University Press.

Collingwood, R.G. (1946) *The Idea of History*. Oxford: Clarendon.

Cooper, H. (1991) 'Young Children's Thinking in History', unpub. PhD thesis, University of London.

Cooper, H. (1993) 'Removing the scaffolding: a case study investigating how whole class teaching can lead to effective peer group discussion without the teacher', *Curriculum Journal*, **4** (3), 385–401.

Dilek, D. and Yapici, G. (2004) 'The use of stories in the teaching of history', History Educators' International Conference, Ambleside, England (www.heirnet.org).

Donaldson, M. (1978) *Children's Minds*. London: Fontana.

Egan, K. (1988) *Teaching as Story Telling: an alternative approach to teaching and the curriculum*. London: Routledge.

Elton, G.R. (1970) 'What sort of history should we teach?' in M. Ballard (ed.) *New Movements in the Study and Teaching of History*. London: Temple Smith.

Ferguson, N. (1997) (ed.) *Virtual History: alternatives and counterfactuals*. London: Macmillan Picador.

Girling, R. (2006) 'A cemetery of secrets', *The Sunday Times*, Magazine, 26 March: 14–18 (www.bbc.co.uk/timewatch).

Harlow, J. (1996) 'Found: site of forgotten battle that decided 1066 and all that', *The Sunday Times*, News, 3, 29 December.

Heaney, S. (1999) *Beowulf: A New Translation*. London: Faber and Faber.

Hexter, J. (1971) *The History Primer*. New York: Basic Books.

Piaget, J. (1926) *The Language and Thought of the Child*. London: Routledge.

Piaget, J. (1928) *Judgement and Reasoning in the Child*. London: Kegan Paul.

Piaget, J. (1932) *Moral Judgement and the Child*. London: Kegan Paul.

Piaget, J. and Ingelder, B. (1951) *The Origin of the Idea of Chance in the Child*. London: Routledge.

Ryle, G. (1979) *On Thinking*. Oxford: Blackwell.

Swanton, A. (ed.) (2000) *The Anglo Saxon Chronicle*. London: Orion, Weidenfeld and Nicolson History.

Vass, P. (2004) 'Thinking skills and the learning of primary history: thinking historically through stories', History Educators' International Research Conference, St Martin's College, Ambleside, England, *International Journal of History Teaching, Learning and Research*, **4** (2). (www.heirnet.org)

Vella, Y. (2004) 'Assessing history talk in a group', History Educators' International Research Conference, St Martin's College, Ambleside, England (www.heirnet.org).

Vygotsky, L.S. (1962) *Thought and Language*. London: Wiley.

Vygotsky, L.S. (1978) *Mind in Society: the development of higher psychological processes*. Cambridge, Mass.: Harvard University Press.

Wheeler, S. (2006) 'And so the years passed . . .' *Spectator*, 25 March: 48.

Wood, E. and Holden, C. (1997) 'I can't remember doing the Romans: the development of children's understanding in history', *Teaching History*, **89**, 9–11.

3

Interpretations and accounts

What are interpretations?

INTERPRETATIONS OF THE PAST are accounts of a period, written in a subsequent period. To try to make sense of the past, historians combine their inferences about sources to create accounts of the past. In Chapter 1 we considered the many reasons why sources may be interpreted differently. In this chapter we shall consider why accounts may differ, but be equally valid, and also why they may be of different validity.

- Sources may be incomplete but they are also numerous and wide-ranging. Historians therefore have to select the sources relevant to their accounts. Selection depends on the focus of their accounts for, as we have seen, there are many types of history, from political, social, economic to sports history, history of music or art, histories of groups or individuals, broad or in-depth.

- Historians also write from their own interests and perspectives: gender, ethnicity, politics, social class. Rowbotham (1973), Beddoe (1983), Boulding (1976; 1977; 1981) and Hill (1989; 1996; 2001) take a female perspective. Fryer (1984; 1989) writes from the perspective of a Black historian and Vishram (1988) from an Indian perspective. C.V. Wedgwood's (1955) account of the English Civil War is different from that of the Marxist historian Christopher Hill (1980). Chinn (1995) takes a working-class and a female, though not necessarily feminist, perspective.

- Accounts reflect the dominant values of the time in which they were written. The Victorians, for example, focused on finding aspects of British freedoms and rights embedded in Saxon laws. In the statue of Queen Victoria and Prince Albert, in the National Portrait Gallery, London, commemorating Albert's untimely death, they are wearing Saxon costume!

Interpretations change with time

History is dynamic. Historians challenge previous interpretations The raids of Bomber Command in the Second World War were seen as necessary and effective for a variety of reasons until Max Hastings (1979) questioned this, saying that the raids were both ineffective and disproportionate. (As a result red paint was thrown over the statue of 'Bomber Harris'.) Anthony Grayling (2006) demonstrated the bombing to be, according to the laws obtaining at the time and subsequently, an essentially immoral activity.

Wild Scots (Fry 2005) challenges the dominant account of the Scottish clearances by pointing out that many Highland landlords were benevolent Tory paternalists who went to great lengths to maintain the ties which bound the people to the land. Dee Brown's *Bury My Heart at Wounded Knee* (1991) challenges the traditional image of the 'Wild West'. Niall Ferguson's *Colossus* (2002) re-examines America's dominance and argues that America really is an Empire, before going on to argue that this is something to celebrate. Churchill once said that he would ensure his place in history by writing it – but historians are still writing it.

Apparently Captain Bligh, immortalised in *Mutiny on the Bounty* as the cause of the crew's spontaneous revolt against a tyrannical captain and cast adrift by his second-in-command, Fletcher Christian, has now been found to have been a sea-faring hero and a humane captain, victimised by Christian when he ran out of laudanum (Hellen 1998).

Interpretations change with place

A letter in *The Times* (30 December 1996) from Dr Olga Ashby illustrates what she describes as 'the cultural divide between the two sides of the Iron Curtain'. She lived in Moscow during the 1980s before moving to England. She recalls how she was taught that the battle described in Tennyson's poem, 'The Charge of the Light Brigade', as lost as the result of the blunders of the British commanding officers was represented in Russia as a triumph of Russian strategy; the 'original nurse' of the Crimean War was not Florence Nightingale but Dasha Sevastopolskata.

Children and interpretations in history books

Children can compare different written accounts at their own levels by comparing different information books on the same historical subject. As discussed above, how has the content been selected? Is the focus on everyday life of rich or poor, or on art and artefacts, on individuals or events? Are there inferences about beliefs and values, thoughts and feelings, and how are these justified? Are statements supported by evidence of why this is thought? Is a book written from the perspectives and interests of children – from different backgrounds? Do they represent and value men and women equally? Are they illustrated with artists' impressions, themselves interpretations, or with photographs of sources? What is not included? How do children's books published at different times in the past differ from those of today, in language, hidden messages, selected content?

Examples of children's understanding of interpretations

Hoodless (2004) has analysed ten- and eleven-year-old children's understanding of the changing attitudes and values revealed in historical stories written at different times in the twentieth century. She found that they were able to identify changing styles of presentation with a subtle understanding that adults' different attitudes are transmitted through historical accounts and stories written in different periods. After reading about Boudicca in Sarson and Paine (1930) and in Deary (1994), the children commented on the way each reflected the values of its time; the earlier text avoided dwelling on death and the embarrassment of suicide. The children thought that, in the romantic style of the earlier text, Boudicca was treated with the respect due to a queen and her husband was considered to have done 'the right thing'. They were conscious that the writer's style was intended for children who were regarded differently from children today, and also of its response to the time in which it was written: 'It seems to come out of that time. It reads like it was written just after the war, all proud about how we defend ourselves.' Another child commented, 'You have an image of what other people thought of her, how she was very brave. The problem with that is that because of the time it was based in you don't know if that's what it was actually like . . . Stories change in the time they're told . . . It can completely change the image of someone.' They recognised that the first version was told as a matter of fact while in the second they were invited to decide between various possibilities. Children commented on how they preferred making their own decisions because 'people's opinions, written up in stories, might be wrong'.

Fictional stories about the past in historical settings are also reconstructions. Children can read these or write their own, identifying what is known and what is 'guessed at' to fill in the gaps.

Interpretations through re-enactment

Accounts of the past are not made only by historians. There is now an enormous variety of forms of interpretation of past times. They may be living reconstructions such as The Black Country Museum (www.bclm.co.uk) or Beamish Museum (www.beamish.org.uk) or re-enactments of events. Kentwell Hall in Long Melford in Suffolk is the setting for a Tudor recreation for schoolchildren for three weeks each year. The surroundings of the redbrick Elizabethan manor are peopled with four hundred 're-enactors' at any one time, for the children to interact with: dyers, woodsmen, weavers, chandlers, alchemists, cooks, pedlars, seamstresses, musicians and gentry.

A long list of living history re-enactments is given on www.reenact.com. Reconstructions may be static museum reconstructions, for example the Prehistory galleries in the Museum of London, or reconstructions such as the Iron Age Village at Butser in the Queen Elizabeth Park, Hampshire. Such reconstructions are the product of informed historical enquiry or, as with Butser, of historical research (Reynolds 1979). Children can try to find out how such reconstructions were made (what is the evidence?) by asking questions on the site, comparing with other sources or information books, and consider why they were made and their validity.

Less academic accounts are made for different purposes and may have different levels of validity. Benjamin Britten's opera, *Gloriana*, the BBC television serial *Blackadder II* and the BBC film *The Virgin Queen* give very different interpretations of Elizabeth I which are easy for young children to identify and explain (see pages 171–3). Similar stark contrast is provided by a model Iceni village in Norfolk, complete with brightly painted horses' heads and skulls on poles, which is very different from the scientific reconstruction at Butser. The statue of Boudicca on the Embankment in London represents a different interpretation of the period from that in *Asterix in Britain* (Goscinny 2004). New interactive media technologies are making new kinds of historical interpretation possible. It is possible to walk through virtual museums and virtual sites. A great deal of research into virtual museums is being undertaken by Manchester Metropolitan Museum (www.doc.mmu.ac.uk/virtual-museum).There are also BBC interactive TV adventures, for example *Pyramid: Beyond Imagination*, and interactive BBC digital programmes. I was involved as a consultant on a BBC digital history programme for three- to eight-year-olds which is intended to be used either independently or with parents to supplement work in school or playgroup. My job was to ensure that it involved the processes of historical enquiry in activities related to a prehistoric hunt, a castle and an Edwardian street. It raised some interesting problems about creating an interpretation.

Children's accounts through re-enactments

If children can create their own interpretations through reconstructions this is not only fun but helps them to consider how interpretations are created and their validity. They may be reconstructions created through play. Play in historical contexts is discussed elsewhere (Cooper 2002; 2004) and on pages 63, 85 and 126, 131 and 147–157. Older children may create considered historical drama (as seen on TV!) over a longer period, researching character, place, setting, and examining a problem or an issue, considering what is based on research and what needs to be imagined based on what is known. This could link well with literacy objectives. If it were made into a film this would also have ICT objectives and the cross-curricular approach would justify the time spent. Why not add design and technology, designing sets? This would also be a way of 'communicating results of an enquiry'. Or there may be two dramas made, an interpretation from a female and male perspective. (Getting carried away now. Can't wait to get back into a school!) There are companies which provide units of history work resulting in a musical production (www.educational-musicals.com), although I prefer the children's own creations. A range of historical costumes for Key Stages 1 and 2 can be purchased from Charlie Crow Costumes (www.charliecrow.co.uk). We once did a performance of the musical *Oliver!*, and discussed it in relation to factual enquiries about the poor in Victorian London. I have the photograph on my wall still of me dressed as a chimney sweep – because it's fun for teachers to join in too!

Interpretations created could be a series of paintings or murals, maybe as a background to a museum exhibition, depicting aspects of a period studied, based on what can be researched about different aspects of life or different key events; there are links to art here too. Any display is itself a reconstruction in which some things are selected and others neglected; models are reconstructions within a display reconstruction. Making models – Viking boats, Tudor houses, Iron Age huts – is fine as long as, in the process, children find out what they can from sources – and become aware of the problems involved in reconstructing from sources.

Why is it important to understand 'interpretations'?

Understanding how and why accounts of the past are made has been found to be a neglected aspect of historical enquiry in primary schools, yet children enjoy thinking seriously about accounts which can nevertheless be light-hearted and funny. They enjoy accounts made using different kinds of information technology. Since the past and heritage and family and local history are now frequently regarded as popular leisure activities and as entertainment, it is increasingly important that children can evaluate them. There are also more serious reasons for learning why there is no single view of the past and that accounts of the past are dynamic and may vary and change over time. Children are learning to challenge validity and assess validity and to recognise different motives behind creating accounts. For history is the most politically powerful subject in the curriculum and earns constant attention from politicians.

International comparisons

The importance of allowing pupils to discuss alternative interpretations of the past is made painfully real and clear in societies where history is contested, such as Northern Ireland or South Africa. Barton and Cully (2004) emphasise how history plays a contentious role in popular discussion and community conflict in Northern Ireland and one purpose of the school curriculum is to provide alternatives to the sectarian, historical perspectives pupils encounter elsewhere. Their interviews with 253 secondary school pupils demonstrated the strong impact of community influences, especially family members, but they also revealed that pupils consciously and explicitly expected the school to provide alternatives to those influences.

Harnett (2005) analysed how the British Empire and Commonwealth Museum in Bristol attempts to construct the narrative of Empire and takes account of different interpretations and alternative viewpoints within its collection. The museum, reflecting the work of contemporary historians, revises the Victorian view of Empire, epitomised by Cecil Rhodes' remark that 'the British are the finest race in the world and the more of the world they inhabit, the better it will be for mankind' (Cannadine 2001) with contemporary interpretations which reflect current values of equality of opportunity and human rights. (The history of Britain in the nineteenth century and since 1930 at Key Stage 2 is central to the history of Empire, whether viewed from a peripheral or metropolitan perspective.) In Harnett's study primary pupils investigated the lives of different individuals and social groups within the Empire, the challenges of the early settlers, the colonisation of Australia and the experiences of a Caribbean immigrant.

Hilary Claire provides excellent guidance on ways in which stereotypical interpretations of minority cultures and histories can be challenged at Key Stage 2, through art, music and drama. One study focuses on Irish history, one on the New Commonwealth and Caribbean history and one on the Kindertransport (www.multiverse.ac.uk).

In South Africa Gail Weldon (2004) explains how it is the explicit aim of the revised history curriculum to identify and develop values of 'democracy, equality, human dignity and social justice'. She points out, however, that the teachers were conditioned, in varying degrees, to the attitudes and prejudices of apartheid society, and as a result projects have been set up to support teachers and learners in education for human rights and democracy through history, with Nazi Germany and Apartheid South Africa as case studies.

In 1994 Jon Nichol and I set up the History Educators' International Research Network (www.heirnet.org) through which researchers in history education could share their work. We have had a number of successful conferences. The 2005 conference on Museums was about Identity and Citizenship. A number of the papers focused on the extent to which pupils are encouraged to understand that there may be more than one interpretation or that interpretations can change.

In a Portuguese study Barca and Pinto (2005) took children aged between ten and fourteen for a walk through the historic town of Guimaraes. They compared the large new 'castle' constructed in the days of the Salazar dictatorship with an engraving of the original, thirteenth-century castle it had replaced. The children were very articulate in comparing the two buildings, understanding why each had been built and how, and were clear about why they thought this should not have happened.

In Quebec Jocelyn Letourneau (2005) tried to contest the French Canadians' interpretation of Canadian history as a golden age until the British arrived and took it over for their own benefit. The Quebeckers are depicted in textbooks as childlike, dominated by their seigneurs and priests until the British invaders imposed commerce and progress. In 1995 nearly half of Quebeckers voted to split from Canada. Letourneau tried to set up a museum exhibition challenging the partial view of Canadian history but the challenge was not responded to. Alternative interpretations were not accepted. Other examples can be found elsewhere. In Germany there is a different interpretation of the past taught in the former East Germany and West Germany; the former teaches only about the positive values of the GDR and the latter, vice versa. Pupils are not invited to compare and discuss these interpretations.

In the United States of America Rozensweig (2000) has suggested that pupils see themselves as conscripts or prisoners and teachers as drill sergeants or wardens.

Recent work on 'Doing History in elementary schools' (e.g. Levstik and Barton 2000) introduces teachers to the idea that history is about asking questions, that it is interpretive and controversial; you 'get to argue', and 'There sure aren't many facts!'

Young children may not be debating the major issues through comparing interpretations but they are learning that there is more than one version of the past and beginning to understand why.

References

Barca, I. and Pinto, H. (2005) 'How children make sense of historic streets: walking through downtown Guimaraes' (www.heirnet.org).

Barton, K. and Cully A. W. (2004) 'Learning history and inheriting the past: the interaction of school and community perspectives in Northern Ireland', History Educators' International Research Network Conference, St Martin's College, Ambleside, England, *International Journal of History Teaching, Learning and Research*, **5** (1) (www.heirnet.org).

Beddoe, D. (1983) *Discovering Women's History*. London: Pandora.

Boulding, E. (1976) *Handbook of International Data on Women*. Beverly Hills: Sage.

Boulding, E. (1977) *Women in the Twentieth Century World*. New York: Sage.

Boulding, E. (1981) *The Underside of History*. Boulder, Co.: Westview.

Brown, D. (1991) *Bury My Heart at Wounded Knee*. New York: Henry Holt.

Cannadine, D. (2001) *Ornamentalism. How the British saw their Empire*. London: Penguin.

Chinn, C. (1995) *Poverty amidst Prosperity: the urban poor in England 1834–1914*. Manchester: Manchester University Press.

Claire, H. (www.multiverse.ac.uk).

Cooper, H. (2002) *History in the Early Years*, 2nd edn. London: Routledge.

Cooper, H. (ed.) (2004) *Exploring Time and Place Through Play*. London: David Fulton Publishers.

Deary, T. (1994) *The Rotten Romans*. London: Scholastic.

Ferguson, N. (2002) *Colossus: the price of America's Empire*. New York: Penguin.

Fry, M. (2005) *Wild Scots: four hundred years of Highland history*. London: John Murray.

Fryer, P. (1984) *Staying Power*. London: Pluto.

Fryer, P. (1989) *Black People in the British Empire – an introduction*. London: Pluto.

Goscinny, R. (2004) *Asterix in Britain*. London: Orion.

Grayling, A.C. (2006) *Among the Dead Cities*. London: Bloomsbury.

Harnett, P. (2005) 'Exploring the Potential for History and Citizenship Education with Primary Children' at the British Empire and Commonwealth Museum, Bristol, History Educators' International Network seminars, QCA, London (www.heirnet.org).

Hastings, M. (1979) *Bomber Command*. London: Michael Joseph.

Hellen, N. (1998) 'Sex and drugs drove mutiny on the Bounty', *The Sunday Times*, News, 4 January.

Hill, B. (1989) *Women, Work and Sexual Politics*. London: Routledge.

Hill, B. (1996) *Servants, English Domestics in the Eighteenth Century*. Oxford: Clarendon.

Hill, B. (2001) *Women Alone: Spinsters in England 1660–1850*. London: The MIT Press.

Hill, C. (1980) *The World Turned Upside Down: radical ideas during the English Revolution*. Harmondsworth: Penguin.

Hoodless, P. (2004) 'Spotting the Adult Agendas: investigating children's historical awareness using stories written for children in the past', History Educators' International Research Network, St. Martin's College, Ambleside, England, *International Journal of History Teaching, Learning and Research*, **4** (2) (www.heirnet.org).

Letourneau, J. (2005) 'Museums and the (un)building of Historical Consciousness', QCA Symposium (www.heirnet.org).

Levstik, L.S. and Barton, K.C. (2000) *Doing History: investigating with children in elementary and middle schools*, 2nd edn. Mahwah, N J: Laurence Erlbaum Associates.

Reynolds, P. (1979) *Butser, an Iron Age Farm*. London: British Museum Publications (www.butser.org.uk).

Rowbotham, S. (1973) *Hidden from History*. London: Pluto.

Rozensweig, R. (2000) 'How Americans use and think about the past: implications from the National Survey for the Teaching of History', in P. Stearns, P. Sexias and S. Wineburg (eds) *Knowing Teaching and Learning History: national and international perspectives*. New York and London: State University of New York Press.

Sarson, M. and Paine, M.E. (1930) *Stories from Greek, Roman and Old English History*, Piers Plowman Histories, Junior Book 11. London: George Philip and Son.

Vishram, R. (1988) *Ayars, Lascars and Princes*. London: Pluto.

Wedgwood, C.V. (1955) *The King's Peace 1637–1641 (The Great Rebellion)*. London: Collins.

Weldon, G. (2004) 'Thinking each other's History. Can Facing the Past contribute to Education for Human Rights and Democracy?' History Educators' International Research Network Conference, St Martin's College, Ambleside, England, *International Journal of History Teaching, Learning and Research*, **5** (1) (www.heirnet.org).

4

Historical concepts

What are historical concepts?

- Procedural or substantive concepts. Key historical concepts are concerned with the processes of historical enquiry, making deductions and inferences from sources and combing sources to create accounts which trace changes over time. These concepts include: evidence, source, cause, effect, similarity, difference, continuity, change, validity, interpretation.

- Time concepts. Other concepts central to history are concerned with the measurement of time (now, then, decade, century) or with describing periods of time (Victorian, Elizabethan).

- Some concepts used in history are vocabulary no longer used or used very differently today: villa, bailey, common.

- Concepts central to history but not exclusively historical. These are concepts which are at the heart of the process of tracing changes in societies, and their subordinate concepts. Examples are: agriculture (farm, field, crops, etc.); trade (buy, sell, profit, wealth); defence/attack (fight, battle, weapon).

Learning theory and historical concepts

Vygotsky (1962) pioneered research into how we learn concepts, which has been developed subsequently. Firstly, concepts are hierarchical. For example, if children are introduced to, and encouraged to use, the word castle, perhaps on a visit, they may associate it initially with this particular building. Through talking about the visit, the drawbridge, the moat, the mound, the battlements (level 1 concepts), they will be introduced to and use specialised concepts which are all part of an overarching concept, castle (level 2). They will become aware, through the talk and the concrete examples, that a castle was built for defence against attack. This will give the owner power. Hierarchies are not always clear and are often blurred around the edges, so defence, attack and power may all be categorised as level 3. Children do not necessarily learn the most concrete concepts first, but there is evidence that if they are explicitly introduced to new vocabulary at each level and given opportunities to use it, quite young children enjoy using and experimenting with 'hard words' (Chapter 11). Vygotsky showed how concepts are learned through trial and error, in communication with others. A visit to a castle may be followed up by research to find more examples of castles. A peel tower may be rejected because it is 'only a house', which could lead to discussion about whether being fortified justifies its inclusion in 'castles'. Or claims may be made that a monastic ruin is a castle because it is built of similar materials, which would lead to further refining of the concept of castle. A Victorian folly such as Balmoral could extend the discussion further: what exactly is the definition of a castle?

Concepts of time

There has been research both into children's ability to understand temporal concepts and the measurement of time and into their understanding of causes and effects of events and decisions.

Measurement of time

There has been much research into the development of children's ability to understand the sequence of days, months, seasons, between two and sixteen years old (e.g. Thornton and Vukelich 1988). Early research into children's ability to understand historical time (e.g. Hallam 1975; Peel 1967) suggested that understanding the nature of history and the significance of time is a question of maturation, and does not develop until about eleven. Piaget (1956) also claimed that young children had no concept of duration or sequence. This stage-related structure influenced further research, which tried to accelerate children's temporal understanding within a Piagetian framework (e.g. Lodwick 1958; Hallam 1975; Rees 1976). Later researchers (Booth 1994) questioned the relevance of this structure. Their research found that children's thinking about time depended not on maturation but on, for example, teaching strategies, familiarity with the material, relevant experience and interaction with other children.

Recent research (Hodkinson 2003a) suggests that children remember more of what they are taught in history if they have an efficient framework, a chronological framework, within which to place, store and retrieve what they have learned. Hodkinson set out to show that it is the design of the curriculum, focused teaching methods and resources which challenge and progress children's understanding of time, irrespective of such variables as intelligence, reading and mathematical ability. Hodkinson's research (2004) involved 129 Year 4 and Year 5 children. Over three terms a 'treatment group' and a control group studied their locality, the Victorian era and the reasons behind invasions and settlement of Britain. Pupils were encouraged to work co-operatively within activities which enabled open-ended discussion and temporal vocabulary. Activities sought to promote temporal concepts at increasingly complex levels. Historical material was always presented from time present to time past and time-lines were used consistently in every lesson. Specific skills-based activities were also introduced at the beginning and end of each lesson. Although the 'treatment group' developed greater chronological understanding than the control group, Hodkinson admits that in the 'treatment group' there was less time for developing other aspects of historical thinking.

Hodkinson's study (2003b) raised questions about the inconsistency of the National Curriculum for History. Foundation Stage and Key Stage 1 pupils, and less able older children, are expected to use vocabulary describing the passing of time (a long time ago; now, then; before, after). Yet temporal vocabulary is not mentioned in the Year 3 or Year 4 Study units or schemes of work, and the suggested temporal learning tasks, vocabulary and use of resources in other units are, Hodkinson claims, vague and inconsistent. He finds that the use of such terms as 'a long time ago' is confusing. His research found that children's understanding of such a phrase varies from a few years ago to hundreds, thousands or billions of years ago.

So what conclusions can we draw? We need to give more thought to teaching within a chronological framework and hope that this will help children make sense of and remember what they learn? Possibly, but not at the expense of other aspects of historical enquiries or we shall be back to lists of dates. We need to think how to develop a chronological framework based on our own experience in the absence of a consistent National Curriculum and with still rudimentary research. And finally, we must not get hooked on chronology at the expense of other aspects of historical enquiry.

Causes and effects of changes over time

Bage (1999) explores ways in which narrative interpretations of the past can be used to develop historical understanding. He says that children need to criticise, not copy stories. He suggests for example that the story teller plans to suspend the story at points, in order to discuss motives and the causes and effects of decisions and to discuss moral issues; this makes the story motivating, forward looking and meaningful.

The CHATA project (ongoing) has investigated the development of children's understanding of causes and effects in detail. For example, Lee (Lee et al. 2000) shows how children's ideas about explanation in history depend on their understanding of the situation the person was in, on knowledge and on 'historical imagination'. People in the past appeared to do weird things and it is not part of everyday understanding to assume that these made sense. All the 320 children in this study, aged between seven and fourteen, were able to offer rational explanations of why the Roman Emperor Claudius invaded Britain. There was progression in their explanations from simply because 'he wanted to get the gold and tin' at Year 3, to a recognition of his public role as emperor at Year 6: 'He wanted more people to like him', 'He wanted to take over other countries and the world', 'to be a better Emperor than Julius Caesar'. In Year 3 nothing puzzled the children about Claudius's motives, whereas at Year 6 some children argued that he could, for example, have 'stayed at home and had a better life'. By Year 7 pupils were beginning to see that his motives were not confined to personal wants or on what to do as emperor, but also considered the situation he was in: 'He was at peace and had spare soldiers; not all British tribes were friendly to the Romans.'

Putting it all together

Although the three strands of historical enquiry have been discussed in turn, they are, of course, not discrete. Nevertheless, one strand may be the focus of a particular enquiry. The following chapters consider how the history curriculum may be put into practice through whole-school planning (pages 41–69), medium-term planning (pages 71, 137–141, 147–57 and 159–63) and lesson planning (page 170) in imaginative and enjoyable ways.

References

Bage, G. (1999) *Narrative Matters: teaching and learning history through story*. London: Falmer.

Booth, M.B. (1994) 'Cognition in history', *Educational Psychologist*, **29** (2), 61–9.

CHATA Project (Concepts of History and Teaching Approaches at Key Stages 2 and 3) (ongoing), Lee, P., Dickinson, A. and Ashby, R. ESRC funded project, Institute of Education, London University.

Hallam, R.N. (1975) 'A Study of the Effects of Teaching Method on the Growth of Logical Thought, with special reference to the teaching of history', unpub. PhD thesis, University of Leeds.

Hodkinson, A. (2003a) 'History howlers: amusing anecdotes or symptoms of the difficulties children have in the retention of historical knowledge. Some observations based on recent research', *Research in Education*, **70**, 21–36.

Hodkinson, A. (2003b) 'National Curriculum and temporal vocabulary: the use of subjective time phrases within the National Curriculum for History and its Schemes of Work: effective provision or a wasted opportunity?' *Education 3–13*, **31** (3), 28–34.

Hodkinson, A. (2004) 'The Social Context and the Assimilation of Historical Concepts: an indicator of academic performance or an unreliable metric?' *Research in Education*, **71**, 50–66.

Lee, P., Dickinson, A. and Ashby, R. (2000) '"Just Another Emperor": understanding action in the past', *International Journal of Educational Research*, **27** (3), 233–44.

Lodwick A.R. (1958) 'An investigation of the question of whether the inferences children draw in learning history correspond to the stages of mental development that Piaget postulated', unpub. MA, University of Birmingham.

Peel, E.A. (1967) 'Some problems in the psychology of history teaching', in W.H. Burston and D. Thompson (eds) *Studies in the Nature and Teaching of History*. London: Routledge and Kegan Paul.

Piaget, J. (1956) *A Child's Conception of Time*. London: Routledge.

Rees, R. (1976) 'Teaching strategies for the advancement and development of thinking skills in history', unpub. MPhil thesis, University of London.

Thornton, S.J. and Vukelich, R. (1988) 'The effects of children's understanding of time concepts on historical understanding', *Theory and Research in Social Education*, **16** (1): 69–82.

Vygotsky, L.S. (1962) *Thought and Language*. London: Wiley.

Planning and assessment

5

Excellent teaching, enjoyable learning

OUTSTANDING SCHOOLS, WE ARE told, are characterised by high standards in literacy and numeracy and a broad, rich and balanced curriculum. They offer a rich, exciting programme of learning across the full curriculum. They have a distinct identity and ethos and work in close partnership with parents and the community (QCA 2003a: 9–10) and network between schools (p. 71). In order to achieve this, schools are encouraged to take ownership of the curriculum, to shape it and make it their own through cross-curricular links. They can decide which aspects of a subject to empha- sise (p. 17), managing time in innovative ways. Apparently rich creative experiences across the curriculum have been found to raise standards of numeracy and literacy! The use of support staff will free you to plan collaboratively with your colleagues; plans can take any format as long as they have clear learning and assessment oppor- tunities and will be judged by their impact on teaching and learning. There is fre- quent mention of 'creativity'. Blow me down! We consider each of these dimensions in this and the following chapter.

There are a few difficulties, of course. *Excellence and Enjoyment* talks about 'high standards across the full curriculum' (p. 11) and says that support consultants' work will include 'support for the foundation subjects' (p. 30). However, *Excellence and Enjoyment* mentions art, music and sport (p. 9) but nowhere does it refer to history (or geography). Just a slip of the Secretary's brain, no doubt. But if we, as primary school teachers, are serious about a broad, rich curriculum it is up to us to use this opportunity to bring back the excellent work in history which developed after the introduction of the National Curriculum, before it was marginalised to the point of extinction by the impact of the National Literacy Strategy (DfEE 1998) and the National Numeracy Strategy (DfEE 1999a) and the decision that history was not a required part of Initial Teacher Training.

I have no doubt about the important contribution of the National Curriculum in identifying the thinking processes of historical enquiry and the ways in which they interact with content, or with the rigorous analysis of what is involved in develop- ing all the dimensions of literacy and numeracy objectives, in increasingly complex ways. And I am sure that teachers are now sufficiently familiar with both the curriculum and the strategies, firstly to make meaningful connections between subjects and to plan links which recognise the discrete thinking processes of each subject and, secondly, to teach the literacy framework objectives (and sometimes the numeracy objectives) through other subjects. Some teachers may feel unconfident about their subject knowledge in history, as teachers did when the National Curriculum for History was introduced, but enthusiasm and learning with the children (and colleagues) is more important and there are many sources of information available to help, as shown at the end of Chapter 1.

The Futures Programme

The QCA *Futures Programme: Meeting the Challenge* (2005) encouragingly states that, 'Education only flourishes if it successfully adapts to the demands and needs of the time.' It identifies five forces for change and aims to enquire how education should respond to them.

1   How should we respond to changes in society by developing a curriculum that promotes skills and knowledge needed for life?

2   What will a technology rich curriculum be like?

3   What are the implications of our understanding about multidimensional intelligence and the importance of emotional well-being in learning for the way we organise the curriculum?

4   How can we ensure national entitlement yet use the voice of the learner to shape an evolving curriculum?

5   How might we prepare young people to recognise their rights and responsibilities in a global society?

We need to be articulate about the potential contribution of history to these aims. In January 2005 I was invited by the QCA to a summit (!) at the Cumberland Hotel (an inspiring choice with its vast foyer, containing modern art works, futuristic furniture and virtual running water which constantly changes colour). We worked in subject groups to make recommendations. The key recommendations of the history group were:

■   to convince those outside the subject community of the relevance of history teaching and learning;

■   to negotiate with pupils historical enquiries relevant to them;

■   to require all schools to devise a rationale for their approach to history, showing its contribution to pupils' present and future enjoyment and well-being;

■   to put people into the curriculum, what they have done, why, and with what consequences, which contributes to emotional literacy and sense of self;

- to respond, for example, to the *Every Child Matters* agenda (DfES 2003) recognising the contribution of history to understanding identity and diversity, and to relate to other people and cultures;

- to clearly state history's contribution to democracy, through offering different versions of the past, understanding that there may be many and more than one answer to a question;

- to look at the relationship of history to other subjects and dimensions.

The recommendations conclude that such an agenda needs a cultural shift, in which teachers have high self-esteem, trust their own judgements, know that they are trusted by others, are enthusiastic, flexible, adaptable and see history within the bigger picture.

Responding to the challenge

Really we are being given the freedom and responsibility to build on what we already do. The literacy objectives were always intended to be applied across the curriculum. Until the curriculum became overloaded it was assumed that there would be planned links between subjects. All of the challenges above are already embedded in the revised curriculum (DfEE 1999b). The phrases are all familiar. So let us look at each of the challenges and see how they can be integrated into a holistic, and meaningful, broad and balanced curriculum. The important thing is working collaboratively with colleagues, sharing ideas, supporting and leading where appropriate and resolving the difficulties which will inevitably arise.

Planning for history within the curriculum

A shared rationale for history

Everyone in the school needs to discuss this, then support the agreed rationale. It might succinctly encapsulate all of the challenges above, which are explored in this and the following chapters. They may discuss the following ideas:

- The content of history covers all aspects of societies in the past, in different parts of the world (music, art, architecture, science, sport, literature, mathematics, technology), and so makes natural links with other subjects. It contributes to coherent units of learning and contains aspects of everyone's favourite subjects.

- The process of historical enquiry involves making deductions and inferences from sources, listening to the views of others and recognising that two people may be equally correct or that there is no single answer, understanding that there are therefore different versions of the past and that these change over time. This is essential to developing democratic thinking.

- Finding out about the past involves finding out about the history of your culture and other cultures, about the history of the community in which you live and the past of your family. This is important in developing a sense of identity, of where you stand in relation to the past and present world around you.

- History involves trying to understand attitudes and values of people in the past, which may be different from yours; it helps you to try to be tolerant to others and understand yourself.

- History is about all social groups and about men and women, boys and girls and includes everyone, now and in the past.

- It includes all localities and shows how, now or in the past, they have been important in their unique ways, at national and international levels.

- The strands of historical understanding develop at different rates and in different contexts and there are so many variables that everyone can participate in the process, irrespective of ability levels.

This is not a comprehensive list. You may also like to personalise and emphasise some of the points for the children in your school and for the specific industries, buildings, events and famous people of your locality.

Time management

Blocks of time

After a time when head teachers had to itemise each minute of the school day, account for the time spent on each subject and ensure that this tallied with the required hours – and later were expected to insert the literacy and numeracy hours – responsibility for managing the timetable is, to say the least, welcome. This makes it possible to prepare for and follow up a visit over a block of time; it allows children to get really involved, to start planning their own learning as activities evolve and ideas occur, and to conclude with a performance, an exhibition, books or videos which makes their learning meaningful. This makes it possible to assess what has been achieved and to share it with an audience.

I am thinking, for example, of a visit to Kendal Castle in a four-day history and literacy topic, which led to the reconstruction of a medieval banquet (pages 75–80), or of my visits with my Year 4 class to both a local and a 'further afield' site, linked to each of four history units: the Stone Ages, the Iron Age, the Romans and the Saxons (page 188); each unit was cross-curricular and lasted four weeks.

Flexibility

I remember extending time planned when events went in unexpected directions, initiated by the children but still meeting my planned learning objectives. For example, after visiting the British Museum as part of a topic on Ancient Greece one group of Year 5/6 children who had finished their work asked if they could organise a 'dig' on a waste patch of the school grounds. This led to a carefully measured archaeological excavation, which revealed numerous finds (e.g. a piece of an old beer jug, some coins, an old shoe . . .). These were cleaned, measured and drawn, put in probable sequence of age, and displayed with labels suggesting their possible use. (Yes, they should have had tetanus jabs first but fortunately nobody needed one.) Children went on to interview a classroom support teacher who had lived in the area before the school was built and visited the library to find out more. These were entirely their own ideas, mostly carried out at lunch time, but they gave me a clear idea of what they understood about how sources are found and interpreted and communicated. There were so many examples of learning 'outside the box'.

History, personal and social education, parents, the community

In groups, throughout a topic, children made a lunch using receipts from the historical period studied, with the help of a parent. The Iron Age lunch, based on the evidence that they had wild root vegetables and soay sheep, was a mutton stew. Guests were invited to share lunch by each group: the school nurse, the local policeman, a librarian, a school governor. This required social skills, language skills, responsibility – especially when it came to washing up.

Blurring the home/school boundaries

One group set up a travel agency complete with brochures, posters, booking forms, time changes, as part of a cross-curricular project on Ancient and Modern Greece. A lot of the language, mathematics and numeracy was initiated in class lessons, but continued and developed at home and in lunch hours. It is when the boundary between school and home blurs, initiated by the children, that you have evidence for your self-evaluation that they are enjoying their work! I could go on and on!

History and writing

When I showed some recent secondary postgraduate students some of the written work, in a variety of genres and for a range of purposes, which emerged through history topics from this time, they said they had never seen writing of such quality anywhere. These were not extraordinary children, so what can we infer? Enjoyment results in high standards. Amazing! It may be possible to work with a visiting historical story writer, an archaeologist or a real historian on a local project. Of course you cannot devote the entire timetable to visits and performances but some days of blocked time are important.

History and other subjects

Other ways of blocking time might be having two or three linked subjects taught as part of a theme for half a term, then another group the following half term, in rotation, or having whole school weeks given over occasionally to, for example, the arts, the humanities, literature, conservation, sports.

A real danger with the restructuring agenda, however, is that foundation subjects will still be seen as something that classroom support staff can take on in order to allow teachers to spend most of their teaching time on numeracy and literacy. If we refer back to our rationale for the importance of history education, this is not a good solution to time management.

Selecting and sequencing history study units

An eye to the future

There are some recognised problems with the present history curriculum, which will be revised again by 2008. Nichol and Guyver (2005) see these as politicians' concerns with, obsessions, omissions, and narrative problems with British and British imperial history. The Tudor period is isolated between the Vikings and the Victorians; the gaps are intended to be filled in at Key Stage 3. This structure has led to a lack of coherence in pupils' appreciation of the development of Britain into a civic and democratic society which has had a significant impact on the rest of the world. Clearly the current curriculum continues for another two years but it may be a good idea to bear in mind and work towards possible changes. Nichol and Guyver suggest possible new approaches; current teaching may begin to build these into long-term planning. Firstly, they suggest lack of coherence may be addressed through teaching units in chronological sequence. Secondly, they suggest that the variety of perspectives in history referred to in Chapter 3 can be encompassed by mapping four substantive concepts onto four themes. (This is an approach I recommended to QCA years ago but their response then was that it is up to teachers to make these adjustments.) So you could start thinking about focusing one unit on democratic government and human rights (maybe Britain since 1930), one on social, technological and economic history, everyday life, industry, inventions and trade (perhaps the Victorians), one unit linking with relationships with the wider world (this could be any of the British units). A fourth focus could be on diversity and inclusion, different inheritances and their impact on a locality. Nichol and Guyver also suggest that different approaches to history, discussed in Chapter 1, may be modelled by one unit focusing on learning through biography (perhaps the life of Henry VIII and/or Queen Elizabeth I) while another unit may be studied from the perspective of a local historian. The processes of historical enquiry would, of course, remain integral to teaching and learning. *Excellence and Enjoyment* (QCA 2003a) already encourages us to develop innovative approaches and to move between depth and breadth studies, and in response to the *Every Child Matters* (DfES 2003) and the inclusion agenda we also need to find ways of making history relevant to every child. Now that we are allowed, teachers should seize the initiative in response to these bland claims, find the energy to take the bull by the horns, and make them a reality in advance of 2008 in order to receive new guidance with professional and informed criticism.

Deciding which aspects of a unit to focus on

Foundation Stage

The *Curriculum Guidance for the Foundation Stage* (QCA 2000a) is organised into Areas of Learning, with learning goals in each area. Only one learning goal, which is in the area of Knowledge and Understanding of the World, is specifically about the past: 'Find out about past and present events in their own lives and in those of their families and other people they know' (p. 94). However, goals in the other areas of learning are involved in the process of doing this. Other goals introduce children to the past in other ways, through stories, rhymes, role play. Some goals can be applied to the past, for example finding out how old artefacts were used and made. The practitioner's role is to plan meaningful links between the areas of learning. Table 5.1 shows which Early Learning Goals can link with themes exploring past times.

The REPEY project (Siraj-Blatchford *et al.* 2002) found that the most effective early years settings provided teacher-initiated group work, balanced with an open environment in which adults supported children's learning. In good and excellent settings equal numbers of activities were initiated by adults and by children,

TABLE 5.1   Areas of Learning and Early Learning Goals particularly relevant to finding out about the past

Examples of children's talk about time	*Curriculum Guidance for the Foundation Stage* (QCA 2000a) Foundation Stage Profile (QCA 2003b)
Children retell and talk about their own and their family stories, often linked to photographs, birthday cards etc., using the language of time (yesterday, last summer, when I'm five). They can relate their own experiences to stories about growth and change.	QCA 2000a: 94–5 QCA 2003b: 43, 46
They learn to put events in order, ask questions and clarify their thinking (Why? How? Where? When?).	QCA 2000a: 58, 62, 74 QCA 2003b: 21, 45
Children enjoy reading traditional rhymes and stories set in the distant past and learn about sequences of events, motives, causes and effects.	QCA 2000a: 74 QCA 2003b: 20, 23, 27, 28
Children recreate fairy stories, folk tales, stories set in the past through imaginative play.	QCA 2000a: 25, 58, 62, 63 QCA 2003b: 20

suggesting that effective settings encourage children to initiate activities modelled by staff. Children's cognitive outcomes appeared to be directly related to the quantity of adult/teacher planning. Good curriculum knowledge, knowing the questions to ask and the key skills and concepts of a subject were as essential as an understanding of child development.

Children need to have a sense of ownership of their environment. This depends on planning a rich variety of themes, play settings and experiences. Two teachers participating in a project to reflect on and develop their practice (Bennett *et al.* 1997) assessed each of the National Curriculum subjects through play. They integrated play and teacher-directed activities through a topic approach, changing the topic every half term. The children were involved in the decisions. The teachers observed links between what the children were doing in play and what they were doing with another adult. They were aiming for a curriculum model in which adults' observations inform both child- and teacher-initiated activities.

Themes that teachers might introduce include, 'When I was a baby', stories about growth and change in fictional families, oral history fairy stories and folk tales extended as play. Fairy stories and folk tales may not be literally true but they contain old features (coaches and horses, windmills, castles). They are the product of oral history and versions change with retelling. They are about a variety of types of people still to be found today (rich and poor, wicked and good, clever and stupid), and they involve sequence, cause and effect, motive (see Chapter 7). There are lots of opportunities here for meaningful, shared dialogue between children and adults, and for adults to introduce ideas that children can choose to develop or which children might introduce within the theme and adults take up and help them develop.

Stories and family history are loose themes which can be developed, in which children have ownership and which can involve, in embryonic ways, all the aspects of historical enquiry. Table 5.2 shows how selected Early Learning Goals link to the National Curriculum Programme of Study for Key Stage 1; they reveal underlying continuity. Case studies showing how teachers have planned and carried out activities to help nursery children find out about past times can be found in Seward and Boertien (2004), which focuses on personal histories with very socially disadvantaged children, in Robson (2004) on castles and in Moore (2004) on ancient history. More case studies and the theoretical background to 'history' at the Foundation Stage can be found in Cooper (2002).

Key Stage 1

Firstly, although the different strands of historical enquiry interact, it is not necessary to cover all aspects of the knowledge, skills and understanding of the Programme of Study for History in the same topic. Chronological understanding seems particularly relevant in finding out about changes in children's own lives and

TABLE 5.2 Continuity in historical thinking from Early Learning Goals and Areas of Learning (QCA 2000) to National Curriculum for History Year 2 (DfEE 1999b)

ELG CLL: p. 52	Retell narratives; sequence events
NC:1a	Place events and objects in chronological order
ELG CLL: pp. 52, 54	Extend vocabulary
NC: 1b	Use common words relating to the passing of time
ELG CLL: p. 50, KUW: p. 88	Listen to stories, rhymes, songs: ask why things happen
NC: 2a	Recognise why people did things, why things happened
ELG KUW: p. 88	Look at similarities and differences
NC: 2b	Identify differences between ways of life at different times
ELG CCL: p. 58, PSE: p. 42, DD: p. 104	Recreate roles, experiences; understand people have different needs, culture, beliefs
NC: 3	Identify different ways in which the past is remembered
ELG KUW: p. 58	Investigate objects and materials
NC: 4a	Find out about the past from a range of sources
ELG KUW: p. 58	Ask and answer questions: why things happen; how they work
NC: 4b	Ask and answer questions about the past
ELG KUW: p. 90	Build and construct
CLL: p. 58	Recreate roles
CLL: p. 52	Retell narratives
CD: p. 124	Use imagination in art, music, dance
NC: 5	Communicate in a variety of ways
ELG KUW: p. 94	Find out about past and present events in own lives/families
NC: 6a	Changes in own lives, lives of families
ELG KUW: p. 96	Find out about the environment
NC: 6b	Ways of life in the distant past
NC: 6a	Significant people and events

Key
ELG Early Learning Goals (QCA 2000)
Areas of Learning (QCA 2000)
CLL Communication, Language and Literacy (44–67)
KUW Knowledge and Understanding of the World (82–100)
PSE Personal and Social Education (28–43)
CD Creative Development (116–127)
NC National Curriculum Programme of Study at Key Stage 1

those of their families (Pos 6a), and Historical enquiry and Interpretation, to finding out about the more distant past. Perhaps the lives of significant men and women and past events links well to Knowledge and understanding of events, people and changes (Pos 6c).

The ubiquitous Florence Nightingale

Often an ordinary life can illustrate universal themes and throw light on broader aspects of the society of the time. I recently saw a student teacher working with a Year 1 class on Florence Nightingale. Yawn, I thought. Florence again! But this turned out to be an enjoyable lesson. I was amazed that, reviewing what they had learned in the previous lesson, the children announced the dates of her birth and death and of the Crimean war, 'a long war – two years'. I was more surprised when they volunteered the countries on opposing sides and traced Florence's journey on the map on the electronic whiteboard. Oh dear – facts, facts, I thought. Then the student showed them a drawing of Florence in the hospital at Scutari. The children were able to make a number of deductions, and also inferences about how the people in the drawing may have thought and felt. Then the student showed them, using the board, how they were going to make and dress a 'Florence doll', with all her layers of clothing. This involved discussion of class, dress and the role of women. Then they compared Florence's dress with that of a picture of a nurse today. This led to talk about their own hospital experiences and comparing then and now and reasons for changes. While they concentrated on cutting out Florence's underwear (without chopping off the tabs for attaching each garment) the conversation was interesting.

> 'Why do you think she wore corsets?'
>
> 'Probably to look thin; to look beautiful.'
>
> 'Do you think she was fat, then?'
>
> 'No they all did – the rich ones.'
>
> 'What colour should her dress be?'
>
> 'We don't know; they only had black and white drawings.'

This lesson really made me realise how much historical thinking (and lots of laughter, e.g. at the stupidity of the student when he suggested Chelsea colours for her drawers) could take place on a Friday afternoon, using very simple resources.

Beyond Miss Nightingale

How are you going to decide which areas of study to focus on other than Florence? You may consider the resources from the distant past in the locality, which may be close enough for young children to visit: a castle or a church or an archaeological site. You may have links with a resource through parents or the community, a skilled worker from an old industry, an amateur dramatic group who could lend or show costumes and do a bit of hot seating. A Darby and Joan club could maybe teach children old dances and games as well as be willing interviewees, in which case you may spend a lot of time on (Pos 6a) changes in living memory. You may have children whose families are of other cultural heritages who could help select and find out about 'significant men and women' or past events from the wider world (Pos 6c, d). Taking a leaf from the Foundation Stage you may be flexible enough to see where and for how long the children and their resources take the enquiry. You may discuss your options with parents, or the local history or photographic society or, for example, the Cumbrian Wrestlers club! I suggest you don't look at the QCA schemes until you have considered all these options. The schemes might help you to structure your planning, in new contexts, but for goodness sake look at other possibilities, use your local and human resources, and you and the children can ENJOY it!

Key Stage 2

How might you decide what to do in depth at Key Stage 2? This emphasis on depth is important because real enquiry takes time and often does not lead in a straight line from 'A' to 'B'. All that you need to bear in mind in managing an enquiry is that children need to be aware of where the period they are studying fits into a broad chronological framework, to use a variety of historical sources, apart from books, in order to find out about the past, and to help children collate their findings into some form of account: a display, a drama or a video for example. The possibilities are vast. So what are some of the ways you could initiate an in-depth enquiry with the children which all of them will enjoy?

Starting with the children

Southbank International School in Hampstead uses the International Baccalaureate Organisation's Primary Years Programme. This is based on a pupil profile setting out characteristics schools wish to develop and make children aware of in themselves: enquirers, thinkers, communicators, risk-takers, knowledgeable, principled, caring, well-balanced and reflective. Pupils 3–12 play a big role in determining what and how they learn. 'You find out what they know and what they want to learn, then you can shape your unit; it's a big leap of faith sometimes,' the programme co-ordinator said. 'The National Curriculum isn't looking at the bigger picture. It compartmentalises everything.' For a Year 5 unit on the Saxons, for example, children's questions are posted on a bulletin board (as in the Kendal Castle Key Stage 1 visit on page 75). What animals did they have? How did they go to the toilet? If they were wounded what did they do? Did the children go to school? From this starting point the teacher spends some time reflecting with the class on how to answer these questions, using mainly primary sources, and what further questions may arise.

Another way of starting with children might be Tony Robinson's, *The Worst Children's Jobs in History* (Robinson 2005). As Robinson says, 'All children from 5 to 11 can enjoy these stories, those who like reading stories and those who'll just have a laugh at the wee and poo.' The book covers children's jobs throughout time and contains a selection of original primary material for the 'gifted and talented' historian. It could lead on to thinking about issues such as child labour, and give children some sense of the concept of why we are as we are and what has shaped and moulded us.

Starting with the locality

Local events, industries, people

In any period this may be a meaningful way in. Work with the local history library to find out if there were significant local events during this period; these may reflect national events. Was there a time of particular change? Why? Or was there a local industry which maybe flourished and later declined? Why? What was its impact on the community? On the west coast of Cumbria, for example, children took an enormous pride in finding out about the heyday of the copper industry and published a book about it. What was going on at a particular time in a farming community?

Local dialect

Local dialect could also be an interesting starting point. Correct grammar is important but tracing the origins of your own dialect can be fascinating. Melvyn Bragg (2003) has traced the origins of the buried words which he is proud to claim as his Cumbrian dialect: 'Aah's gaan yem.' Gaan was an Anglo Saxon word, to go, and was known to the Vikings; yem means home in Scandinavia, heim in Old Norse. As for 'laik in t beck'; leika is Old Norse for play and bekkr for stream, still beck in Cumbria. He used Anglo Saxon and Celtic words, crag, tor, pen, and some Romany from the annual gypsy fair, which harks back to an Indian dialect of Sanskrit, gadji for man and parnee for rain. One Cumbrian school started looking for Viking words in their own speech, then went on to a place-name study as a beginning of a unit on the Vikings.

Local Heritage site

Pat Lewis, a teacher in Blaenavon in South Wales, makes clear to her pupils that their town has the same historical status as the pyramids or the Great Wall of China (Saunders 2004). Blaenavon is a Heritage site recognised for the dynamic part it played in the world's first Industrial Revolution, the powerhouse of the British Empire. It had coal, iron ore, quarries, furnaces and a primitive railway system. 'It's the part they and their families have played and are playing that makes it so special,' she said. The children have family histories, stories, photographs and artefacts. Following a cross-curricular project which included history and science (exploring types of forces and energy), art (working with an artist to produce costumes, flats for the school play and paintings of the locality), music (taking part in the Eisteddfod), Citizenship (exploring regeneration plans) and language of different genres, children took part in a *son et lumière* held through the town, playing the parts of nineteenth-century children. To prepare for the event children invited historians and archaeologists into the school to help them research the history of iron and its impact on the Industrial Revolution. Useful resources about the Blaenavon iron and coal industries can be found at www.newportsouthwales.net/revolution.

Local Remembrance Day

Keyworth School in Kennington had a Reminiscence Day attended by dozens of parents and elderly relatives. After researching the bombing and rebuilding of Kennington they have designed a Second World War garden with an Anderson air-raid shelter and an allotment where they grew vegetables for the recipes their guest, Marguerite Patten, the wartime ministry of food advisor, helped them prepare. This was a National Lottery Funded Heritage Initiative.

After school club: local military history

The 43 members of the Stephenson Way Primary School After School Club in County Durham won an Our History My Heritage English Heritage competition for restaging and video-recording an attack on the Durham Light Infantry, on Primrose Bridge, during the Allied Invasion of Sicily in 1943 (Jones 2002). They hit on the topic after a visit to the Durham Light Infantry Museum. They extended their research by reading, interviewing families and getting first-hand accounts of war from veterans of the Normandy landings and the Gulf War. Adults, including a teacher, a parent and the chair of governors, also got into role and accepted the leadership of the pupil in charge. They also worked across the age range and with some pupils from the local secondary school. Watching the video helped them to see how relationships different from those in the classroom fitted together.

Working with a local museum and the community

Lancaster City Museum's projects of, for example, the Vikings bring together the museum exhibitions, historical re-enactments and visits to a specially created longhouse. These involve local schools. The school visits are preceded by a special Viking weekend, to which people of all ages are invited, in order to take education into the community. After listening to one gory tale one grandmother said, 'That's the best story anyone has told me since I was a tiddler!'

Cross-curricular local projects

Goetre Infants' School focuses on local history (Brooks 2004). In an area where children do not get off their estate much it is considered important to take them out and let them enjoy what is out there. Local history is the focus of the curriculum and of key skills development. Each year the Year 2 teacher, Alison Hocking, picks a person, a place or an era and creates lesson ideas that will stimulate work for several weeks. 'The history part is easy,' she says, but you become adept at finding innovative and relevant ways to cover all areas of the curriculum.

The National Grid for Learning local history trail is a free on-line event to help children and adults use the internet to uncover people, places and events that have made their locality what it is today (www.ngfl.gov.uk/localhistory).

History for different interests

Since history involves every aspect of life in the past we can find out a lot about a particular period from a chosen theme. Individuals or groups of children can select their own theme to research the same questions – for example, how did this change over the period? What were the causes and effects of the changes? – then combine their enquiries to draw overarching conclusions. Tracing changes in popular music and songs from 1930 will involve finding out about changes in technology, in society (e.g. the impact of the Second World War), finding out where new styles (e.g. jazz) came from and why, and making inferences about changing values and ways of life. Similarly an interest in clothes might lead to an interest in changes in dress. Here Joanne and her friend in Year 3 are discussing a wedding photograph taken during the war: 'They didn't have much money in the war. They couldn't have new dresses. She's wearing a normal dress like you'd wear to a party. She's got a small bunch of flowers and no veil. They had short dresses so they could run down the shelters.'

Other themes might be cars or planes. Such themes reflect wide-ranging social changes and children make connections about how they interact, and contribute to broad patterns of change, for example, before, during and after the war.

Flexibility lets children do things 'their way'

Here is an exemplary tale which illustrates how children, given the flexibility, will turn a teacher's plans into something which actually interests them – and still meet the teacher's objectives. I was an advisory teacher doing a local study with a Year 6 class based on four buildings in the locality, one of which was the church. 'What do we have to do this for?' two recalcitrant boys dragging along at the end of the line asked, as we trudged through the rain. 'I thought you might like to make a model,' I replied brightly. 'Nah.' Yet a few weeks later they had created a wonderful model of the church, with an indicator board which lit up and explained different parts of the church and its history, 'stained glass' windows which could be illuminated from inside, accompanied by a tape recording explaining the images and church music which played. What makes such activities part of an historical enquiry is the questions we ask – what do they tell us about the people who made and used them? – and seeking other evidence, perhaps from books, which may extend or verify our inferences.

Starting with the family

'To forget one's ancestors is to be a brook without a source, a tree without a root.'

Old Chinese proverb

Given the internet resources now available, researching family history has become very popular amongst adults and might become a way into a history topic for all the family. A useful website for young people is www.ffhs.org.uk/general/youngpeople.htm.

Tania Braga and Maria Auxiliadora Schmidt (Schmidt and Garcia 2004) in an ambitious experiment, Teaching History Based on Documents and the Brazilian Family, helped a primary school to write the history of their own town, using maps, family histories and photographs, which was published as a hardback book (Schmidt and Garcia 2003).

History that encompasses different cultures

Sensitive issues need to be dealt with in an atmosphere of trust by sensitive teachers. A democratic model needs to be set up where everyone is free to speak, subject to an understood code of conduct. Draw out similarities and differences slowly, as you go, and make sure that the lessons are structured and grounded in the curriculum. Evaluate the effectiveness of the cultural diversity aspect by asking children to reflect on changes in their thinking.

Probably because of the limited resources available to support non-Anglo-centric dimensions of the history study units they are rarely a subject of in-depth focus. Yet the Programme of Study for History (DfEE 1999b: 105 2b) states that 'pupils should be taught about the social, cultural, religious and ethnic diversity of societies studied, in Britain and the wider world'. 'Pupils should learn about change in their own area and in other parts of the world.' Hilary Claire points out that the Race Relations Amendment Act of 2000 means that 'teachers must pro-actively strive in the curriculum towards inclusion of minority cultures, take responsibility and work to reduce racial tension and prejudice, paying more than lip service to a wider inclusive curriculum which challenges racism and Euro-centrism' (Claire 2002; 2003; 2005).

This means giving every child, and particularly children in mono-cultural environments, a sense of their own identity and worth, tolerance of diversity, and understanding of local, national and global connections. Children need to learn about their own, and other children's, heritage, about life in the places their families lived before, and why families move around.

Citizenship issues and history

Claire (2005) says that through history children can consider notions of 'progress' and how progressive measures sometimes have a downside, learn about how society can be changed and consider the historical instances of violent and non-violent resistance to change. She suggests that, in history, children can consider how earlier societies and different civilisations took responsibility for the sick, the elderly, the unemployed and the less privileged. In history children can deal with sensitive issues at one remove before moving into a contemporary perspective. Older children can debate or role-play different perspectives.

Citizenship dimensions

Citizenship, local, national and global, is not an 'add on'. It should permeate everything we think and do. It has been found that this dimension is best taught in primary schools where the curriculum is integrated. Developing an awareness of citizenship requires us to have knowledge and understanding of social responsibility, social justice, peace and conflict and respect for diversity. It involves skills of critical thinking, the ability to argue effectively, to challenge injustice, and values which include empathy, a sense of self-esteem and identity, respecting people and things (Oxfam 1997). It is not difficult to identify ways in which to link history with discussing citizenship issues and it may be easier to discuss issues which remain today, distanced by time.

Questions for discussion

Discussion can relate to any Key Stage 2 historical period, particularly the Tudors (protests at the dissolution of the monasteries, by Thomas More, or Catholic protests in Elizabethan England), the Victorians (Victorian protests about water supplies in the big cities, for example) and Britain since 1930 (the Jarrow March and similar protests in the 1930s).

At Quarry Bank cotton mill in Cheshire the National Trust staff, in role as mill owner or worker, talk about how their lives have been changed by the Industrial Revolution. Then the pupils are divided into groups: handloom weavers and spinners, mill workers and mill owners. They explore issues such as the mill owner whose profits are falling following a slump in business. Does he lower wages or sack workers? What do the weavers and spinners do, threatened by the new water technology? Do they sell up and go to the workhouse, apply for a job at the new mill or protest and break up the machinery? If they do the last, what will happen? With no police force the army will come in as at Peterloo and they may be killed. The discussion involves questions of social responsibility, political, spiritual, moral and cultural values, empathy, debate and conflict resolution.

In Southwell Union Workhouse, recently bought by the National Trust, social change, human rights and responsibilities, employer and employee rights, conflict resolution and moral and social dilemmas are debated by the children in role as workhouse inmates. In prioritising wants and needs they need to consider where to place freedom of expression or freedom to practise their own religion. They debate issues such as child labour, adopting the role of mill owners, pauper children and social reformers. The exercise is illustrated with case studies, statistics and contemporary photographs.

Sometimes it is easier to approach issues through historical fiction. There are several series which do this. The Short History series (www.theshortbookco.com/kidsbooks.asp) has such titles as *Anne Boleyn,* and *Ada Lovelace, the computer wizard of Victorian England.* Sparks series (www.wattspub.co.uk) has *Escape from Germany, Sid's War* and *Bodies for Sale.* Coming Alive series (www.evansbooks.co.uk) has *Dear Mum, I Miss You, What if the Bomb Goes off?* and *Princess Elizabeth Are You a Traitor?* My Stories series (www.scholastic.co.uk/zone) offers *Mill Girl* and *Battle of Britain.* Survivor Series (www.hodderheadline.co.uk) offers *Everything to Live For,* about Northern Ireland and *Only a Matter of Time,* about Kosovo. Finally, Flashback Series (www.acblack.com) has *Gunner's Boy* and *A Slip on Time.*

Claire suggests some significant events which could be explored through enquiries, concept maps, role play, letter and speech writing. Would you, without hindsight, have voted for Attlee's untried Labour government in 1945? How were the campaigns of Gandhi conducted? What might it have been like to be a child on the Kindertransport? (Britain since 1930). How did people work for the emancipation of slaves in the nineteenth century. What of the reformers who tackled the conditions of child workers such as Annie Besant and the match girls' strike in 1888? What might it have been like to be born into a poor Irish family in the 1840s? (Victorian Britain). What might it have been like to be a slave taken by the Romans (the Romans in Britain), a Mexican child in Tenochtitlán when the Spanish came (the Aztecs). Would you have hidden a Catholic priest? How do Indian galleries in the Victoria and Albert Museum illustrate the rich cultural influences of India on Elizabethan England, in clothes, buildings and garden design? (Britain and the wider world in Tudor times). What might it have been like to be a Roman soldier invading Britain? (most of them came from the Middle East, as evidenced by artefacts in the Museum of London, the British Museum and the Temple of Mithras on Hadrian's Wall) (Roman Britain). The Assyria and Mesopotamia study units could extend these links with the Middle East. Examples of such ideas incorporated into Claire's case studies can be found on www.citzed.info.

Other perspectives

The struggle to succeed has faced each generation of immigrants: Ancient Britains from Central Europe (40,000 BC), Celts (7000 BC), Romans (AD 43), the Norsemen, the Normans, the two thousand Black people living and working in Elizabethan London, seventeenth-century Huguenots, nineteenth-century Irish, Russians and Jews. Perhaps we can help to make the process of assimilation easier by teaching children about their past. Penelope Harnett (page 29) describes interesting approaches to cultural diversity based on the Museum of Bristol.

Insider/outsider?

The Parekh Report into the future of multicultural Britain (2000) has suggested that the position of the Irish in Britain as 'insider/outsiders' is uniquely relevant to the nature of Britain's multicultural society; the experience of eight million citizens of Irish stock has been neglected owing to the myth of homogeneity of white Britain. This can be a particularly useful introduction to cultural diversity where there is not much cultural mix in schools.

Year 3 children can easily relate to the plight of a woman (in role) as an Irish mother during the famine and this understanding can be extrapolated to other areas of famine (O'Sullivan 2003). An Irish dimension to a Tudor study can be cross-curricular at Key Stage 1 or 2, focusing on the female pirate Grace O'Malley, the battle for Ireland, Spencer's poetry on Ireland, and the bards who chronicle Gaelic history then realise that now these foreigners have come something terrible has happened. There is also Irish song and dance.

Marcia Hutchinson, inspired by the stories of her Jamaican mother, produced a photographic exhibition of men and women who left the Caribbean to live in the UK after the Second World War (Brooks 2003). This led to her book, *The Journey*, about ten personal stories of people who settled in West Yorkshire (Hutchinson 1999), and then to *The Journey Learning Resource* (Hutchinson and Tidy 2003) which provides cross-curricular materials (history, geography, literacy, drama, personal social and health education). Hutchinson says that it is intended for all sorts of schools and has been successfully piloted in all-white schools in leafy suburbs. Other resources for giving a voice to an unrepresented section of society are www.100greatblackbritons.com, www.everygeneration.co.uk and an excellent site with general histories and oral histories, http://les.man.ac.uk/rrarchive/trust/documents/Britainsincethe1930s.pdf.

At Wilberforce School Year 2 children worked with Hilary Claire and their teachers, using role play, to discuss three significant Black people: the Black aviator Bessie Coleman, Ruby Bridges, who went to an integrated school during the American civil rights movement, and Frederick Douglass, a slave who escaped to become an important figure in the abolition movement (Ward 2002). The older children tackled issues such as racism with help from visitors who talked about their own childhoods. One arrived in Britain from the Caribbean in the 1950s and the other was a refugee from Nazi Germany.

Artefacts from other cultures

The Victoria and Albert Museum and the British Museum have artefacts which can be used to illuminate rich cultures and histories: African, Asian, Indian Native American and Islamic (www.britishmuseum.co.uk). It is important to look at modern and historical works in order to avoid misrepresentation or stereotyping. However, art from non-western cultures can extend children's understanding of the purposes of art. But should we have these artefacts in British museums?

Publications for active learning about the Indus Valley at Key Stage 2 and replica artefacts can be found on www.harapa.com/teach and from hec@harapa.com. Resources include cross-curricular activities such as making and testing terracotta wheeled toy carts, board games and a DVD made when Mohenjo-Daro became a world heritage site. Ilona Aronovsky (2003) gives suggestions for teaching the Indus Valley unit.

Gender issues

Pounce (1995) reminds us that it is important to be aware that women are still seriously under-represented in school books and when they do show women the sources are rarely interpreted from a female point of view. Osler (1995) suggests that teachers are careful to acknowledge great women alongside men of the past and also to encourage children to study the experiences of ordinary women. Children should consider why women have been invisible and undervalued and discuss how they are portrayed. The Women's History Network at the Centre for Women's Studies at Lancaster University publishes useful information relating to women's history.

Working with parents

How can we ensure that children's individual interests inform how they choose to undertake a history topic? I used to tell children and their parents what the study unit on the school's long-term plan would be and discuss possibilities of what we could focus on, teaching approaches we could use, what might be particularly interesting to the children and what parents and their community contacts might be able to offer. From this it was possible to frame a group of key questions and possible ways of investigating them. This would feed into an overarching enquiry, a medium-term plan within which smaller studies by individuals and groups could contribute in different ways, concluding with some form of account, display, presentation or drama for parents and others involved. Everyone would understand and monitor the learning objectives of the medium-term plan and how these were broken down into learning objectives for the smaller studies. If the unit was taught over a number of weeks the children and adults could review and modify the medium-term plan weekly. Even if the unit was taught as a block, perhaps preparing for and following up a visit, there were constant instances of children deciding to do things differently. When they continue it at home, as previously said, you know they ARE enjoying it!

I remember one eight-year-old child who had to get herself off to school because her parents were at work, telling me that she had read her 'Beowulf Poem' to the milkman (hem), and another child who had given her grandparents an impressive guided tour of Norwich Cathedral, modelled on a class visit to Canterbury, and a boy who, when told by his mother about a television programme on Maiden Castle that she had watched the previous evening, said, 'But what was the EVIDENCE for that?'

One day which 'bridged the gaps between the generations' was a reconstruction of Breugel's 'Children's Games' (1560) in which 180 children from a small French village, who were in the last year of primary school, with their teachers and their families, recreated the painting in the town square. They walked through the town singing old French songs, rolling hoops, standing on their heads, turning somersaults, riding a hobby horse, playing with stones, sticks and barrels, and at intervals silence fell and they transformed themselves into the living image of the painting. The children had looked closely at the picture, analysed and discussed the symbolism of games as idle pursuits, carried out research on the painting, the artist and his times, learned about the games, compared them with those of today, chosen one of the people in the painting to re-enact, collaborated with the community in rehearsals, prepared costumes and props and worked on aspects of scenery. The day was a great success. Maybe there are paintings, even of your own area, which you could study in the same way as a community endeavour.

Planning for links between history and other subjects

'History has many cunning passages, contrived corridors.'

'Gerontian', T.S. Eliot

English, mathematics and information and communication technology are communication systems which can run through any subject. How they might link to history is considered below. This section considers ways in which links can be made between history and foundation subjects. The selection and sequence of history study units must be a whole-school decision (page 41). The statutory requirement is that during Key Stage 2 pupils should study local history, three of the British history study units, one of the European units and one of the world history units specified. The QCA schemes of work are models of possible ways of planning units, but if used, need to be modified to meet the aims of the *Excellence and Enjoyment* strategy. Since the content of history to be studied, and to a lesser extent of geography, is, despite flexible interpretation, quite precise, it seems reasonable that art and music, science, design and technology and physical education should at times be planned in relation to history units, rather than vice versa. There seem to be three kinds of links.

1 Combined units within a history theme. Activities may be planned with learning objectives from either of the subject areas. For example, at Key Stage 1 the life of a famous person commemorated in a local statue might be explored through history learning objectives and also as part of art unit 1C, What is sculpture? (QCA 2000b).

2 Sequenced units. Units with some related content may be taught discretely, possibly by different teachers with particular expertise, but enhance each other. For example, a local history study could be linked to Britain since 1948. These could be followed or preceded by (QCA 2000b) religious education units 6F, How do people express their faith through the arts, and possibly by What is the

role of the mosque, 6B, and other units on Islam, or by 4D, What religions are represented in our neighbourhoods, or by 4A, How and why do Hindus worship at home and in the Mandir?

3 A unit with a history focus may draw on particular parts of units in other subjects. If the planned link is substantial it can be recorded as covered; otherwise it could be regarded as reinforcement. For example, a Key Stage 1 history study of our locality could draw on design and technology unit 1D, Homes, art unit 2C, Can buildings speak? and geography unit 1, Around our school, the local area (QCA 2000b).

It is demanding, and a team activity, to explore such links but the possibilities of making themes coherent and meaningful are enormous, particularly if you do not stick rigidly to schemes of work, at least in some subjects. But if the National Curriculum Programmes of Study are taken as the starting point, possibilities for coherence are endless. Table 5.3 indicates possible links based on the schemes and the National Curriculum Programmes of Study and their QCA sequence, although

TABLE 5.3 Examples of some possible links between history schemes and schemes for other subjects (QCA 2000b)

History unit	Possible connections to schemes for other subjects
1 How are toys different from those in the past?	Science 1A–D Grouping materials; 4 Physical processes: forces and motion Design and technology 4A, C How mechanisms make things move
2 What were homes like a long time ago? (Changes in my own life, NC 6a)	Design and technology 1D Homes Art and design 2C Can buildings speak? Science 4 Physical processes: electricity, light and dark Art and design 2A Use photographs to explore an event in their lives
3 What were seaside holidays like in the past?	Science 2 Life and living processes Geography 1, 2 What is it like to live in this place? 4 Going to the seaside Art and design 5 Explore range of starting points for practical work using range of materials Music 5D A range of recorded music from different times and cultures PE 7 Games activities
6ABC Why have people invaded and settled in Britain in the past?	Art and design 4C Journeys: Use mixed media to communicate ideas about journeys through signs and symbols; 5C Explore tradition of making vessels and containers Geography 6 Investigating our local area Art and design 1B Investigating materials: weaving, colour, texture Geography 9 Village settlers

(cont'd)

TABLE 5.3   cont'd

History unit	Possible connections to schemes for other subjects
8 What were the differences between the lives of rich and poor in Tudor Times?	Art and design 5C Talking textiles in different times and cultures; 4B What chairs tell us about everyday life; 3B Investigating pattern; 3A How paintings and other images communicate ideas about relationships Music 5A–E Music from different times and cultures Design and technology 5C Food technology
9 What was it like for children living in Victorian Britain?	Art and design 4B Take a seat; 3B Investigating pattern; 3A Investigating relationships in photographs, paintings etc.; 6C A Sense of Place Design and technology 5C Food technology Music 5E Music from different times and cultures Geography 19 How and where do we spend our time? (inferences from maps)
11 How has life in Britain changed since 1948? 12 Who were the Ancient Greeks?	Music 5E Music from other times and cultures Art and Design6C Observations through photography and 2D work 3A Portraying relationships in photographs and paintings, other images
13 How can we find out about the Indus Valley civilisation?	Geography 10 A village in India; 22 A contrasting locality overseas; 24 Passport to the world Art and design 3B Textiles from different times and cultures; 5C Talking textiles
15 What were the effects of Tudor exploration?	Art and design 4C Journeys Design and technology 5C Food technology

they can of course be modified for other age groups. Suggestions for cross-curricular planning which are not based on QCA schemes can be found on pages 48–58, 65.

Integrating core values

Table 5.4 shows a synopsis of the references made to history activities which were seen to contribute to children's social, moral, spiritual and cultural development in the section on history in Ofsted inspection reports. Such activities can be identified in medium-term plans.

Creativity

We are expected to be 'creative and innovative' but what is meant by creativity? According to Arthur Koestler creativity is the defeat of habit by originality. Ralph Caplan sees one of the hallmarks of a creative person as the ability to tolerate

TABLE 5.4 A synopsis of the references made to history activities which will also contribute to the development of pupils' social, moral, spiritual and cultural development. The references were made in the section on History in the Ofsted inspection reports

	Aspects of history being taught	How are the history lessons promoting pupils' SMSC development?	History Pos or Key Elements
SOCIAL	– Older pupils know that they can find out about the past by . . . asking their parents and grandparents. – The school regularly asks older citizens about days gone by. – By the age of 7, pupils know famous people and their contribution to social development. – Recent work on the Second World War involved pupils talking with members of the local community about their wartime experiences.	– School encouraging pupils to relate effectively with others. – Citizenship. – School encouraging pupils to participate in the community.	**Key Element 4** – Finding out about the past through adults talking about their own past. **Key Stage 1** – Area of Study 2 – Pupils should be taught about the lives of different kinds of famous men and women. **Study Unit 3b.** Britain since 1930 – Britons at war.
MORAL	– They knew something of the stories of Grace Darling and Guy Fawkes. – Pupils recognise there are reasons why people in the past acted as they did, e.g. pupils were able to discuss Guy Fawkes and his actions. – A study of the journey of Grace Darling considering the view points involved. – Displays in classrooms include high quality artefact collections which pupils treat with care and respect.	– Providing pupils with opportunity to express moral values.	**Key Stage 1** – Area of Study 2. (As above.) **Key Element 1** – Using artefacts – put in chronological order. **Key Element 4** – Historical enquiry – use artefacts to find out about aspects of the past.

(cont'd)

TABLE 5.4 cont'd

	Aspects of history being taught	How are the history lessons promoting pupils' SMSC development?	History Pos or Key Elements
SPIRITUAL	– A study of the journey of Grace Darling. – Visit to York Minster to experience atmosphere. – Year 6 visit to local church.	– Gain understanding on reflection of other peoples' beliefs. – Opportunity for reflection – awe and wonder.	**Key Element 4** – Finding out about aspects of the periods studied from buildings and site.
CULTURAL	– Pupils wrote briefly about why we wear poppies. – They know something of the history of the local lighthouse. – They have used the school Log Book to find first-hand evidence of the opening of the school in 1940. – Year 6 visit to local church. – Upper KS2 pupils are learning about historical development of Carlisle. – The pupils in Y1 make good progress in learning about their own personal history when completing own time-lines. – At KS1 they begin to learn about chronology by learning about recent events within their own families and in the community. – At KS2 pupils extend their understanding of chronology . . . learning includes key facts about local history. – Visits to museums and historic buildings linked to their studies also help to broaden their horizons. – Attainment in history is enhanced by the good use made of the historic setting of the school. – The school organises visits to places of historical interest to deepen pupils' insight and understanding.	– Developing knowledge of the nature and roots of their own cultural traditions. – Have a sense of their own identity and belonging within and have value for local, regional and national cultures. – Positive contributions made to pupils' cultural development through visits to museums and other historic sites.	**Key Stage 2** – Study Unit 3b, Britain since 1930. **Key Stage 2** – Study Unit 5, Local History. **Key Stage 2** – Britain since 1930. **Key Stage 1** – Area of Study 3 – notable and local events. **Key Element 1** – Chronology – time-line. **Key Stage 1** – Area of Study 1a – changes in their own lives and those of their family or those around them. **Key Element 4** – historical enquiry.

ambiguity, dissonance, inconsistency, things out of place. For Robert Gudrin the ways of creativity are infinite: the ways of formal learning are numbered. (All are quoted, *TES* 17 August 2004.) The National Advisory Committee on Creative and Cultural Education (DfEE 1999c: 27–39) defined creativity as:

- multidimensional, involving all fields of activity;
- 'playing with ideas' in all areas of work, for example conducting experiments in mathematics or science or acquiring insights by writing stories;
- involving imaginative and affective as well as cognitive dimensions, expressing ideas, values, feelings;
- purposeful, and directed to achieving its own objectives.

This does not seem such a tall order. Yet when I searched the National Curriculum in Action website (www.ncaction.org.uk/search) for examples of creativity in history at Key Stage 1 and 2: 'This search matches **0** examples of pupils work . . . Choose back and try a different refinement.' Oh dear . . .

Historical thinking is creative, using the NACCCE definition.

- It is multidimensional; it involves all aspects of a society and making connections between societies.
- It involves 'playing with ideas'; making possible inferences from sources.
- Historical imagination is integral to the process of historical enquiry.
- Historical enquiry must be purposeful; sources must be combined to construct and communicate accounts of the past.

A Year 6 'Egyptian Day'

I visited on the very last day of these children's time in primary school, and the culmination of a project on Ancient Egypt reflected all of these aspects of creativity in history (Capita *et al.* 2000). The children and teacher were elaborately dressed in costumes they had made at home by copying wall paintings or artists' illustrations in books. The girls had spent much time on exotic eye make-up; one explained how the cone on her head was designed to drop perfume throughout the day! Anubis had to remove his dog's head to speak and a rich merchant proudly displayed his replica jewellery and his slaves. They were working in rotating groups to investigate a variety of questions about Ancient Egypt. It was multidimensional and involved 'playing with ideas' in mathematics, language, art, science and technology. James was using 3D shapes to try to find out how pyramids were constructed, Shelley and John were making puppets of an Egyptian prince and princess in order to re-enact a story written by an Egyptian scribe three thousand years ago in which the son of an Egyptian king wooed and won the daughter of the King of Naharin by leaping high enough to reach her in her tall tower.

Paul and friends were playing senet. Andrea, Jack and James were designing mummy cases, looking in books to get ideas for the sort of patterns they used. Levi made a model shaduf and Jason was sitting in the sunshine grinding seeds using a quern. Laura and her friends were writing a diary account of a farming family over ten years, suggesting how their lives might have been affected each year by different levels of flooding of the Nile, which were determined by a dice game.

Another activity involved a group of girls using sources found in wall paintings, books, video and the internet to construct an account of an Egyptian banquet which was audio-taped for a 'radio programme' – 'Ancient Egypt'. When I met them they were discussing the myth of Isis and Osiris and, in particular, with eleven-year-old knowingness, how Isis became pregnant.

> 'After all Osiris had died – AND he was away a lot; we shall never find out.'
>
> 'There are different versions. In one version she turned into a kite and flew over his body. We didn't believe that one!'

I was visiting the school with a Romanian colleague who was fascinated. 'The English teacher's approach to teaching Ancient Egypt is quite different from classroom practice in Romania,' she later wrote, 'mainly because the students are involved in the activities. The use of drama stimulates much more discussion than debate and the use of primary sources as a basis for drama re-enactment is interesting and is able to satisfy scholars' demands. Students team up and develop a holistic approach to history. The student-centred perspective allows them to develop their own perspective on a topic. Pupils use information which is relevant to their interests and the "abstract" character of history is avoided. The development communication skills should, in my opinion, underpin activities.' It really is refreshing to hear from a Romanian perspective, how Carol, the teacher, in spite of the constraints in 2002, was meeting the aspirations of *Excellence and Enjoyment*.

King of the Nile

One Year 4 teacher explored gender in contemporary and ancient societies as well as spirituality, following a visit to the school of the Twisting Yarn Theatre Company who presented *The Queen Who Would Be King*. This is the story of a working man who became a scholar and a queen who became a king. It tells the story of Senenmut, the clever son of a peasant family, who rises through his scholarship to become the royal tutor to Hatshepsut, the ambitious queen who becomes Pharaoh. Another teacher, following the visit of the company, worked on Egyptian multiplication, and made parchment scrolls and stage backdrops with her Year 5/6 class. (RealPapyrus can be bought from www.pyramidcrafts.com.) They became so inspired that they wrote and performed their own play, *The Eye of the Pharaoh*, based on a scheme of work from MADD (literacygoesmadd@aol.com). The Twisting Yarn Theatre Company (twisting.yarn@bradford.gov.uk) worked with the Egyptology Department of Manchester University Museum to produce the narrative. A useful website is Kahun, a joint project between Manchester Museum and the Petrie Museum of Egyptian Archaeology, University College London (www.kahun.man.ac.uk).

Richard Rowe, head teacher of Holy Trinity School in Guildford, has 'moved his school on' to the ethos of a topic-based curriculum which involves working hard and having fun. His school was one of 32 included in the Ofsted Report, *The Curriculum in Successful Primary Schools* (Ofsted 2003). He recognises that 'this type of creativity does not just happen' but believes that any school can achieve it. 'You have to work really hard at it' (Ward 2002). For example, all 93 Year 6 pupils became inventors, explorers, biologists or missionaries in their investigation of 11 countries in the former British Empire. This concluded with a recreation of the Great Exhibition of 1851 in the school hall.

Museums and historic sites are already organising visits based on cross-curricular approaches, which could be a starting point for planning a unit of study. For example, at Norwich Cathedral there are opportunities planning a visit which includes history and also involves studying the different materials used in the building, the effects of chemicals and weather on stone and glass, considering how flint and limestone were formed, by looking for fossils in the stonework, then making comparisons with modern materials and technologies. There is also a herb workshop in the Benedictine herb garden, English and drama activities, art and religious education, planned appropriately for particular groups (www.cathedral.org.uk). One of the many other examples of cross-curricular programmes which are adapted to suit teachers' requirements is the Hat Works, Stockport where children not only make felt at different levels of sophistication but observe the machinery in action, find out about the lives of factory workers in the past and try on lots of hats which reflect jobs and status in the past! The museum offers science, design and technology courses, personal, health and social education and 'literacy specials' in which storytelling and 'big book work' is linked to museum artefacts (www.hatworks. org.uk).

The Tower of London includes a programme of science options. After visiting the 'Bloody Tower' where Sir Walter Raleigh was imprisoned, children can carry out a distillation experiment, which he apparently invented while in the tower, to find out how men could survive at sea if all the fresh water ran out. 'I couldn't believe my eyes when the salt and dirty water turned into plain!' said Farzana Sulthans in Year 3. This is a lead into 'changes of state and solutions'. A replica of Henry VIII's longbow and mail armour are used as a basis for work on 'materials' at Key Stages 1–3. 'Astronomy is awesome' is offered in conjunction with the Royal Observatory Greenwich and 'Diet and disease' with the . . . Florence Nightingale Museum.

Planning and assessment

Foundation Stage

At the Foundation Stage the time dimension of Knowledge and Understanding of the World (QCA 2000a) may be integrated into other Areas of Learning piecemeal, through talking about stories, birthdays, grannies, babies (see Chapter 7). They will therefore feed into many aspects of the *Foundation Stage Profile* (QCA 2003b), especially literacy and communication, and personal and social education. Table 5.5 shows an example of planning and assessment for a topic with a time focus.

Key Stages 1 and 2

It is made clear in the *Excellence and Enjoyment* programme that teachers' plans need only sufficient detail to enable them to teach effectively. Long-term school plans need to show the curriculum areas covered by each age group each year. Medium-term plans need to show learning objectives for each curricular area with exemplar, differentiated activities which will allow children to achieve them and demonstrate that they have done so. Medium-term plans could be created by identifying cross-curricular sub themes, which may be different group enquiries as on pages 87–91, 137–41, 147–56 and 159–63, then listing the learning objectives and differentiated activities which will enable children to achieve them separately for each subject. This would make it simple to see exactly what had been covered in each subject wholly or partially and what might need reinforcement (see pages a, b). Alternatively, the cross-curricular learning objectives could be combined on a single plan. Weekly plans need to show which aspects of the medium-term plan will be taught, and at what times, each week. The medium-term plans need to be annotated and modified as the topic progresses, in response to new ideas and children's progress. There are examples of medium-term plans for the Foundation Stage on page 67, Key Stage 1 on pages 137–41 and for Key Stage 2 on pages 159–63. There is an example of a lesson plan and self-assessment proforma on pages 170 and 175.

Assessment in history, as we saw in Part 1, can only be 'broad brushstroke', because children progress in different strands of historical enquiry at different rates and because there are so many variables in the complexity of sources used and of questions asked. Progression in history is not as simply hierarchical as the National Curriculum may suggest. However a synopsis of the broad progression within the National Curriculum is shown in Table 5.6.

The QCA Innovating with History website (www.qca.org.uk/history) emphasises that knowledge, skills and understanding are integrated in history and lists characteristics of progression at Key Stages 1 and 2.

- Asking and answering more complex questions.
- Making links and connections between different areas of learning.

TABLE 5.5 Medium-term plan (weeks 1–4) for Knowledge and Understanding of the World – Nursery and Reception ('Toys and Games, Now and Then').
I am grateful to Elizabeth Hart and Sarah Spink for allowing me to use their plans

Week	Learning objectives	Activities	Links to Early Learning Goals, Knowledge and Understanding of the World	Assessment opportunities
1	To sustain attentive listening, responding to what they have learned with relevant comments, questions or actions.	Each day children will describe a favourite toy, explain what it is made of, why they like it, demonstrate how it works.	Show interest in the world in which they live. Investigate objects using all their senses as appropriate. Find out about and identify uses of everyday technology.	(Focus Children) can speak with confidence, show awareness of listeners, take turns to speak.
2	To develop and stimulate interest in and awareness of the past; changes over time, reasons for changes, and continuity.	Each day a parent or adult working in the class shows and describes a favourite toy from their childhood; invites and answers questions. Range may include e.g. teddy, doll, bricks, toy car, fort/doll's house.	Talk about similarities and differences between children's favourite toys and parents' favourite toys. Raise questions and suggest reasons for differences.	(Focus Children) ask questions, identify similarities and differences between their favourite toys and parents' favourite toys.
3	To work as part of a class, sharing fairly, understanding need for agreed values and codes for adults and children to work harmoniously together. Extend vocabulary. Use everyday words to decide position; more/less; size; sets.	Collect information about parents' teddies. Collect information about parents' favourite toys. Set up a 'teddy bear museum' of 'old' and 'new' teddies using parents' and children's teddies. Agree rules and labels for museum. Make word bank to describe old and new teddies.	Find out about past and present events in their own lives and in those of their families.	Children and parents work together to complete information sheets on favourite toys and on teddies. Children use teddy museum according to agreed rules. Use appropriate adjectives to describe old and new teddies. Parents visit toy museum with children.
4	To move with confidence, control and co-ordination; to use imagination in music, dance, role play.	Children will learn about and participate in a variety of outdoor games from the past in outdoor play area: hopscotch, hoops, marbles, Oranges and Lemons. Poor Mary lies a-weeping, The Farmer's in his Den, The Grand Old Duke of York.	Find out about past and present; similarities and differences.	Children understand that these games were played by children a long time ago. Children participate. Demonstrate understanding of roles in games.

TABLE 5.6 Synopsis of progression in history from the Foundation Stage to Key Stage 3.

UNDERSTANDING	NURSERY-RECEPTION	KEY STAGE 1	KEY STAGE 2	KEY STAGE 3
Areas of Study	■ family ■ locality ■ artefacts ■ events ■ perspectives	■ lives and lifestyles of people in the recent past ■ famous people and events from the more distant past ■ use variety of sources	■ four specified dimensions: local, national, Europe, global ■ coherence within a period: impact of personalities and events on everyday lives of men, women, children	■ four dimensions integrated: locality, Britain, interacting with Europe and global contexts
Chronology, time concepts; cause/effect; motive; similarity/difference	■ sequence objects ■ talk and ask questions about changes over time	■ sequence events and objects ■ use time vocabulary to identify differences, give reasons for causes, effects, motives	■ sequence using appropriate periods ■ use vocabulary of time measurement to identify characteristics of periods, using specific characteristics, explain changes	■ use dates and specialised terms to describe changes over time ■ analyse and explain relationships between periods, recognising trends and patterns
Historical Interpretation		■ identify different ways in which the past is represented	■ identify different ways in which the past has been represented and subsequently interpreted	■ know how and why historical events, people, situations and changes have been interpreted differently ■ evaluate interpretations
Historical Enquiry	■ ask questions to gain information about why things happen; how things work; re family, locality, objects	■ ask and answer questions about a greater range of sources (e.g. pictures, photographs, eye-witness accounts, ICT)	■ select and record sources relevant to a focused enquiry; additional sources: documents, printed sources, music, sites, records	■ evaluate sources; reach conclusions ■ use range of out of school sites, additional sources: oral, media
Organising and Communication Information	■ recall in talking	■ increased means of recall (e.g. writing, drawing, ICT)	■ select information ■ use historical vocabulary	■ prioritise information ■ use historical, chronological conventions ■ more emphasis on structure and explanation

- Understanding more general and specific historical concepts.

- Growing understanding in and use of historical skills.

- An increasing ability to apply skills across different areas of learning.

- Increasing independence in learning.

The expectations at the end of each key stage reflect the knowledge, skills and understanding set out in the Programmes of Study. It is difficult to give examples of each characteristic because the sources and the questions may be of different levels of complexity.

References

Aronovsky, I. (2003) 'Teaching the Indus Valley Civilization in the 21st Century', *Primary History* **33**, 22–3.

Bennett, N., Wood, L. and Rogers, S. (1997) *Teaching Through Play: teachers' thinking and classroom practice*. Buckingham: Open University Press.

Bragg, M. (2003) *The Adventure of English*. London: Hodder and Stoughton.

Brooks, Y. (2003) 'Finding a voice', *Times Educational Supplement*, 14 February.

Brooks. Y. (2004) 'Built to last', *Times Educational Supplement*, 17 August.

Capita, L., Cooper, H. and Mogos, J. (2000) 'Children's thinking and creativity in the classroom: English and Romanian perspectives', *International Journal of Historical Learning, Teaching and Research*, **1**(1), 31–8.

Claire, H. (2002) 'Why didn't you fight Ruby?' *Education 3–13*, June.

Claire, H. (2003) 'Dealing with controversial issues with primary teacher trainees as part of citizenship education'. www.citized.info/pdf/commarticles/hilary_claire.pdf).

Claire, H. (2005) 'Learning and teaching about citizenship through history in the primary years', in *Leading Primary History*. London: The Historical Association.

Cooper, H. (2002) *History in the Early Years*, 2nd edn. London: Routledge Falmer.

Cooper, H. and Twiselton, S. (2000) *Art and Artists: Impressionism (7–9)*, Reading for Information Series. Leamington Spa: Scholastic.

DfEE (1998) *National Literacy Strategy*. London: DfEE.

DfEE (1999a) *National Numeracy Strategy*. London: DfEE.

DfEE (1999b) *The National Curriculum: handbook for primary school teachers in England and Wales, Key Stages 1 and 2*. London: DfEE.

DfEE (1999c) *The National Advisory Committee on Creative and Cultural Education*. London: DfEE.

DfES (2003) *Every Child Matters*. London: DfES.

Hutchinson, M. (1999) *The Journey*. Huddersfield: Primary Colours.

Hutchinson, M. and Tidy, P. (2003) *The Journey Learning Resource*. Huddersfield: Primary Colours.

Jones, S. (2002) 'Bombs and battalions', *Times Educational Supplement*, 29 November.

Moore, H. (2004) 'Ancient History, things to do and questions to ask', in H. Cooper (ed.) *Exploring Time and Place Through Play: Foundation Stage to Key Stage 1*. London: David Fulton Publishers.

Nichol, J. and Guyver, R. (2005) 'In my view: the debate upon the English National Curriculum for History', *Primary History*, **42**, 8–10.

Office for Standards in Education (Ofsted) (2003; 2005) *The Curriculum in Successful Primary Schools.* www.ofsted.gov.uk.

Osler, A. (1995) 'Does the National Curriculum bring us any closer to a gender balanced history?' *Teaching History,* **79**, 21–4.

O'Sullivan, J. (2003) 'Gael Force', *Times Educational Supplement,* 4 July.

Oxfam (1997) www.oxfam.org.uk/coolplanet/teachers/globciti.

Parekh Report (2000) 'The Commission on the Future of Multi-Ethnic Britain', Runnymede Trust.

Pounce, E. (1995) 'Ensuring continuity and understanding through teaching of gender issues in History 5–16', in R. Watts and I. Grosvenor (eds) *Crossing the Key Stages of History.* London: David Fulton Publishers.

QCA (2000a) *Curriculum Guidance for the Foundation Stage.* London: QCA.

QCA (2000b) *A Scheme of Work for Key Stages 1 and 2.* London: QCA.

QCA (2003a) *Excellence and Enjoyment: A Strategy for Primary Schools.* London: QCA.

QCA (2003b) *Foundation Stage Profile.* London: QCA.

QCA (2005) *The Futures Programme: Meeting the Challenge.* London: QCA.

Robinson, T. (2005) *The Worst Children's Jobs in History.* London: Macmillan.

Robson, W. (2004) 'Kings, Queens and Castles', in H. Cooper (ed.) *Exploring Time and Place Through Play: Foundation Stage to Key Stage 1.* London: David Fulton Publishers.

Saunders, T. (2004) 'History on your doorstep', *Times Educational Supplement,* 12 March.

Schmidt, M.A. and Garcia, T.M.B. (2003) *Recriando historias de Campina Grande do Sul.* PR: UFPR/PMCGS.

Schmidt, M.A. and Garcia, T.M.B. (2004) 'Teaching history based on documents: a social experiment with Brazilian children', *International Journal of History Teaching, Learning and Research,* **4** (2).

Seward, D. and Boertien, V. (2004) 'All about us', in H. Cooper (ed.) *Exploring Time and Place Through Play: Foundation Stage to Key Stage 1.* London: David Fulton Publishers.

Siraj-Blatchford, I., Sylva, K., Muttock, S., Gilden, R. and Bell, D. (2002) *Researching Effective Pedagogy in the Early Years,* Research Report 356. Annesley: Department for Education and Skills (www.dfes.gov.uk/research/).

Ward, H. (2002) 'Bringing historical conflicts to life', *Times Educational Supplement,* 7 June.

6

History, the curriculum and communication skills

THIS CHAPTER CONSIDERS HOW the *National Literacy Strategy* (DfEE 1998), aspects of the *National Numeracy Strategy* (DfEE 1999a) and information and communication technology can be integrated with teaching and learning in history.

History and literacy

I have above my desk the original pen and ink drawing which accompanied a piece I wrote for the *Times Educational Supplement* (Cooper 1996) when a National Literacy Strategy was first proposed. It depicts a large, very angry black bull, nostrils flared, branded 3R, raging through a china shop – or rather a museum of show cases containing fragile ceramic plates decorated with historical icons and models of key historical figures. His little white eyes are full of menace. Well, this bull has certainly caused havoc over the past few years. The rich and imaginative history developed when the National Curriculum was introduced has been smashed to smithereens.

Yet the National Literacy Strategy was never intended to be taught only as a discrete session. Its objectives were intended to be applied across the curriculum and to extend outside the hour. There is no aspect of the strategy which cannot be applied in any subject, including history. For many understandable reasons it was not interpreted in this way. Subsequently it was found (surprise, surprise) that pupils' extended writing, speaking and listening skills and even reading for pleasure were suffering. Here are some examples of how literacy can be linked to historical enquiry, using literacy skills for a purpose, in meaningful contexts and increasing the time available for history.

A sequence of Key Stage 2 sessions with shared history and literacy objectives culminating in an exhibition

Conferences were organised in York and in London to model for teacher trainers how the literacy objectives could be applied to a range of subjects. I was invited to write materials for literacy and art, based on work I had recently published (Cooper and

Twiselton 2000). Our intention had been to develop a sequence of literacy sessions on the theme of 'The Impressionists', linked to practical work in art which would conclude with an exhibition of work in an 'art gallery', created by Year 4 children. I have modified this project to focus on an exhibition of historical sources which could lead towards a class museum exhibition. This would be most suitable for work on the Victorians or Britain since 1930 because artefacts and photographs are available. For other periods it might be an exhibition of relevant art for an art gallery exhibition. Visitors to the school could be given plans, information leaflets, guided tours, audio tape recordings. The extensions to the suggested activities are endless. Of course, other history and literacy would flow outside this sequence as well.

These sessions require children to access information in books and on the internet, record information in note form, evaluate, form opinions, and discuss and record them. The objectives come from the National Literacy Strategy for Year 4 and the National Curriculum Key Stage 2 Programme of Study for History. It is only possible to give a flavour of the session plans, which can be developed in relation to particular history topics.

Plan 1 Making inferences about artefacts

Objectives

History 4 a, b

To understand that opinions about artefacts differ; to form and express opinions

NLS Y4 T1

Word level

Define familiar vocabulary in own words

Text level 19 and 20

To understand and use the term opinion

To identify use of voice and of headlines

Outline

1 Discuss an obscure artefact: how was it made, used, what was its effect on people who made and used it.

2 Groups: using different Victorian artefacts and writing frame if necessary, write labels stating what object is made of, opinion(s) about how it may have been used and why they think so. Focus group write short article, possibly for audio tape recording.

3 Plenary: list opinions on flip chart; rephrase those which are not opinions.

Plan 2 Describing key features of a Victorian artefact, painting, photograph

Objectives

History 2a, b, 4b

Understand features and diversity of period

Find out from sources and select and record information relevant to an enquiry

NLS Y4 T2

Word level

To use alternative words and expressions that are more interesting or accurate than obvious choices

Sentence level 1

Revise and extend work on adjectives, constructing adjectival phrases

Text level 21

Make short notes, abbreviating ideas, selecting keywords, recording in diagrammatic form (focus group continuous prose)

Outline

Explain we are going to look at a painting in detail and write brief notes recording what information in the picture tells us about what Victorian life was like using adjectives to describe things. Make spidergram around picture, indicating place in picture with ruled lines and arrows. Groups use Victorian paintings or photographs showing different aspects of Victorian life using postcards on A3 paper. Underline adjectives.

Plenary: share, evaluate.

Plan 3 Instructions for Victorian activities

Objectives

History 2, 4 and 5

Understanding about people in the past

Ask and answer questions about sources

Communicate knowledge and understanding in a variety of ways

NLS Y4 T1

Sentence level 2

To revise work on verbs

Text level 22

To identify features of instructional text including noting intended outcome at the beginning, listing materials, clearly setting out sequential stages, language of command, imperative verbs

This could focus on creating instructions about how to do anything in the period studied: a dance, learning a song, cooking a recipe, using an old artefact such as a washboard, riding a penny-farthing

Outline

Model creating instructional text, emphasising verbs, imperatives, sequence, using children to carry out, then evaluate and change instructions. Groups write instructions for other activities using differentiated historical sources.

Plenary: try to carry out instructions; evaluate, correct.

Plan 4 Writing captions for the exhibition

Objectives

History 3

Recognise that the past is represented in different ways and give reasons for this.

NLS Y4 T1

Sentence level

Reread own writing and check for grammatical accuracy; identify errors; suggest alternative constructions

Text level 17

Identify features of non-fiction text in e.g. headings, captions, which support the reader in gaining information efficiently

Outline

Children collect (photocopy) different interpretations of Victorian period, e.g. *Villainous Victorians* (Deary 2004), old children's textbook, cartoon, a video clip, picture of reconstruction in a museum or living history reconstruction.

Where do we find captions? (museums, galleries, illustrated books) Who are they written for? What purpose do they serve? Read caption. What does it tell us? (fact, some background information), intended to be read in conjunction with the interpretation. Conclude, purpose to inform and interest reader, help to understand a little more; note economical language, headings, quick to read limited information. Model creating a caption for one of the interpretations using writing frame if necessary (title, name of creator, where found, description, purpose in making it, how valid as information about period?).

Groups write captions for other interpretations. Guided group devise catalogue to record categories of information, using ICT so that entries can be word-processed for exhibition.

Plan 5 Advertising the exhibition

Objectives

History 5 a, b, c

Organisation and communication

NLS Y4 T1

To understand fact and opinion

Y4 T3

Text level 18

Investigate how style and vocabulary are used to convince

Text level 19

Evaluate advertisements and their impact, appeal, honesty

Text level 25

To design an advertisement

Outline

What information is on a poster? What is it for? What is main heading, subheading? Which text is trying to persuade us? Are there reviews quoted? (speech marks and opinions).

Is it brief, informal, colourful? Identify need to create poster with title, factual information (price, time, place, transport). Are there persuasive text reviews? Make best copy using word-processing (variety, different fonts, colours, digital photographs).

Kendal Castle 1998

In order to define precise links between learning objectives for history and for English in the National Curriculum, five student teachers worked intensively for three days with a Year 1/2 class in Stramongate School, Kendal. They visited Kendal Castle, and found out more about castles from other sources in order, firstly, to create a role play of what a medieval banquet in Kendal Castle may have been like and, secondly, to make a children's information board for the castle, since they found that the board on the site, written for adults, was difficult for them to understand. This project (Cooper 1997; 1998a; 1998b) preceded the national literacy framework, so it is interesting, though not surprising, that each of the activities had both National Curriculum for History (2000) learning objectives and National Literacy Framework text level objectives (Table 6.1). It could therefore have been taught over a longer period through a sequence of literacy hours.

TABLE 6.1 Activities with combined National Curriculum History and National Literacy Framework Learning Objectives. Kendal Castle

History NC	NLF
FINDING OUT ABOUT THE CASTLE 2b *Concept Map of Castle* Identify differences between ways of life at different times	write captions 1.1.14 labels for drawings/diagrams 1.2.22 to explain, describe 1.3.21
4b *Questions* to investigate about the past . . .	Write simple questions 1.2.24 1.3.22
Site Visit – notes 4a Find out about past from sources 5 Communicate in writing; drawing	make simple lists for planning, reminding etc. 1.1.15 assemble information from our experience 1.2.25 use headings; sub-headings 2.3.20
4a. *Inferences from brass-rubbing* Find out about the past from a range of sources	describe characteristics, behaviour, simple profiles of characters 1.2.15 write character profiles, simple descriptions 2.2.14
5. *RECONSTRUCTING A BANQUET IN THE CASTLE FROM PRIMARY AND SECONDARY SOURCES*	
Communicate awareness of the past in different ways; talking, writing, drawing Invitation to banquet	Substitute and extend patterns from reading 1.2.13
Theme for banquet Programme for entertainment	simple lists 1.1.15 organise in lists 1.2.25 read for information and record answers 1.3.22 use models from reading to organise sequentially 2.1.16 make simple notes from non-fiction texts 2.3.19
Story for banquet: Sleeping Beauty The banquet	use patterned stories as models using basic conventions 1.1.10 represent outlines of story plots 1.2.14 write stories, based on reading 1.3.14 use the language of time 2.1.11 use the language of story . . . 2.3.10
Use primary and secondary sources to ask and answer questions about the past; communicate information:	simple non-chronological reports 1.2.25 using language of texts read as models for 1.3.20 writing 2.3.21
The kitchen Plan	use diagrams, drawing, labelling 2.1.17 instructions 2.2.19

First the children were asked to 'draw and label a picture of a castle: the ideas that come into your head when someone says "castle" '. Students scribed for younger children. This was in order to find out what children already knew (and possible misconceptions); what images they had of castles. Some children had a lot of factual knowledge, about moats, drawbridges, arrow-slits; others were dominated by fantasy – garlands of flowers around the turrets; Max, from *Where the Wild Things Are* in a boat on a rescue mission across the moat (Sendak 1970).

Then the class were told that they were visiting Kendal Castle in the afternoon and asked what they would like to find out about it. Their questions were listed on a flip-chart and grouped into four focuses:

- now and then: what can you see from the castle mound now and what would you have seen a long time ago – certainly; possibly?
- attacking the castle: why was it built here; how could you attack? where?
- daily life: where did they cook; wash; get water; have banquets?
- survey of the site: measure curtain wall, windows, doorways; note materials, where did they come from?

In the afternoon the children worked in groups on the site to record information in notes and lists. Some children organised their notes under headings, others recorded as small drawings, with labels scribed for them where necessary.

Next day preparations began to reconstruct a banquet at Kendal Castle in the time of Catherine Parr, who had lived there as a child. In order to find out how to dress, children made rubbings of replica medieval brasses, including one of Catherine Parr. This gave them lots of information about ladies' headdresses, 'belts with tassels', patterns on dresses; about knights' chain mail, armour, helmets, swords, coats of arms on shields. Then each child chose a small item of dress from their rubbing, a necklace or a shield, for example, and made a replica, from card, fabric or shiny paper, which they could wear to the banquet.

They found the rest of the information they needed to plan the banquet from books – usually from illustrations, either artists' reconstructions or contemporary pictures. *The Medieval Cookbook* (Black 1992), although an adult book, has splendidly vivid pictures of medieval feasts to accompany the recipes: killing the boar, baking the bread, roasting birds on spits, etc. Invitations were sent (modelled on familiar party invitations), menus were written and programmes for entertainment devised. These were divided into subheadings; during the meal – stories, jesting, lute – and after the meal – singing, jesters, dancing and tournaments. Samantha's drawing of the joust (Figure 6.1) and accompanying writing (Figure 6.2) show how the interpretation of medieval people on the brasses was brought to life by her further enquiry using information book illustrations of knights, which informed the joust role play following the banquet. Stories were written, to be read during the meal,

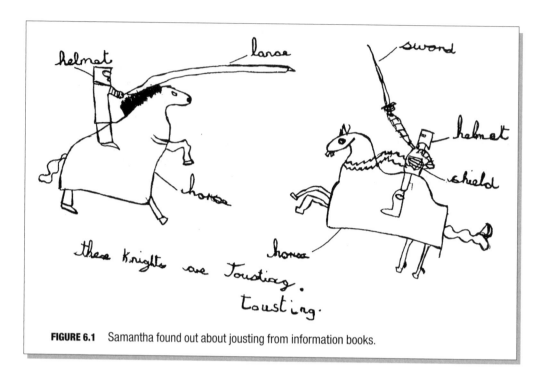

FIGURE 6.1 Samantha found out about jousting from information books.

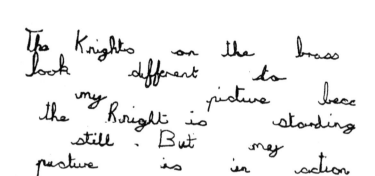

FIGURE 6.2 Knights on brasses look different from illustrations in books.

modelled on the familiar conventions of fairy stories about princes and princesses. Jokes were remodelled suitably for medieval jesters: why did the chicken cross the drawbridge? Replica food was prepared (finding from their researches that squirrels were eaten, as well as boars' heads, a lugubrious pig's head and some surprisingly perky-looking squirrels were carried to the table with great care on a large silver salver). Following the banquet jugglers caught most of the balls, everyone laughed at the jesters' riddles, and Baron Dorset, looking remarkably like the head teacher, joined in the dancing to the viol, the harp and the crumhorn of the Past Times tape.

The various examples of non-chronological writing on the children's information board (Figure 6.3) were an excellent assessment of the enormous range of detailed information the children had acquired over the intensive three-day project and the site plan of Kendal Castle, with its topographically accurate key to the plan of the castle, showed a significant development from the fairy-tale fantasy castles of the initial concept maps to a factual labelled diagram.

If this project were repeated as a series of literacy hours the sessions may be structured differently, with planned work at word and sentence level, more explicit

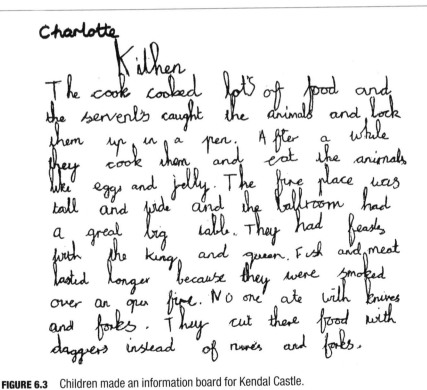

FIGURE 6.3 Children made an information board for Kendal Castle.

emphasis on modelling the story, jokes, invitations, menus, and on analysing the characteristic features and purposes of captions, labels, notes, diagrams. The literacy objectives might be made more explicit, but certainly the motivation to do the work would be intrinsic, rather than as with some literacy hours, a collection of discrete exercises. This case study is a good example of the way in which the literacy framework makes more explicit, but does not change, the National Curriculum for English.

Abbot Hall Museum, Kendal (1999)

The following year another group of students, Alex, Alison, Sarra, Suzanne and Laura, volunteered to work on a two-day project in Stramongate School to investigate how more precise links could be made between history learning objectives and the literacy hour (Cooper and Twiselton 1998; 1999). Both Year 2 and Year 5 were studying the Victorians and were going to visit Abbot Hall Museum in Kendal where rooms are furnished as a nineteenth-century bedroom and kitchen. It was decided that the focus of the literacy hours for both classes would be the museum visits in order to see how museum work on artefacts could be linked to the literacy framework at two different levels. 'Alphabets' was chosen as a theme for the museum visits for several reasons. Learning the alphabet by rote was a key feature of Victorian Board schools, and alphabet books were written for middle-class children to read at home. Both provide opportunities for discussing phonics and phonemes, for using patterning, rhythm, rhyme and picture clues to predict meaning; for shared reading; for modelling writing. They provide opportunities for discussing the meaning of archaic words such as vintner, squire and oyster-wench. The three alphabets selected also reflected changes in attitudes to children over the century. 'A was an Archer' (in Opie and Opie 1980) made few concessions to childhood; Kate Greenaway (Ernest 1968) romanticised it; Edward Lear (Sampson 1977; Alderson 1975) enjoyed it!

The literacy hours were supported by a variety of history-focused activities. The reasons for attempting to make links between the literacy hours and the history topic were firstly, to create curriculum coherence and, secondly, to give the literacy hour activities a purpose and an audience. However the conclusion reached at the end of this case study was that although literacy hours may sometimes meet history objectives their focus must be on literacy.

The project began, for each class (at different times) with the visit to Abbot Hall Museum, where the children were shown an amazing, hand-painted cloth alphabet book, made by a Kendal woman, Mrs Clara Walker, for her two-year-old daughter Mary in 1891, and photographs of Mrs Walker and Mary. 'What is this?' they were asked, 'Who made it? How? Why?' After reading and marvelling at Mrs Walker's book they were asked the same questions about other intriguing Victorian artefacts set out on the tables: butter pats, bellows, curling tongs, etc. Then the Year 2 children were divided into five groups. Each group was given five (non-consecutive) letters of the alphabet and asked to list as many artefacts as they could find in the bedroom and kitchen beginning with 'their' letters. This was made easier by the labels on many artefacts and competition was fierce. 'I've got 10–23–30'. 'Does cast-iron cauldron count for two?' 'If you say ragged rag-rug is that three?'

Literacy hour (Year 2, Term 2)

Whole class: text level

Learning objectives: to reinforce word level skills (T1); use phonological contextual grammatical and graphic knowledge to check and predict meanings of unfamiliar words (T2); identify and discuss patterns of rhythm and rhyme (T9).

After discussing the cloth alphabet book they had seen in the morning, Alex showed the children a printed version of an old alphabet book, *The Nursery Companion* (Opie and Opie 1980), to give them some more ideas about how they could make their own Victorian alphabet book. They began reading 'A was an Archer' together.

> A was an Archer
> And shot at a frog
> B was a butcher
> And kept a great dog . . .

Alliteration, similar sentence structure, rhyme, rhythm and pictures all helped to predict the meaning of unfamiliar language: nobleman, tinker, watchman.

Whole class: word level

Learning objectives: identify phonemes in speech and writing (W2); apply phonological and graphic knowledge, through guided writing.

After more explicit discussion at word level Alex wrote the alphabet on a flip-chart and helped the children to put the names on 'their' artefacts, seen in the museum with 'their' letter, discussing spellings as she did so.

Independent group work

Learning objectives: to identify phonemes in speech and writing (W2); secure use of simple sentences in writing (S9).

The children wrote simple sentences, modelling those on the flip-chart for 'their' artefacts, e.g. D is for dolly tub, with the potential for an explanatory clause, 'for washing the clothes'.

Guided group (Alison)

Learning objectives: common spelling patterns (W2); split familiar words into component parts (W4); use structures from poems as a basis for writing (T15); comment on and recognise when reading a poem aloud is effective (T10).

This group read and were captivated by the rhyming pattern of the Lear alphabet – a pattern which was nonsense but followed conventions. They used their artefact words to construct nonsense alphabet entries, an interesting way of looking at patterns and exceptions in the meanings, sounds and visual appearance of words.

> Bottle
> Tottle
> Mottle
> Gottle
> Jottle
> Big blue medicine bottle

Plenary

Learning objectives: read own poems aloud (T8); comment on and recognise when reading aloud makes sense and is effective (T10).

The children read their poems and alphabet entries in order. They recorded their work on tape. As a postscript many chose to redraft their efforts for a second recording later in the day, accentuating the alliteration and rhythm they could hear in the first recording. This version was illustrated and collated into the children's own 'Victorian Alphabet Book'.

Literacy hour 2

The following literacy hour followed the theme of pattern and rhythm, in Victorian street cries, using the *Victorians, Music from the Past*, text and audio tape (Longman 1987).

Whole class: text level

Learning objectives: identify and discuss patterns of rhythm, rhyme and other features of sound in different poems (T).

After playing a tape of Victorian street chants, Alex led a discussion building up a vivid picture of a Victorian market scene and the use of chants to sell goods. She talked about the need for the chants to be memorable and easy to repeat, making use of rhythm, rhyme and snappy slogans to do this.

Whole class: word and text level

Learning objectives: discriminate orally syllables in multi-syllabic words (W5); comment on and recognise when the reading aloud of a poem makes sense and is effective (T10); use structures from poems as a basis for writing (T15).

The class read the street cries together, looking for rhymes first, and underlining them, before focusing on the rhythm. They also made up their own market chants (based on their letters) orally, which were then written down.

Group work

(W5; T10; T15)

The children were each given a chant and worked in pairs, tapping out the rhythm of their given chant with a pencil. They tried doing the various chants as a round, before constructing their own. There was discussion of the use of speech marks, exclamation marks and question marks, which they employed effectively in their writings.

Plenary session

Learning objectives: read own poem aloud (T8); comment on and recognise when the reading aloud of a poem makes sense and is effective (T10).

The children performed their street chants to each other, with discussion of what made them effective.

More Victorians

Work in the literacy hour in Year 2 was linked to a rich variety of other history-focused activities, planned by the students. One group used photographs of a Victorian parlour, a family living in one room, a school and an ironmonger's shop. They were given a sheet of A1 paper divided into four boxes and tried to find clues to differences between now and then for each box. In the ironmonger's box they wrote 'the packaging was darker than today's', and 'customers had to ask for things then. Today we don't'.

One group found out more about artefacts borrowed from Abbot Hall in order to label them for a class museum. Greg found out about button hooks. 'Gaiters have a sort of key with a hook on the end, and a hole at the end to put your thigh in.'

Some children coloured (photocopied) line drawings from Kate Greenaway's *Colouring Book*, imitating her delicate colours and writing interpretations of the pictures. 'They're collecting flowers to sell at the market.' 'It's lavender to make lavender bags.' 'They're wild flowers.' Others followed instructions to make Victorian peg dolls, then made up a 'Victorian story' which they wrote in tiny books, like the miniature books they had seen inside Kate Greenaway's *Treasury*. The peg dolls acted out the story.

Another group made a replica Pollock's theatre, like the one the student had bought in Pollock's Toy Museum and decided to write and perform the story of the Minotaur.

Year 5, Term 2

When Year 5 visited Abbot Hall they also discussed Mrs Walker's cloth alphabet book and artefacts in the handling collection, but they were encouraged to use conditional language (if, then, should, might) and conjunctions (and, but). 'If you had an ostrich feather fan, you might have been rich, because ostrich feathers had to be imported, but the feathers might have been more common then!' Then each child was given one letter and asked to find an artefact in the museum beginning with their letter, draw it and write notes describing it and explaining how it worked, how it was made, who might have used it and why.

Literacy hour, Year 5, Term 2

Whole class: text level

Learning objectives: locate information confidently and efficiently through (i) using indexes/headings (ii) skimming (iii) scanning (iv) close reading (T17).

After an introductory look at 'A was an Archer', the Victorian alphabet (in Opie and Opie 1980) Suzanne contrasted this with a modern dictionary to establish what children already knew about dictionaries. It was explained that they were going to write a dictionary of Victorian artefacts. They were then given photocopied pages from a variety of modern dictionaries and discussed definitions, and the use of abbreviations to denote nouns, verbs, adverbs and plurals.

Whole class: word level

Learning objectives: use dictionaries (W3); search for, collect and define technical words (W9); evaluate text critically by comparing how different sources treat the same information (T18).

Suzanne explained that not all dictionaries have so much information, and she asked for feedback from the children on what was in the different dictionaries in front of them. This led to a series of dictionary games where words were suggested and children had to race to locate them and find all the information on them available in the dictionary they had.

Group/Individual work

Learning objectives: to convert personal notes into notes for others to read, paying attention to appropriateness of style, vocabulary, presentation (T21); search for, collect and define technical words (W9).

The children were asked to write dictionary entries for artefacts they had drawn and written notes on in the museum.

Plenary

Definitions were read and evaluated.

In the second literacy hour Laura and the class read Edward Lear's *A Book of Bosh* (Alderson 1975) together, then discussed the ways in which this was a shift from the other more literal Victorian alphabets. They noticed the difficulties of reading alliteration at speed. (It was explained that they were going to write their own Victorian 'Book of Bosh'.) For word and sentence level work they chose the letter P and wrote as many words as they could think of beginning with P on separate cards, then tried to make sentences with them, rearranging and substituting them. Then they worked in pairs. Each pair was given a pile of blank cards and asked to experiment with 'bosh' sentences about the Victorian artefacts they had drawn in the museum, constructing them in different ways by reordering (S8), then writing in a final form (T13).

In the plenary children enjoyed listening to and making constructive comments on each other's efforts (T24).

Flighty footmen fancied feather-fans . . .

Even more Victorians

To consolidate what else they knew about the Victorians, the Year 6 children worked in groups to construct spider diagrams about photographs of Victorian subjects – a parlour, a shop, a beach, for example – showing ways in which life in Victorian times was different from today and suggesting why. When they shared their diagrams they found that each group had organised their analyses in quite different ways, creating a variety of 'spiders'.

In one session children studied photocopies of Victorian illuminated letters. The class then made their own Victorian illuminated letters. Half of them used scraps of fabric, velvet, silk, lace, beads, as this was identified in one of the pattern books as a popular early Victorian pastime. These contrasted with the cardboard prints of birds, leaves, fruits and vines inspired by William Morris designs which the rest of the class made as a background for their superimposed letters. This was an interesting example of using historical sources to illustrate how patterns, colours and textures reflected changes in nineteenth-century design.

In another intense session children used information books to find out about aspects of Victorian schools: reading, writing and arithmetic; drill; playground games. As a class they decided on four key words for each topic; in groups they were given 20 minutes in pairs to list questions related to each set of key words and try to find out the answers.

Then, each group worked on a short role play on their topic, using these facts (History KE3, 4 a, g; English 2c). Tables were recited and very hard arithmetic problems were posed, to which only the inspector knew the answer, probably because 's' (shillings) and 'd' (pence) were incomprehensible (but, like his Victorian counterpart, the inspector had an answer book). Drill was rigorous. At playtime 'The Big Ship Sailed up the Alley Alley O'; and of course the alphabet, chanted and painstakingly copied onto slates, played a major part in the reading and writing lessons. Dunces were reprimanded; and certificates were awarded for graphic and phonic skills, and for definitions of 'Gradgrind' accuracy: 'K is for kettle; noun; made of metal; hangs over the fire; used to warm water.'

Role play – A Victorian street, with a school on one side and a grand family house on the other (English AT 1 a-c; History KE3, 5c).

On the third afternoon, the Year 2 and Year 5 classes waited quietly, facing each other in the hall, to share what they had learned about the Victorians. A hunched figure, barefoot and enveloped in a vast paisley shawl, walked between them. She had a strange accent. She seemed to think she was in a London street. She said she could see a tall, grey building on one side of it – 'A three-decker, big high windows – it must be one of them new schools.' She peered inside. 'Can you see all the children inside? I thought you could; you've got magic eyes like me – cor – innit strict?'

Everybody suspended disbelief and looked in turn at the various activities going on in the school. Then they all agreed that on the other side of the street they could see a grand house, with its brass knocker and railings and red velvet curtains. They could even peep into the parlour where the children were performing a puppet play, Theseus and the Minotaur. A peg-doll play about Queen Victoria was then presented by the children in the big house.

Following this, the cries of street sellers were heard approaching – some cries were familiar; others were new.

> White tur-nips, white, young tur-nips white!
> Fine car-rots O! Fine car-rots O!

Then

> Red raspberries red, fresh raspberries red!
> Clothes, clothes, any old clothes?

And

> Who'll buy my sweet, red roses
> So fresh and sweet as night?
> Who'll buy my hot spiced gingerbread?
> Smoking hot and good to eat?

Then a sweet-seller appeared.

> Jelly beans, liquorice, who'll buy my liquorice?

Everyone was rewarded.

Can history and literacy objectives be achieved within the literacy hour? (2000)

The cohort of history specialist students who met in January 2000 listened to accounts of the case studies undertaken by their predecessors. In the first there had been concurrent National Curriculum and literacy objectives but not within the literacy hour format. In the second the literacy objectives dominated the literacy hours but these linked by content to the history activities of the study unit on the Victorians. The challenge for the students in this workshop was to explore ways in which history and literacy objectives might both be an integral part of a literacy hour. The focus was on reading and writing non-fiction from Reception to Year 6.

Each group of students was given a text and a list of pre-selected history objectives and literacy hour objectives at text, sentence and word level for a given year and term and asked to draft a literacy hour plan combining as many of the objectives as possible. The plans they produced could be translated into a variety of other contexts. Here are some examples.

Finding out about Victorian washday: reading and writing instructional text at Year 2, Term 1

This could be applied to explaining how any artefact was used.

History objectives
1b Use common words or phrases related to passing of time.
2b Identify differences between ways of life at different times.
4a Find out about the past from a range of sources.
5   Communicate awareness and knowledge of history.

Literacy hour objectives
Text level
T13 Read simple instructions.
T14 Note structured features: statement of purpose at start, sequential steps in list; direct language.
T15 Write simple instructions.
T16 Organise sequentially (lists, numbers) each point depending on the previous one.
T18 Use appropriate register (direct; impersonal).

Sentence level
   Reread own writing for sense and punctuation.
   Use simple organisational devised to indicate sequence (arrows), boxes, keys.

Word level
New words linked to particular topics.

Victorian washday: literacy hour plan (Year 2, Term 1)

Whole class: text level
Show wash tub, scrubbing board, postle, iron, line, pegs, soap.
H1b ■ What were these things used for? When?
H2b ■ Why? What do we use today?
H4a ■ By whom? Who does the washing today?
H4b ■ How do you think the scrubbing board was used? Can you follow Mrs Tiggy-Winkle's washing instructions?

   To Wash a Shirt
   You will need:

- A scrubbing board
- A wash tub
- Hot water
- Soap

Half-fill wash tub with hot water

Put in dirty clothes

Stand scrubbing board in the wash tub

Stretch dirty shirt across scrubbing board

Rub the shirt with soap until it is clean

Wring out soapy water

Rinse the shirt in clean water

Hang on outdoor clothes line to dry with pegs, or on clothes horse by kitchen fire, it if is raining.

T13   ■ Child mimes as instructions are read from flip-chart (or overhead transparency).

T18   ■ Were they good instructions? Why?

       Identify   *statement of purpose

                  *sequential steps; each point depends on previous one

                  *direct impersonal language.

Whole class: word level

T10   ■ Do you know what the other things are called? (label)

      ■ How do you think you use the postle?

      ■ Child mimes as class read scrubbing board instructions, changing as necessary for postle.

      ■ Explain class are going to make a book of Mrs Tiggy-Winkle's washing instructions.

Independent groups

T15   ■ You are going to write instructions for using the postle.

T16   ■ Either write the instructions as for the scrubbing board, or draw pictures or a diagram with labels.

      Remember: purpose, sequence, register.

Focus group

T15   ■ We are going to explain how to use a flat iron (key instructional features, but new information).

Plenary

S4   ■ Read instructions for using postle and iron; child mimes.

H5   ■ Evaluate for inclusion in Mrs Tiggy-Winkle's washday book.

What were Ancient Egyptian houses like? Year 4, Term 2

This model could be used to find out about a key aspect of any area of study from a variety of reference books.

History objectives

H4a,b Asking and answering questions about the past, using variety of sources.
H3 Understanding why there are different interpretations of the past.

Literacy hour objectives

Text level

T15 Appraise a non-fiction book for its contents and usefulness by scanning (e.g. headings, contents list).
T16 To prepare for factual research by reviewing what is known, what is available and where one might search.
T17 To scan text in print or on screen to locate key words or phrases, useful headings and key questions and to use these as a tool for summarising text.
T18 Mark extracts by annotating and by selecting key headings, words, sentences.
T20 Identify key features of explanatory text (e.g. to answer a question, use of illustrations and diagrams).

Sentence level

1 Use cues (phonic, graphic, grammatical knowledge, context when reading unfamiliar texts).

2 Understand that vocabulary changes over time (e.g. discuss why some words have become little used).

Egyptian houses: literacy hour plan (Year 4, Term 2)

Whole class: text level

Show OHT photocopy of a page about an Ancient Egyptian house from a reference book.
T16 What do you already know about houses in Ancient Egypt?
H4a,b How can we find out more? (Archaeological remains, tomb, book.)
The information in books comes from making deductions and inferences about archaeological sources; different books may say different things. We are going to see what we can find out from these books: what is the same/different; how useful the books are.
T15 Where can we find out about Egyptian houses in this book? (Contents, index.) Find text.
T17 Read page (an OHT).
T18 Mark key information. List on flip-chart under headings.
T20 Discuss usefulness of text, illustrations, diagrams.

Whole class: sentence level

S1   Discuss unfamiliar vocabulary: brewery, bakery, silo, granary.

S11   Do we still use these words today? When? How has their meaning remained the same/changed?

Independent group work

Groups given other reference books at appropriately differentiated levels.

T15   Find reference to Egyptian houses.

T21   List key words/information.

Plenary

T23   Whole class list what they have found out on flip-chart, adding under original headings.

H4   Note differences between books; discuss reasons.

T24   Reorganise list under headings, sub-headings, numbered points.

Hilaire Belloc's cautionary tales. *Matilda, Who Told Lies and Was Burned to Death* (1991). Humorous verse, Year 3, Term 3

History objectives

H2a,b Characteristic features of period and experiences of middle-class child.

H4   Find out about the past from a variety of sources.

      Discuss clues in illustrations about when poem written:

      – tea in the drawing room – servants.

      About Matilda's life:

      – fire engine

      – street scenes

      – clothes

      – carriages.

Literacy hour objectives

T4   Consider credibility of events.

T6   Discuss character behaviour.

Text level

T6   Compare forms of humour, e.g. cautionary tales.

T7   Prepare, read aloud and recite by heart, poetry that plays with language or entertains; recognise rhyme and patterns of sound that create effects.

T8   Compare and contrast works by the same author.

Sentence level

S4   Use speech marks and other dialogue punctuation.

Word level

W4   Discriminate syllables in reading and spelling.

W12   Collect new words from reading and work in other subjects.

Matilda: literacy hour plan (Year 3, Term 3)

Whole class: text level

T4   Read poem: what is it about? Is it likely? True?

T5   Is Matilda reasonable? Brave? Foolish?

H4 T6 Discuss clues in illustrations about Matilda and her life; similarities with and differences from children today. Introduce concept of 'cautionary tales'.

T7   What makes it fun? Identify rhythm. Mark a photocopied page (OHTs).

T8   Introduce other Belloc cautionary tales to read at another time.

Whole class: sentence level

S4   Identify speech and punctuation marks: 'Matilda's house is burning down!' using photocopied page (OHT).
      They only answered 'little liar'.

Whole class: word level

W4   Tap out syllables (using OHT page).

W12   Reread. List any new words (e.g. gallant, frenzied).

Independent/group work

W4

T7   Give children photocopied pages to read; to mark rhymes; syllables; prepare to recite.

Guided group work

T15   Give children sheets marked with lines of eight dashes (one per syllable). Help them make up their own, modern, cautionary verse.

Plenary

T1   Class recite their pages, to read complete poem in sequence. Guided group read their poem. H2d T2 Discuss what makes them effective. How is Victorian poem the same/different from modern version?

Advertisements

Persuasive Text. Year 4, Term 3.

Commercial advertisements can be read as an historical source. They both mirror and influence the ways of life, aspirations and social values of men, women, children and the ways in which these change from decade to decade. Children are familiar with the concepts of advertising and can understand them as persuasive interpretations. Text is minimal, supported by clear picture clues and illustrates a range of linguistic features. The History of Advertising Trust is an excellent resource (www.hatads.org.uk): posters for whole-class work; calendars which children can work on individually or in groups. Their collection on 'Women in Advertising – from Victorian Times to Today' was used to plan for the following learning objectives.

History objectives

H4a,b Ask and answer questions from sources about life in the 1890s; 1930 to the present.

H2a   Characteristics of periods and societies, attitudes and experiences of men, women, children.

H2b   Social diversity.

H2c   Reasons for situations and changes.

H2d   Make links between situations, changes, within and across periods.

Reasons why the past is represented and interpreted in different ways.

Literacy hour objectives

T18   From examples of persuasive writing investigate how style and vocabulary can be used to convince the intended reader.

T19   To evaluate advertisements for impact, appeal, honesty, focusing on how information about the product is presented: exaggerated claims, tactics for grabbing attention, linguistic devises; puns, jingles, alliteration, invented words.

T25   To design an advertisement making use of linguistic and other features learned from examples.

S3   To understand how the grammar of a sentence is altered; statement to question; question to order; positive to negative.

W15   To use a range of presentational skills, e.g. print script for captions, headings for posters, range of computer-generated fonts.

The opportunities to use these skills in order to discuss and evaluate messages of old advertisements, and compare them with those of today offer an exciting variety of possibilities.

Diary of Anne Frank (21 August 1942) (OHT)

Diaries and journals recounting experiences and events (Year 6, Term 1).

History objectives

H4   Find out about the past from a variety of sources.

H2a,b Characteristic features of periods and beliefs, attitudes and experiences of men, women and children; social, religious, cultural, ethnic diversity.

Literacy hour objectives

T3   Personal responses to literature, identifying why and how a text affects the reader. Prepare a short section of the story as a script.

T11 Distinguish between biography and autobiography, fact and opinion, implicit and explicit point of view.

T14 Develop skills of biographical and autobiographical writing in role of an historical character through describing a person from different perspectives, e.g. police.

T15 Develop a journalistic style; consider balanced ethical reporting.

S4 Identify connectives to convey sequence; causal connectives.

Anne Frank: literacy hour plan (Year 6, Term 1)

Whole class: text level

H2a,b What do you know about Anne Frank? Put diary extract in context; use website, photo scrapbook of story of her life, brief history of the Holocaust, and tour of the rooms where she lived (http://www.annefrank.com).

H4a Read diary entry.

H4B What more does this extract tell us (weather, hiding place, holiday . . .)?

T11 What is special about a diary (not written for others; personal views, feelings, perspective, language)? What does it tell us about Anne's feelings, relationships, what sort of person she is?

S4 How does Anne explain the time sequence (first three days, now, at present, already, now).
Identify causal connectives (because a lot of houses had been searched; because we all knocked ourselves in the doorway).

T15 List on flip-chart what you would need to consider in writing:
- a newspaper article about the discovery of the diary
- a police account of the search for the hiding place.

Independent group work

HSa,b,c (i) Write a newspaper account of the discovery of the diary.

T14 (ii) Write a police report on searching for the hiding place.

T3 (iii) Read/write another entry from Anne's diary.

Guided group work

H5a,b,c Prepare a diary extract as a film script.

Plenary

H3 Compare interpretations; discuss fact/opinion; point of view, validity.

After sharing these literacy hour plans, which used a variety of texts across a wide age range, and encompassed both literacy and history objectives, the students agreed that they would have a go at developing these models in other contexts during their coming block placements in schools.

Analysis of links between the National Literacy Strategy and historical thinking

The UK School Museums Group Conference (1999) invited a short paper on links between history and the literacy strategy, which they could use to ensure that discussions of their artefact collections with primary school children and the information labels, brochures and follow-up activities which they provide (quizzes, trails, worksheets) reflect and develop the objectives of the literacy framework. They felt that this would enable them to justify to schools the time spent on visits to museums; a parlous situation – but an interesting exercise. The resulting analysis could also be used as a starting point for developing similar links in school.

Types of non-fiction texts

The summary of the range of non-fiction given in *The National Literacy Strategy* (DfEE 1998: 66–72) lists a variety of types of text which can be used in historical contexts, and which move from simple description and instruction in Year 1 to discussion and debate in Years 4 to 6.

Information texts						
Signs, labels, captions, lists	Y1					
Non-chronological reports	Y1	Y2	Y3	Y4		Y6
Observations	Y1		Y3	Y4	Y5	
Reports, articles	Y1		Y3	Y4		
Describe and classify				Y4	Y5	
Formal writing: public information, documents etc.						Y6
Instructional texts						
Instructions	Y1	Y2	Y3			
Rules, recipes, directions, instructions showing how things are done						
Processes, systems, operations					Y5	
Explanations		Y2		Y4		Y6
Puzzles, riddles			Y3			
Viewpoints, fact/opinion, discussion, debate				Y4	Y5	
Discussion texts						Y6
Chronological texts						
Recount events, activities (visits)					Y5	
Observations which recount experiences over time						Y6

Technical vocabulary

The technical terms which should form part of pupils' developing vocabulary for talking about language (DfEE 1998: 69–77) can be used in the discussion of and writing about artefacts or other historical sources. Again these develop from simple questions and instructions, an old recipe, how to play a simple Victorian game or use a butter pat at Key Stage 1, to the language of probability, opinion and argument in Year 4 and of hypothesis and perspective in Year 6.

Y1   Question, label, instruction, list, non-chronological writing.

Y2   Explanation, fact, notes, skim, scan.

Y3   Definition, bullet points, past tense, legend, myth.

Conjunction: if, so, while, though, since, when; time – first, then, after, meanwhile (Y3, T3, sentence level 5)

Y4   Connection: conditional – 'if . . . then'; 'on the other hand'; . . . 'finally'; 'so' (Y4, T3, sentence level 4)

Argument

Debate

Discussion – argument for and against

Opinion

Y5   Chronological sequence

Point of view

Y6   Word derivation

Hypothesis

Viewpoint

Sight vocabulary, writing and spelling

The same pattern is embedded in the high frequency vocabulary children are expected to learn to recognise in context, through shared work, practice and exploration from Reception to Year 2, and to learn to use, write and spell correctly in Years 4/5 (DfEE 1998: 60–3). These words, with which children are expected to become very familiar, reflect the key questions, deductions and inferences of historical enquiry in increasingly complex ways.

Questions, Deductions and Inferences	R–Y2 Sight recognition	Y4–5 Write and spell correctly
Key Questions	What	Used
What is it?	Where	
How was it made?	Who	
Used?	People, their	
What did it mean to the people	Make, made	
who made/used it?	Name	
	House, home	
Probability	If	Almost
Distinguish between what is known,	May	Know, knew
possible, probable;	Or	Why
Hypotheses	Should	Think, thought
	Would	Might
		Sometimes
		Sure

Questions, Deductions and Inferences	R–Y2 Sight recognition	Y4–5 Write and spell correctly
Explanations, Opinion	Because So	
Chronology, Change Similarity/difference, cause/effect	After, again, just, last, new, now, next, old, once, then, time, when	Always, before, began between, change, different, during, first, follow(ing), often, still, stopped, suddenly, through, today, while, year

Scaffolding children's historical thinking

Bruner's notion (1966) of devising scaffolding frameworks for supporting and developing children's thinking processes has been applied to thinking in history through research and in published history resources (Counsell and Thomson 1997). The National Literacy Strategy has generated many further examples (e.g. Wray and Medwell 1998). Many of these writing frames can be used to enable children to develop the literacy skills defined in the technical vocabulary in historical contexts.

Children can use them to write structured reports about artefacts or sites; this report is about . . .; detail a, b, c, d; conclusion. They can write explanations of historical events, or of why people in the past may have behaved in a certain way: I want to explain why: reason i) ii) iii) iv); so now you see why . . . They can use a series of steps to sequence instructions ranging from how to make a peg doll to how to navigate a course to the East Indies in an Elizabethan ship. They can use a template to identify an issue, list arguments for/against, and write a conclusion. If the writing frames are linked to ICT this allows the flexibility to reorganise text, to work collaboratively, and it gives a structure for comparing responses.

History, literacy and fiction

There has recently been a renewed exploration of ways in which story and in particular fiction set in the past can help children to develop historical understanding (Hoodless 1998; English Heritage 1998a; Bage 1999). When a group of Year 3 BA QTS students worked in pairs on the National Literacy Strategy Summary of Fiction and Poetry (DfEE 1998: 66–8), brainstorming texts they had actually used, they found that between them they had already used each of the genres specified for each year group in their history teaching. One interesting fact to emerge was that all kinds of historical texts and genres had been adapted for use at a range of levels: the Year 1 spidergraph for example recorded that five-year-old children taught by these students had worked on Egyptian and Greek myths and legends, Saxon and Viking sagas and Chaucer. Year 6 children had worked on extracts from Dickens, Leon Garfield and Rosemary Sutcliffe and written their own scripts after hot-seating as factory owners and child workers.

One student, Hannah Dewfall, said that 'it was my own delight in historical fiction that fuelled my enjoyment of history'. But she was also aware of the dilemmas of teaching history through fiction.

> While English teachers often see historical fiction as a minor genre history teachers often see it as an inaccurate view of historical events. If an historical novel is to be used to teach history, social conditions and public events must be thoroughly researched, free from anachronisms and an integral part of the text.

She went on to explore ways in which literacy hour objectives for fiction might deepen children's historical understanding. Her Year 5 class were reading *The Machine Gunners* (Westall 1975). She focused on two statements to discuss how the central character, a child, is presented through dialogue, action and description and how the reader responds to him through examining his relationship with the other characters (NLS Year 5, Term 1, Text 3).

> Chas watched them as if they were ants, without sympathy, because they were a slummy kind of family.

and

> Besides the dead German would scare the silly little cow. She wouldn't interfere in men's business again.

She used these statements to help the children discuss reasons for attitudes to class, race and gender now and in the past, and why these might change over time.

Another student read extracts from three stories about the Second World War. *Rose Blanche* (McEwan 1985) a fictional story about concentration camps, *After the War is Over* (Foreman 1995) a story about real children and events in the history of a village and the *Diary of Anne Frank* (Frank 1989), an eyewitness account.

Through focused discussions her Year 6 children considered how the authors handled time and conveyed the passing of time, and the influence of the viewpoint of narrators on the readers' view of events as well as differences between fact, opinion and fiction (Year 5, Term 1, Text 2; 11; Term 2, Text 1); we need such creative teachers who are proactive in responding to change and interpreting requirements in ways which give them ownership and reflect their professional judgements. We do not want passive, mechanistic teachers who are targets for political manipulation. We need literacy to be taught not by teachers who enable children to read, write and cipher by rule and recipe but in ways which provide children with new tools for thinking.

History, non-fiction and the literacy strategy

Baldwin (2003) has identified literacy strategy objectives in comprehension throughout Key Stage 2, which can be used in connection with interpretations in history. These range from distinguishing between fact and fiction and comparing the way information is presented, in Year 3, to comparing how different texts treat the same information, in Year 5. He also lists non-fiction writing composition objectives which can be applied to interpretations in history, ranging from presenting a point of view in Year 4 to describing a person from different perspectives in Year 6. Taylor (2001) describes how her Year 6 class learned history within the literacy framework through a topic on Charles Dickens. They researched his character in order to write a biography and a CV. They watched the beginning of the film *Oliver Twist* to compare their lives with his, then used dialogue from the text to write a play script. They read a description of Coketown from *Hard Times*, (underlining and finding the meaning of unknown vocabulary), to find out about the impact of the Industrial Revolution. This led to paintings and poems describing a walk through Coketown and discussion of the benefits and disadvantages of industrialisation.

Engaging in fictional and non-fictional writing

The children's author Stewart Ross worked with Year 6 at St Illytd's School in Swansea, using the internet, as part of the Adopt an Author Scheme funded by the National Endowment for Science, Technology and the Arts (Nesta) (Ross 2004). The aim of the project was to give children, and particularly boys, an insight into the way professional writers operate. He was working on *Tales of the Dead: Ancient Rome* (2005a) and began by asking the children to compose their own storyboards, twenty frames of words and pictures, that would be their smaller version of the book he was preparing for Dorling Kindersley. He sent them some of the roughs which they used as a guide for spreads of their own, choosing subjects from the agreed book map. They were invited to write attention-grabbing openings and develop them to a cliffhanging end. At the end of the project the teacher said that the children had looked at fiction and non-fiction in depth, confronted issues such as slavery, seen that writers are normal human beings, and had their confidence considerably reinforced.

Historical fiction

A sense of other times and experiences may be more successfully drawn from fiction, a more nourishing food for the imagination than many 'historic experiences' available. Some recent historical fiction is humorous and instantly readable. *The Silver Spoon of Solomon Snow* (Umansky 2004) is the story of a foundling's journey in search of his true identity, with terrific verbal and visual jokes on the way. *Jammy Dodgers on the Run* (Sivers 2004), set in the Victorian underworld of Seven Dials, is gruesome in places but also full of fun. *Joshua Cross and the Queen's Conjurer* (Redmond 2003) is a time-slip adventure set in Tudor times. *Tread Softly* (Pennington 2004) is historical fiction about Elizabethan plotting and intrigue on a more serious level and *Anne Boleyn and Me: the diary of Elinor Valjean* (Prince 2004) presents, in diary format, the reactions of a young Spanish woman to Henry VIII's rejection of Catherine of Aragon.

Older classics for children such as *Tom's Midnight Garden* (Pearce 1976) may be read simply as stories which take you to other times, or they could be used to explore what they also tell us of the times in which they were written. Do they reflect a nostalgia to retrieve vanishing ideals or a community outliving the transience of individuals? Dan Dare, hero of the post-Second World War *Eagle* comic, can also be seen as representing the values of the Festival of Britain: liberal (slightly evangelical) nationalism. It is interesting to compare the predictions for space technology of the time with reality, which turned out to be far more advanced – although Dan was able to relieve the rationing crisis with food from Venus. Dan Dare can tell us lots about the 1950s.

Narrative Matters (Bage 1999) looks in depth at the use of story in history. *History and English in the Primary School* (Hoodless 1998) is a theoretical examination of case studies which link the two subjects. The Literacy Through History Project (Nichol 1998, Lewis and Wray 1988, Nichol 2000) makes links between a discrete literacy hour and history.

Speaking and listening

The Primary Strategy has a strong emphasis on speaking and listening as part of assessment for learning. Speaking and listening are crucial for extended thinking and clarifying and embedding new concepts. There are, of course, many contexts for speaking and listening in history: group discussion, discussing interpretations of sources, justifying statements, problem solving and evaluating learning.

Drama

Drama, in its different forms, extends and clarifies thinking through speaking and listening in role. I watched a Year 1/2 class responding to a student in three separate roles. A Roman sandal had been lost and was now in a museum show case (under an upturned aquarium). The student used different signifiers for each role. She was in turn the Roman child who had lost the shoe, the archaeologist who discovered it and the museum curator. The children listened and questioned her in each role without difficulty and with great interest.

Steve Mynard decided to take a break from teaching and set out to explore some ideas of his own about rejuvenating the curriculum with the intention of putting 'some of the creativity and imagination back' into professional development. He runs a Living History Course which is held all over England (steve.mynard@blueyonder.co.uk).

This year I was asked to run a session to 'tell a group of postgraduate distance learning students all they need to know about history'. Hmm. I used a session my colleague, Mike Huggins (1997), had written about, which required me to give an arresting knock on the door with my stick and appear bent, wearing my second-best long black dress and wrapped in a piece of hand-dyed and woven cloth I had found in Ireland, in role as a Kendal woman in 1589. This caused a sensation. There is no space to recount this interpretation in detail but it involved the students in each choosing a name, photocopied from the parish records of the time, and responding in role. They chose a house from a contemporary map and a lifestyle indicated by the places named on the map (e.g. tenters' field). From a series of contemporary woodcuts they each chose an occupation. I developed the scenario, reporting from key documents throughout the year which record how the plague arrived, its effects and the problems the inhabitants faced in knowing how to deal with it, what to do with those who were ill, whether to close the market . . . The role play started as great fun as people developed their roles and addressed each other each time by name. But what astonished me was how the atmosphere gradually changed, became muted until some people were practically in tears. It ended with a reading from the vicar's sermon at the end of the year when the plague had subsided, attributing it to the misdeeds of the people, living and dead, and looking forward to returning, chastened, to their previous happy community.

The session involved making inferences from maps and a variety of primary written sources, and statistics, considering problems from the points of view of those living at the time, beginning to understand how different people may have felt, and filling in the gaps, by extrapolating from evidence of what was known and tracing the events chronologically through the year. Everyone felt relaxed about talking freely in role. The session was also very informative. There had been no reading or writing but a great deal of speaking and listening.

Oral history

Claire (2004) gives excellent guidance on how to plan for oral history. She also refers to Howarth (1998), an excellent book for teachers interested in developing their personal understanding of oral history, and to practical books on oral history in schools: Hewitt and Harris (1992) and Redfern (1996). She suggests putting 'Oral History' into Google for a wealth of websites.

History and mathematics

It is recognised in the *National Numeracy Strategy* (DfEE 1999a: 16, 17) that mathematics contributes to many subjects which may form the starting point of a mathematics lesson or be applied in the context of other lessons. Examples of contexts in history using Numeracy Strategy objectives from Reception to Year 6 are given in Table 6.2

TABLE 6.2 Examples of links between the National Numeracy Strategy and historical contexts for mathematics

	Numeracy Strategy	History contexts
Reception	Use number names in familiar contexts. Use language such as more or less; heavier, lighter. Sort into sets	My sister is two, I am four Old iron is heavier, new iron is lighter Old/new
Year 1	Count on and back, in ones and in tens; addition and subtraction; mental calculations Compare, measure in non standard units: two lengths masses capacities Everyday language to describe 2D and 3D shapes	Time-line calculations Old/new building Old/new artefacts Old recipes Doors, windows, tiles, brickwork
Year 2	Count, read, order numbers to 100; count on or back Estimate, measure, compare Sort shapes Use mathematical vocabulary to describe position, direction, movement	Time-line calculations Describe artefacts in class museum, costumes, gloves; buildings, recipes Tiles, bricks, mosaics Journeys, maps
Year 3	Read, write and order numbers to 1000; count on and back Use units of time and understand relationship between them: hour, day, week, month, year Solve given problem organising and interpreting numerical data	Time-line calculations Calculations: journeys, letters, newspapers, diaries, timetables Census, street directories, graveyard studies, population statistics, trade figures, questionnaires and surveys
Year 4	Know and use relationships between familiar units: length, mass, capacity Use appropriate number operations to solve problems	Recipes, diet, loads carried, weight of artefacts See Year 3 suggestions
Year 5	Understand, calculate area e.g. of rectangle Use all four operations to solve simple word problems involving numbers and quantities, including time	Maps, changes in land use, sites and buildings How long? Longer, shorter, before, after, how many?
Year 6	Measure acute and obtuse angles to nearest degree Use appropriate operations involving numbers and quantities Extract and interpret information in tables, diagrams, charts	Journeys, buildings Trade, population See data presentation Year 3 onwards

History and the numeracy hour

Achievement

While the key learning objectives of the numeracy hour must clearly be to develop confidence and competence in mathematics it is often possible to do this in the context of an historical topic. The concepts of measurement, scale and the properties of 2D and 3D shapes could be taught by making and describing models through a sequence of structured numeracy hours (National Numeracy Strategy 6, DfEE 1999a: 102–5). Key Stage 1 work on counting, sets, number sequences in relation to money and real-life problems could be linked to role-play on Victorian market sellers (NNS 5: 2, 4, 6).

A Victorian market

Mike and Edward, both aged six, devised their street cry in a literacy hour on Victorian street cries but might equally well have done so in a numeracy hour (see Figure 6.4).

> Oranges, oranges, roll up, oranges
> 5p for 1, 10p for 2, 15p for 3, 20p for 4, 5 for 25p!
> All your oranges!

At other times, as with some history-literacy hour links, the mathematics calculation may also be an integral part of an historical investigation. This is particularly relevant to making time-line calculations in order to consider sequence, duration and causes and effects. Numerical calculations are also fundamental in organising and making probabilistic interpretations of data: for example making inferences about reasons for changes in population size, occupations, movement, family size in your locality, and the extent to which they reflect national changes (NNS 6: 113–17). Children could devise techniques to analyse the proportions of Palladian buildings in photographs to see how accurately they reflect the 1 : 1.6. proportions of the Golden Rectangle in order to demonstrate the influence of Greek architecture on subsequent buildings. *A Teacher's Guide to Maths and the Historic Environment* (English Heritage 1998b) is packed with further ideas, and museums such as the Weald and Downland Open Air Museum are developing structured numeracy programmes linked to museum visits.

The examples given in Chapters 7, 8 and 9 of opportunities to develop mathematics concepts through historical enquiries remain appropriate (NNS 1: 40). They have been linked to the key objectives of the numeracy framework from Reception to Year 6 (Table 6.2). The numeracy strategy explicitly states that 'you need to look for opportunities for drawing mathematics experience out of a wide range of children's activities. Mathematics contributes to many subjects of the curriculum, often in practical ways' (NNS 1: 16). It identifies opportunities to collect data, by counting and measuring of all kinds, to relate ratio, scale, position, direction and coordinates

written by Edward and mike
· pictures by Edward and mike

"Oranges oranges get your oranges!"

"Oranges oranges roll up oranges"

"5p for 1, 10 p for 2, 15p for 3, 20p for 4, 25 for

"all your oranges"!

FIGURE 6.4 Mike's and Edward's street cries written in a literacy hour could easily have been part of a numeracy hour.

to maps, to relate problems to the measurement of time, in days, weeks, years, decades, centuries. The National Curriculum also identifies opportunities to make these links. With imagination they can be developed both within the numeracy hour and extend beyond it. Historical questions can be identified and data collected from a site visit: measurements, gravestone information, shapes and patterns in buildings and fabrics. Key knowledge and skills in mathematics can be developed through teaching and activities in the numeracy hour, and linked to work in other subjects in the plenary session (NNS 1:14); founded on sound understanding of the skills required, investigations can extend well beyond the numeracy hour, if they are interesting, and enhance relevance and coherence in a creative curriculum.

History and the numeracy hour: two examples

Besides applying mathematical calculations to historical enquiries children can gain historical insights by finding out how people in the past represented numbers and worked out arithmetic. Robin Foster, a colleague who lectured in primary mathematics education, made this point when I discussed this section of the book with him. 'The arithmetic we take for granted as simple or trivial taxed great minds in the past,' he explained. 'Making children aware of how mathematics developed, and how others too found it difficult can be supportive and illuminating.' It was not long before he was persuaded to put his theory into practice. Here are his plans for two numeracy hours he taught to a Year 2 and a Year 6 class.

Year 2, tens and units in a Victorian classroom

Resources:

Picture of a Victorian school room (e.g. Robson 1874)
Picture of a Victorian abacus, Robson 1874 (Figure 6.5)
A modern two-pronged abacus
Worksheets with empty two-pronged abaci for children to complete

FIGURE 6.5   A Victorian abacus.

Desired learning outcomes

At the end of the session the children will have

- used vocabulary relating to the passing of time; identified similarities and differences between their classroom and a Victorian classroom using visual sources (H 1b, 2b, 4a, 6b/c);
- have seen ways of representing tens and units and relate this to particular numbers.

Mental activity

Have a piece of wire or string with six beads on it. Show the children the beads. *How many beads are there?*

Separate and cover up some of the beads with your hand. *How many are hidden? How many can you see?*

Repeat this for other values of beads. Talk about how in earlier days children did not have much equipment to help them with their mathematics.

Main session

- Show the children the picture of the Victorian classroom

The picture is in black and white, is it a photograph? Imagine the scene in colour. How is it different from our classroom? How is it the same? What do you think the object in the picture is for? What is an abacus?

- Show the children the close up picture of the Victorian abacus

How could you count using this? What happens if I wanted to show 23? Demonstrate how you could have 23 beads or use 20 (as two tens) and three as three ones. Show a simplified idea of using a two-pronged abacus to show numbers up to 99.

- Individual or group work

Supply the children with pictures of two-pronged abaci and ask them to represent particular numbers. (Vary the numbers according to the individuals.) Use the abacus to show 56. *If you had five beads, what number could you make? Which is the biggest/ smallest?*

- Plenary

Relate their answers to the Victorian abacus. Allow them to compare their results. *What about numbers which are greater than 99?*

Year 6, Elizabethan multiplication

Gelosia algorithm – background information

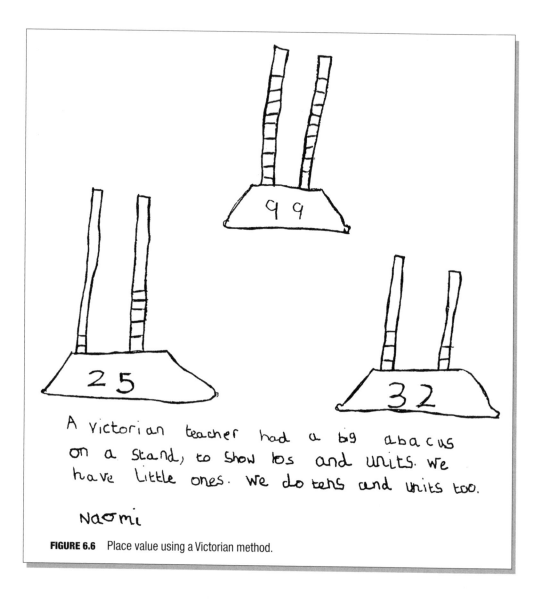

A Victorian teacher had a big abacus on a stand, to show tos and units. We have little ones. We do tens and units too.

Naomi

FIGURE 6.6   Place value using a Victorian method.

This method, which was used in the reign of Queen Elizabeth I to multiply two-digit numbers, was probably introduced from India. The example shows how it is used to multiply 13 by 49 (Figure 6.7).

- Draw a lattice grid of 2 × 2 cells; divide each cell with a diagonal line as shown.
- Put the numbers to be multiplied above and to the right.
- Multiply each digit on the top by each digit on the right; record the tens part of the number at the top left of the cell and the units in the bottom right of the cell.

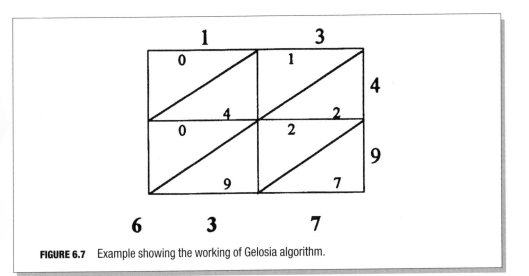

FIGURE 6.7   Example showing the working of Gelosia algorithm.

$1 \times 4 = 04$

$3 \times 4 = 12$

$3 \times 9 = 27$

$1 \times 9 = 09$

- Add the digits diagonally starting from the bottom right to obtain the final multiplication result of $13 \times 49 = 637$.

Careful consideration of the place value will reveal that the only units in the result are in the bottom right-hand part of the grid. The next three digits above and to the left are the tens digits, the next diagonal represents the hundred digits and so on. This is an indication of how the algorithm works, but is not really a requirement of anyone successfully employing it.

Year 6, Numeracy hour: designing and working some 'Tudor' calculations

Resources:
   Worksheets with empty Gelosia grids

Desired learning outcomes
Children will:

- have considered possible multiplication problems people in Elizabethan times may have needed to solve; that they used a calculation method different from those taught today which was probably introduced from India (H H2a, b);
- be able to compute these problems using an Elizabethan method (Gelosia).

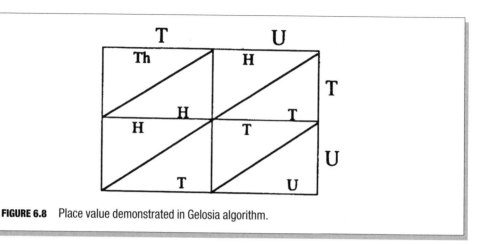

FIGURE 6.8 Place value demonstrated in Gelosia algorithm.

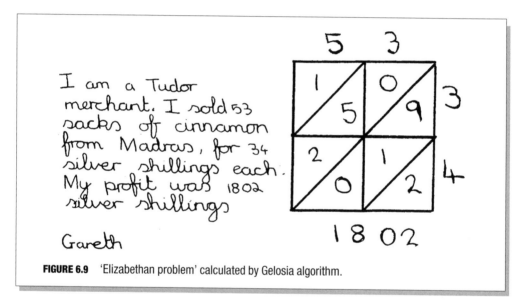

FIGURE 6.9 'Elizabethan problem' calculated by Gelosia algorithm.

Mental activity

Oral multiplication questions (e.g. 7×3)

Teacher records answers on board using lattice-type grid

Main session

Brainstorm possible two-digit multiplication problems people in Elizabethan times might have needed to calculate (e.g. English pirates capture Spanish mule train of 52 donkeys in Central America, each carrying 25 bags of silver coins; profit from 30 sacks of peppercorns from Madagascar sold at 63 shillings a sack; 1 quart of beer per day for a ship's crew of 45 on a 30-day voyage; distance of a 25-day voyage, average speed 25 knots each day).

List problems on flip-chart

Demonstrate how to use the Gelosia method to calculate answers to some of the problems. Supply children with blank grids. Ask individuals or groups to work out remaining problems (or design others) using Gelosia algorithm.

Plenary

Individuals demonstrate particular examples.

Compare results and lattices for 37×25 and 25×37. *Are the results the same? Look carefully at the tens place of the answer. How was it worked out?*

Discuss the place value aspects of this method of recording.

Developing investigations

Clearly the teacher also has a management role in supporting and extending an investigation through a sequence of activities identified in the medum-term plan and in preparing classroom organisation to maximise existing resources, by allowing children to plan and develop computer work while away from the computer. Working together to construct and interrogate a database and discuss and interpret findings is one example of planning over time and organising limited resources.

Databases

A database involves collecting information (records), with shared characteristics (fields), in order to look for patterns and trends. These can be recorded graphically as pie or bar charts, graphs or Venn diagrams. In the context of an historical investigation, such sources may be:

1. street directories, census and parish records of births, deaths, age, sex, occupation, address;

2. other statistics relating to population (illness, height, diet);

3. trade figures (cattle sold at Smithfield, price, weight, numbers);

4. information about buildings or archaeological sites with some shared characteristics (e.g. plans of Roman villas, recording shape, size, hypocausts, mosaic pavements);

5. place-name endings in an area indicating time and date of settlement (Roman, Viking, Saxon).

Such sources could be investigated through asking questions about change and about the causes and effects of change and interpreting the findings in the light of incomplete evidence, uncertainty, probability and what is known of the period. Each child can collect information for at least one record – a gravestone, for example – as part of a churchyard study, complete a 'record sheet' on paper, categorising the information in fields to ensure that s/he can structure the information in this way, then type the record onto the database. Next, when all the information has been collected, each child can fill in a second sheet setting out a question and the correct format for asking this question of the database. When children have the responses to their questions they can fill in the last part of the sheet, saying what inferences they can make from them. This tried and tested method ensures that everyone understands how to use the database, and has equal access to creating and interrogating it in a short time, although the complexity of the questions and sophistication of the deductions can vary considerably. Alternatively children could interrogate an existing database, each constructing a question, finding the information, then trying to interpret it. One interesting finding from a local workhouse database was that most of the inmates were described as paupers; one of the few other groups was 'female school teachers'. Deductions? Another finding was that there were few girls in the workhouse but a lot of young boys. Reasons?

History and information and communications technology

The programmes of study for ICT across the curriculum

Children are required to use information technology sources to support and develop their enquiries in history, to select and analyse information, to share ideas as part of this process, and to organise and communicate their findings (DfEE 1999b). At Key Stage 1 they might gather information (text, images, sound) from a range of sources (CD-Roms, videos, television), use and create databases; at Key Stage 2 these sources might be extended to include the internet, with more emphasis on selecting suitable sources, and working with others to interpret, analyse and check relevance.

This investigative process may be developed at Key Stage 1 by planning and writing instructions, exploring real or imaginary situations through simulations; at Key Stage 2 there may be more emphasis on bringing together and cross-referencing text, images, sound or tables and on reviewing ideas in the light of what others have done.

The findings of the investigation might be presented as a display at Key Stage 1; and at Key Stage 2, through writing brochures, posters, animations or internet publication on the school website, with a sense of appropriate audiences – other pupils, parents, a wider and impersonal audience. All of these are generic requirements taken from the Programmes of Study for ICT.

ICT and history: decisions

The Programmes of Study for History at Key Stages 1 and 2 suggest that the most appropriate ways to use ICT are as sources of information and to make it easier to organise and communicate findings, but clearly this can involve all the other key elements of historical thinking: knowledge and understanding, chronology and interpretations of the past. The wealth of opportunities to use ICT to develop children's historical understanding is daunting and clear decisions need to be made about how this is planned and organised.

Recent imaginative examples of using ICT in history

Interactive whiteboards make possible the interaction between resources such as CD-Roms, website pages, Word documents and PowerPoint slides. They can be used to model how to complete tasks, to gather the views of a class, and to shuffle up and move around text and pictures by dragging and dropping. Pupils can play with ideas using frameworks such as circles or rectangles to create interactive exercises, hierarchical ordering schemes and thinking organisers; this helps them to memorise concepts and ideas, which might not otherwise stick in their minds.

Modelling how to analyse characteristics of a period

The teacher could model for the whole class how to sort a variety of images of a given period using one set of criteria, for example, 'rich' and 'poor'. The children could then work in groups on their laptops or desk machines sorting the images according to other criteria: men/women, adults/children, town/country or whatever criteria they may devise. The whole class could share the work of all the groups and work out what they could deduce and infer about the period.

Modelling concept development

A variety of images of, for example, Victorian houses, could be collected then sorted into categories: semi-detached, detached, terrace. Groups could sort according to other criteria: part of the country, materials made from, size, town or country. This would involve further research and inferences. Sharing their findings children could discuss: Why were they built? Where did the money come from? Similarities and differences in 'Victorian houses'. This would stimulate far more complex thinking than 'a model of a Victorian house'. They might then look at Victorian houses in their locality.

Modelling sequencing activities

The teacher could model with the class the kinds of discussion and reasoning involved in deciding how to sequence, for example, types of transport since 1930. How do we decide which came next? What changes are illustrated? What caused these changes? What were the effects on people's lives? Do changes occur at equal intervals? Can we find by dating them and linking the images to a time-line?

In groups children could repeat the activity with other key features: clothes, houses, leisure activities, jobs. Then the whole class could consider interactions between changes and reasons for them. This would work well for the nineteenth century too: inventions, factories, transport, trade, town sizes.

Modelling place-name analysis

The teacher, with the whole class, might identify place names with a particular Viking (or Saxon) ending on a map (e.g. beck – a stream). In groups the children could identify other Viking endings (e.g. thwaite, how, rigg), possibly using maps of differentiated scales. The information could be combined to find out where the Vikings settled and why they chose those places.

Using a data projector to discuss artefacts, paintings, photographs

This is particularly useful for discussing small artefacts as a class. A small coin, for example, could be put on a table and projected onto the screen. Or the detail on a larger artefact could be zoomed in on, in order to discuss: what we know, what we can guess, what we should like to know.

The teacher could show the class how to explore a painting or photograph by moving around the image with a mouse or graphic pen pointer and magnifying small details. This could be radio connected and passed around the class. Crowd scenes, such as Frith's Railway Station, come to mind. Or two different interpretations could be compared, contrasted, explained, or two images which illustrate changes over time. A whiteboard with a graphics tablet could be used in the same way and would be a cheaper option.

Virtual tours using PowerPoint

Stuart Roper's class used an interactive whiteboard to look at the Victorans through the eyes of the 1851 Great Exhibition (Roper 2006). On a PowerPoint file he placed a plan of the Crystal Palace, and a picture of the inside of the building (www.vam.ac.uk/vastatic/microsites/bg_teachers_packs/supp_info/supps7.htm). Pupils were asked, for example, to find something few people had used before. In turn, using their floor plans, they looked for the place on the whiteboard. Each correct spot had been given a hyperlink. Pressing on the link took pupils to a picture which they could discuss: how was it made, who used it, how did it impact on their lives? The people in the picture were made to ask questions by pressing a sound recording inside a speech bubble. The pupils were individually asked to pretend they were standing next to the person and record an answer. This model could be used imaginatively in any setting or period.

Labelling, clueing and information gathering using PowerPoint

This activity could be used in preparation for or as follow-up to a visit. If it follows a visit the children could take it in turns to collect their own images using a digital camera. This would teach them that there are decisions to be made about what to include and what to leave out in creating accounts and documentaries.

A hyperlink in PowerPoint can be created by clicking and dragging a shape over the portion of the picture you want to be linked to another file. Click on the 'slide show' and on the menu click on 'action settings'. In the dialogue box that appears, highlight the 'hyperlink' option. By pressing on the scroll down arrow you are presented with the option of linking to another PowerPoint slide or any file, page or sound. Choose where you want the link to take you to review the slide show. Once thoroughly tested, use 'line' and 'fill' colour option from the drawing tool bar to hide the link; select 'no fill' and 'no line' to make the shape completely transparent. (Hint: use very specific windows.) The shape needs to have no fill-in colour and no line. This means it is a hidden link.

This could be used for labelling, and adding information. For example, make a square over the portcullis so that when a child clicks on it a label saying 'portcullis' appears. Or it could reveal a clue, pose a question, or link to another page of information. By moving the mouse over the image at random the child may accidentally find other information.

You could create a virtual tour of the building in this way, prior to a visit, opening different doors inside a building, to familiarise children with the place or to help them to plan an investigation in advance of a visit.

Creating a sound recording in a PowerPoint document

Another possibility would be to insert sound into an image. Sailors on a picture of a Tudor ship might explain their diet, their role on board ship, the purpose of their voyage . . . An image of a job or craft which no longer exists could be explained by a former practitioner. Clips from an archive of speeches could be linked to images of the speakers.

Plug a microphone into the computer. From the menu select 'movies and sounds'. Click on 'record sound'. A dialogue box appears that allows you to record your own voice. When finished click on 'OK' and the speaker icon will appear in your file. To run as a slide show, click on the icon for playback.

Using a desktop to compare interpretations

You could put visual information into a photo-editing program (Windows/ digital/photo-edit/paint), in order to show why there are different interpretations of what a derelict place or ruined building may have been like in the past; for example a Roman villa, a ruined castle, a disused Second World War airfield. Children could look at a picture of the ruin, draw their own interpretations of what different parts may have been like, print these out and compare and evaluate them. (Why did you think it was like this? Which seems most likely? Why?) Then they could see artists' interpretations and compare them with their own. This is a way of scaffolding children's historical imagination.

Making reconstructions using technology

Foundation Stage

I recently visited a nursery class when the children dug up 'treasure' which the teacher had previously buried: 'jewels', 'silver' spoons, a golden box. The children were more excited than articulate as they dug the treasure up with great energy. Children watching video-recorded the event, with a little help. Later, after time for reflection, the children were able to watch the video and were very articulate about how the treasure might have been buried, by whom and why.

Key Stage 1

Hugh Moore helped Key Stage 1 children to manipulate digital photographic images to convey what they thought their own area looked like in the distant past (Moore 2004). They took a digital photograph of an area where they could see houses and a road but also plenty of trees and green. Then he used a photo-editing program (PHOTOSHOP) to cut and paste trees, green, marsh and so on all over the houses and roads. (Do not resize or crop.) The children then used PowerPoint to 'dissolve' or 'fade' transitions to make all the buildings and roads seem to disappear from the original photograph. This was done by matching up the before and after images on consecutive slides in PowerPoint, the modern photograph first. When children viewed the show and clicked on the mouse button to bring on the next slide, the houses and roads seemed to disappear but the areas of the photograph not worked on remained.

Key Stage 2

Russel Tarr (2006) suggests many advantages in encouraging children to make their own digital videos. Windows PCs now come with Microsoft Moviemaker as standard and it is possible to get a digital camcorder for little over £100. Tarr suggests video-recorded role play can be used for assessment and self-assessment and peer assessment.

At Key Stage 2 children may, for example, make a video which is the culmination of a long-term role-play project, with settings, characters and events gradually built up through research. Pupils may take on roles as directors, editors, artists, musicians, camerapersons, researchers and scriptwriters as well as actors.

Tarr suggests that, on a site visit which pupils record, they will use their cameras to record key aspects of the day and furiously scribble down accompanying notes. On their return they can edit their film and so reflect upon the day more than they would otherwise.

Then and now

Elaine Dawe, a primary school teacher, has described how she uses word-processing or desktop publishing software across the primary age range to help children compare 'old' and 'new' in their locality (Dawe 2003). Children can, for example, identify images which are old or new in a photograph and add a text box to explain why as a basis for discussion, and also for assessing progression in chronological understanding.

'Ready-made' resources for teachers

There are, of course, many complete kits available for the less confident, which can be modified. A resource pack from the Museum of Antiquities in Newcastle upon Tyne on Romans and Celts on the Northern Frontier contains lesson plans and additional resources (www.museums.ncl.ac.uk/reticulum).

Creating a website

Coventry's Herbert Art Gallery invited Year 3 pupils to create a website about significant periods of Coventry's history (Ross 2005b). The children became 'experts', looking at notable websites and explaining the use of objects. They dressed in costume for the launch. They were consulted about their own knowledge and opinions (www.theherbert.org/learning/).

Examining artefacts on line

David Mason says that artefact databases give us access to information and stimulate children to ask genuine questions, like historians, and to discuss interpretation through whole-class investigations using a data processor or group enquiries using a computer, or by annotating the images on an interactive whiteboard (Mason 2002). He describes using www.britishmuseum.co.uk. This contains three thousand artefacts. Children click on 'explore', then on 'compass', then type a keyword into the 'quick search' box. 'Sutton Hoo' will bring up all the artefacts associated with Sutton Hoo; a click on 'thumbnails' will tell you more about each artefact. But there is still much to conjecture about. Children's inferences about the Sutton Hoo purse can be collated under headings, for example evidence of wealth, imagination and technical skill, extensive trade links, use of a range of materials; they could speculate about the possible symbolism of the decorations. It is seen in Chapter 10 that such activity models the process of asking questions and making inferences about sources which, with time, children become able to do independently. The ability to download the British Museum into your classroom stimulates both teachers and children.

Virtual interactive tours

These may be DVDs, for example, 'Pyramid: beyond imagination' (BBC Interactive Factual and Learning) or virtual tours on the BBC interactive website (www.bbc.co.uk/history/multimedia_zone).

Relatively simple syndication (RSS)

This is useful to capture those moments when you are watching something just perfect for your next project. If you have Broadband you click on the RSS button and save the clips on your desktop.

Pod casting and parents

Of course, parents can be involved in all of the above activities but with pod casting they can also go on visits, share parts of lessons and become involved in work at home. For example, you could make a movie of the local area which you are studying, or of a lesson or visit, with suggestions for how to follow it up, and pod cast it. It will then be permanently available on your server for anyone given access to it to download when they are able to.

The golden rule is only to use ICT if this is the best way to achieve your learning objectives. Is it allowing you to access sources which are better than is otherwise possible? Looking at a real object or painting in a museum conveys the feel, the texture, the size and weight of an artefact better than an image on screen. Is this the best way to develop children's historical thinking in a particular context? Sometimes scribbled diagrams on a whiteboard are a more immediate response to a question than a beautifully crafted PowerPoint presentation. Sometimes drawing on a site or in a museum forces you to observe and reflect much more carefully and to remember better than a more wide-ranging video recording. Does the interactive whiteboard or a video recording stimulate more discussion than would otherwise occur or does it encourage passive viewing? On the other hand, technology is seen as 'cool'!

Recommended rich source websites

I am grateful to Ben Walsh (2003) for the following recommendations and for his teachers' booklet on using the Learning Curve to teach history through ICT (www.learningcurve.gov.uk/howto/teacherict.htm). He sees ICT as a powerful tool to enable pupils to locate, analyse and interpret data. It allows teachers to teach topics outside the mainstream. The difficulty, however, is knowing what is out there.

The National Portrait Gallery (www.npg.org.uk/live/search)

Ben Walsh recommends the National Portrait Gallery's collection of thumbnail portraits. Pupils can access a range of different portraits of the same individual, at different ages, in different clothes and possibly conveying different messages. Kings and Queens are an obvious example. Children could research a question such as 'How did this person want people to see them?'

The Public Record Office website, the Learning Curve (www.learningcurve.gov.uk)

The Snapshots section is particularly good for Victorian homes, prisons, schools. The Learning Curve, launched in 1999, has come top of the poll. Only digital cameras were ranked as useful as the Learning Curve amongst the best ICT resources for history teachers. It is structured to fit in with the National Curriculum. As well as the source material there are interactive quizzes. Pupils can, for example, joust with each other or take a tour around an Elizabethan garden.

The British Museum (www.thebritishmuseum.co.uk/compass/index.html)

This is useful for the Romans, Vikings, Anglo Saxons and Egyptians. Walsh (2003) has seen this used very effectively by pupils planning a museum exhibition on Ancient Egypt. Pupils used the Compass to select a range of objects to go into the museum and wrote accompanying notes based on the curator's notes provided.

The Smithsonian Institution (www.si.edu/)

This site has specialist exhibitions in under-resourced areas such as the African Voices Exhibition and good archaeological resources.

Cadbury's and Sainsbury's (www.cadburylearningzone.co.uk/history) (www.j-sainsbury.co.uk/museum/museum.htm)

Walsh recommends these for literary and visual sources for the Victorian period and Britain in the twentieth century.

The British Film Institute and the Public Record Office (www.bfi.org.uk) (www.learningcurve.gov.uk/onfilm/default.htm)

These are moving image sources. These resources are trailblazers and promise to be an exciting development. Newsreels can be found on www.britishpathe.com.

Census material

This can be used in all sorts of ways to research and present information about, for example, occupations in a locality, life expectancy, family size, movement into the area, employment.

Anglo Saxon burials (www.gla.ac.uk/Acad/Archaeology/resources/AngloSaxon/cemetaries/index.htm)

This site shows Anglo Saxon grave goods. Pupils could make graphs of numbers of different types of grave goods, brooches, rings, javelins and so on, and make inferences about the beliefs of the people buried with them. This would link well to mathematics (see pages 100-110).

Manuscripts

These can be found on www.pro.gov.uk/education.

Other websites

Steve Mynard, who runs living history sessions and workshops for teachers, recommends the following websites:

- www.britarch.ac.uk/yac the home page of the Young Archaeologists Club;
- www.bbc.co.uk/history/forkids/ for its loads of interactive material;
- www.spartacus.schoolnet.co.uk for your own research purposes;
- www.seasidehistory.co.uk for its photographs and archive material;
- www.local-history.co.uk;
- www.familyrecords.gov.uk which has a useful beginners' guide to tracing family history.

Support for teachers

The Historical Association (www.history.org.uk) offers excellent support for the teaching of history 5–11, including the opportunity for teachers to share good ideas and experiences and ask questions.

English Heritage (www.english-heritage.org.uk/education) helps teachers to use the environment as a resource, supported by a huge resource catalogue of books, videos and photopacks.

Museums and galleries online

These sites are recommended by Jo Peat (Walsh 2003).

The twenty-four-hour museum (www.24hourmuseum.org.uk) provides information on museums and galleries countrywide, with interactive activities for teachers to download, such as trails, useful for children's project work.

Virtual Library Museums Page (http://icom.museum/vlmp/) is suggested for regional studies. An enormous range of relevant websites can be found by searching for 'primary history' on the new Becta website (http://contentsearch.becta. org.uk/search/index.jsp?clear=y). The schools liaison website (www.schoolsliaison. org.uk/) has been created by a team of teachers who work with pupils when they visit museums. Peat also recommends particularly the Museum of London, www.museumoflondon.org.uk/MOLsite/learning/. But she warns about the downloading time, inactive links, and the importance of teachers allowing themselves plenty of time before deciding what to use with pupils.

References

Alderson, B. (ed.) (1975) *A Book of Bosh, Edward Lear*. Harmondsworth: Kestrel Books/Penguin.

Bage, G. (1999) *Narrative Matters, Teaching and Learning History Through Story*. Lewes: Falmer Press.

Baldwin, G. (2003) 'Questions you have always wanted to ask about . . . historical interpretations', *Primary History*, **33**, 20–2.

Belloc, H. (1991) *Matilda, who Told Lies and was Burned to Death*. London: Red Fox.

Black, M. (1992) *The Medieval Cookbook*. London: British Museum Press.

Bruner, J. S. (1966) *Towards a Theory of Instruction*, 7th edn (1975). Cambridge, Mass.: Harvard University Press.

Claire, H. (2004) 'Oral history: a powerful tool or a double edged sword?' *Primary History*, **38**: 20–3.

Cooper, H. (1996) 'Threat of the basics instinct', *Times Educational Supplement*, History Extra, 6 September.

Cooper, H. (1997) 'History in its own write', *Primary English Magazine*, 3 (2), 14–17.

Cooper, H. (1998a) 'History in its own write (2)' *Primary English Magazine*, 3 (3), 16–18.

Cooper, H. (1998b) 'Writing about History in the Early Years', in P. Hoodless (ed.) *History and English in the Primary School*, pp. 157–78. London: Routledge.

Cooper, H. and Twiselton, S. (1998) 'Victorian alphabets: a sampler for the Literacy Hour?', *Primary English Magazine*, 4 (2), 7–11.

Cooper, H. and Twiselton, S. (1999) 'Victorian alphabets: a sampler for the Literacy Hour? (2)' *Primary English Magazine*, 4 (3), 18–21.

Cooper, H. and Twiselton, S. (2000) *Art and Artists: Impressionism (7–9)*, Reading for Information Series. Leamington Spa: Scholastic.

Counsell, C. and Thomson, K. (1997) *Life in Tudor Times*, Cambridge Primary History Series. Cambridge: Cambridge University Press.

Dawe, E. (2003) 'From past to present', *Times Educational Supplement*, 4 July.

Deary, T. (2004) *Villainous Victorians*. Leamington Spa: Scholastic.

DfEE (1998) *National Literacy Strategy*. London: DfEE.

DfEE (1999a) *National Numeracy Strategy*. London: DfEE.

DfEE (1996b) *National Curriculum for England*. London: DfEE.

English Heritage (1998a) *Story Telling at Historic Sites*. Northampton: English Heritage.

English Heritage (1998b) *A Teacher Guide to Maths and the Historic Environment*. London: English Heritage.

Ernest, E. (1968) *The Kate Greenaway Treasury*. London: Collins.

Foreman, M. (1995) *After the War is Over*. London: Pallion.

Frank, A. (1989) *The Diary of Anne Frank*. London: Pan Books.

Hewitt, M. and Harris, A. (1992) *Talking Time: a guide to oral history for schools*. London: Learning by Design, Tower Hamlets Education.

Hoodless, P. (ed.) (1998) *History and English in the Primary School*. London: Routledge.

Huggins, M. (1997) 'Helping primary pupils access archive material in the context of Tudor local history', *Teaching History*, **87**, 31–6.

Lewis, M. and Wray, D. (1998) 'Bringing literacy and history closer together', *Primary History*, **20**, 11–13.

McEwan, I. (1985) *Rose Blanche*. London: Jonathan Cape.

Mason, D. (2002) 'Hoodunnit', *Times Educational Supplement*, 15 November.

Moore, H. (2004) 'Ancient history: things to do and questions to ask', in H. Cooper (ed.) *Exploring Time and Place Through Play: Foundation Stage to Key Stage 1*. London: David Fulton Publishers.

Nichol, J. (1998) 'Literacy Through History Project', *Primary History*, **20**, 14–17.

Nichol, J. (2000) 'Literacy, text-genres and history: reading and learning from difficult and challenging texts', *Primary History*, **24**, 13–18.

Opie, I. and Opie, P. (1980) *The Nursery Companion*. Oxford: Oxford University Press.

Pearce, P. (1976) *Tom's Midnight Garden*. London: Puffin.

Pennington, K. (2004) *Tread Softly*. London: Hodder Children's Books.

Prince, A. (2004) *Anne Boleyn and Me: the diary of Elinor Valjean*. Leamington Spa: Scholastic.

Redfern, A. (1996) *Talking in Class: oral history and the National Curriculum*. Colchester Oral History Society.

Redmond, D. (2003) *Joshua Cross and the Queen's Conjuror*. Cambridge: Wizard Books.

Roper, S. (2006) 'Crystal clear', *Times Educational Supplement*, The Teacher, 13 January.

Ross, S. (2004) 'Watch me write', *Times Educational Supplement*, 17 August.

Ross, S. (2005a) *Tales of the Dead: Ancient Rome*. London: Dorling Kindersley.

Ross, S. (2005b) 'Paperback writers', *Times Educational Supplement*, 25 February.

Sampson, B. (ed.) (1977) *Edward Lear: an Alphabet*. The Windmill Press.

Sendak, M. (1970) *Where the Wild Things Are*. Harmondsworth: Penguin.

Sivers, B. (2004) *Jammy Dodgers on the Run*. Basingstoke: Macmillan Children's Books.

Tarr, R. (2006) 'Film focus', *Times Educational Supplement*, 17 March.

Taylor, J. (2001) 'History with a twist', *Times Educational Supplement*, 30 November.

UK School Museums Group Conference, St John's House, Warwick CV34 4NF.

Umansky, K. (2004) *The Silver Spoon of Solomon Snow*. Harmondsworth: Puffin.

Walsh, B. (2003) 'A complex empire: National Archives Learning Curve takes on the British Empire', *Teaching History*, **112**, 22–7.

Westaff, R. (1975) *The Machine Gunners*. London: Macmillan.

Wray, D. and Medwell, J. (1998) *Teaching English in Primary Schools: a handbook of teaching strategies and key ideas in literacy*. London: Letts Educational.

Examples from practice

7

Teaching about the past at the Foundation Stage

WHEN I WAS ASKED to find out from a nationwide sample of early years practitioners what support they would like in teaching the strand concerned with the past, in the area of Knowledge and Understanding of the World in the *Curriculum Guidance for the Foundation Stage* (QCA 2000), I was astonished by some of their responses. In some cases they were very angry responses. 'History at three – over my dead body!' was one memorable example, followed by many reasons why this was quite inappropriate for young children. Yet learning about the passing of time, changes over time and stories set in the past are an important aspect of traditional early years experiences. Maybe we just need to tease out how this links to the processes of historical enquiry identified in Part 1 – but maybe not call it 'history'. We also need to show how finding out about the past supports children's holistic development, in terms of both emotional and social development and the development of communication skills across all the Areas of Learning.

Time: why should we regard time as so important?

Adults working with young children have always helped them to explore the past and the passing of time, although they may not call this history. We talk to children about changes in their own lives and in the lives of their families, why things change and their implications – moving house, a new baby. We help them to tell us about events in their lives, to sequence and explain them. We talk about ways in which the past was different – when you were a baby, when Granny was little. We help children to measure the passing of time: birthdays, seasons, months, weeks, days. The language of time is integral to such talk: before, after; then, now; yesterday, tomorrow, next week. Witherington and Neate (2003) show how children's own stories can extend to finding out more about grandparents and great-grandparents.

Time and change in stories

Everyone loves a story and stories have always been at the heart of early years education. Indeed Bage (2003) suggests that the whole curriculum should be organised around stories. Children can relate their own experiences of time to stories in picture books about other children and families. Kingsbury (1998) lists a variety of such books. Children can also relate to the many fictional stories about growth and change: *When I Was a Baby* (Anholt 1998), *Grandpa* (Burningham 1984), *The Old, Old Man and the Very Little Boy* (Franklin 1992). Woodhouse (2002), Barkham (2002) and Rogers (1995) show how children's personal biographies and those of people they meet can be used as a starting point for exploring the past through their direct experience.

Stories about the more distant past

Stories are inevitably concerned with sequencing events over time, with discussing causes and effects of events and with motives, why people behaved as they did: 'because, so . . .' Young children can engage with true stories from the past. Salter (1996) describes how, in role as Grace Darling, she told her Reception class the story of the brave daughter of a Victorian lighthouse keeper, which they were able to retell two weeks later to a 'reporter'.

Fairy stories, folk tales, myths and legends

A myth is part of a jigsaw of tales in which gods and goddesses mirror the activities of the cultures that create them. They speak of social behaviour and our spiritual longings. In a fairy story human beings and supernatural beings meet; human beings are often rewarded or punished for disrespect. Folk tales illustrate our day-to-day lives, with all their hopes, fears, small challenges, rewards, punishments, dangers and absurdities. Legends are mixtures of history, memory, fact and fiction. Myths and legends help children to decode the mysterious and sometimes threatening life they are growing into.

Traditional stories are derived from oral history. They tell us how there have always been wise and foolish people, good and evil, rich and poor, in all societies. They tell us of ways in which life in the past was similar to ours: people bought and sold things, went on journeys, had celebrations, had hopes, fears and disappointments. And we see how things were different, in a world of chimney sweeps, cobblers, woodcutters, goose girls, baronial feasts, of castles and windmills. Woodhouse (2001a) suggests ways in which nursery rhymes can be used to develop historical skills and understanding.

The same myths, legends and folk tales have spread throughout the world. They give insights into how people lived long ago in many places and their shared human characteristics. The Welsh tale of King March who had enormous ears, which he could not keep a secret from his barber, is thought to be linked to the horned helmet of Alexander the Great and to the Ancient Greek tale of King Midas; other versions are found as far apart as Ireland and Africa. This story reflects the common human difficulty in keeping a secret. *The Barefoot Book of Fairy Tales* (Doyle 2006) contains a broad selection of stories from around the world. Recurrent themes and characters promote universal understanding.

Fairy tales, myths and legends also link the generations more precisely in a continuity of experience. They are the stories of our grandparents and the stories of our grandchildren. Traditional tales help children to develop logic and predictive thought, to consider cause and consequence. They also tell us that we are in many ways all the same but also show us how different we all are, because we are individuals from different ethnic groups, religions, cultures and geographical areas.

The past and identity

Developing an awareness of the past, in the context of our own lives and through stories about the more distant past, is important in understanding who we are and how we relate to others. It enables us to consider why people behave as they do, to infer from their actions how they may feel and think, why things happen. Such discussion involves core values. Bracey (2003) says that it is essential that, from the very beginning, children learn to discuss stories critically. He quotes Ben Okri (1996): 'Stories are the secret reservoir of values: change the stories individuals and nations live by and tell themselves and you change the individuals and nations.' It also develops imagination, an aspect of children's developing thinking which is sometimes ignored (Meadows 1993). Langley Hamel (2002) shows how, from Reception to Year 2, children are increasingly able to retell and modify traditional stories in ways which integrate their own experiences; this helps them to make sense of their lives as part of a continuum of human experience (QCA 2000: 62).

Finding out about past times, then, makes an important contribution to personal, social and emotional development. It helps children to respect cultures, be aware of their own needs and feelings and of those of others, discuss what is right and wrong, consider consequences of actions (QCA 2000: 34, 38).

Finding out about the past and holistic learning

'The past' involves all aspects of human life and finding out about it cannot be a discrete process. Woodhouse (2001b) explains how developing a sense of time encompasses a broad range of Early Learning Goals (QCA 2000). The explicit goal in Knowledge and Understanding of the World, states that children should find out about their own lives and those of their families and those around them (p. 95) This is reinforced by asking for evidence of experience in the *Foundation Stage Profile* (QCA 2003).

Personal, social and emotional development

Many other Learning Goals provide imaginative opportunities for developing historical understanding. They should, for example, understand that people have different needs, views and cultures (QCA 2000: 42); use talk to organise, sequence and clarify ideas, feelings, events (p. 58); retell narratives in sequence and understand how information can be found in non-fiction texts to answer such questions as, where, who, why, when (p. 62); look closely at similarities and differences (p. 88).

Communication skills

We can only find out about the past through developing communication skills. This requires interacting with others, enjoying listening to spoken language – stories, rhymes, music, songs from past times – and using language to recreate roles and stories in play; exploring new words (haystack, tuffet, piper; then, now, until).

Mathematical development

Measuring time involves counting (candles on birthday cakes, months of the year, a long/short time), ordering events in sequence, solving number problems (how much older are you than your sister?). Finding out about the past may require measurement (how much heavier is the flat iron? How far around the moat?) and classification (old/new; similar/different). It may involve discussing what things were made of, exploring how they work, how they were used and their impact on people's lives. Finding out about the past is an ideal context for working with parents, and with the local community.

Play

Play, long cherished by educators as the richest and most powerful vehicle for early learning, provides a splendid opportunity for children to engage with past times. Winnicot (in Bruce 1991: 71) suggested that adults are able to relate to powerful events, hero figures, music and paintings if they have related to them and merged with what is important through play. Erikson (1965) found that if children are encouraged to reconstruct exciting scenes from folk tales through 'let's pretend play' they serve as metaphors for their lives, concerns and interests and help them to engage with the mainstream of human emotions in other times and places. Bruce (1991) describes how a group of five-year-olds heard stories about the Black Prince and King Arthur which led to extensive play about princes and princesses, how Hannah, five and Tom, three, used a rough script based on St George and the dragon as a basis for play and how a teacher added wings to a child's toy pony to retell the story of Pegasus. Garvey (1977) emphasised the importance of play which reconstructs stories about other times and places since it involves experimental dialogue and allows children to explore emotions, relationships and situations, times and places outside their experience. Woodhouse and Lomas (2002) describe how a play area can be organised to develop historical thinking in a Year 1 class.

The Foundation Stage and Key Stage 1

Helping children to find out about the past creates opportunities for the development of rich and complex language skills in meaningful contexts which are central to the traditional early years curriculum. It is also important to see how such an integrated approach, with play at its centre, can be the foundation for good practice at Key Stage 1. Woodhouse (2001b) cautions against ignoring the Foundation Stage in planning this continuum. But this requires an explicit understanding by early years practitioners of the process of historical enquiry and of how this can be part of a continuum across the 3–7 age range.

What exactly is 'historical thinking' for the Foundation Stage?

An explicit awareness of the types of questions to ask and of how they may be answered makes it possible to maximise children's ownership of their learning, yet to intervene appropriately to extend their thinking, to engage with them in sustained shared thinking (Siraj-Blatchford et al. 2002). Young children implicitly develop concepts of time. Wendy Scott (2005) has explained that a wealth of brain research shows that from birth young children construct a world of time, change and sequence. She recognised evidence of this working with children from the age of two in the Fortune Park Day Centre in Islington. Children keep profile books of photographs and are able to articulate differences between the time when a photograph was taken and the present.

But if we are to build on these skills in focused ways, and extend them, it is important to have a clear and explicit understanding of the processes involved in finding out about the past.

'Guesses' about things which remain

Finding out about the past involves making inferences (good guesses) about sources, that is, traces of the past which remain. Sources may be visual: photographs or paintings, advertisements. They may be music: songs, dances, games from past times – whether pop groups from Granny's youth or Victorian street cries. They may be oral: When Auntie lived in Lancaster . . . The lollipop lady said . . . Rogers (1995) suggests voluntary organisations which may be contacted to liaise with older people. Sources may be things which were made in the past, ranging from buttons to castles, found at home or in museums. They may be written; for very young children these include baby tags, birthday cards, old picture books, names on statues and memorials.

Creating meaning from sources

To create meaning from sources we need to ask questions about what they are made of, who made them, why, how were they used, what did they mean to the people who made and used them, are there others?

Since sources cannot give us a complete picture of the past because only some remain and we cannot know the thoughts and feelings of those who made and used them, our responses to these questions must be hypotheses, reasonable guesses based on what we know of human nature and past times. With maturity and greater knowledge children's guesses become more likely to be valid; in line with what is known and likely. But it is important to embark on the process of offering a variety of possible ideas from the beginning, to engage imaginatively in 'what if' thinking which will be refined with maturity. This is an ideal context for learning to develop an argument and explain a point of view ('I think . . . because'), to learn to listen to the views of others, to accept that they may be equally valid ('perhaps', 'maybe'), and that often a question has no single 'right' answer. It is a context in which everyone, including the adults, can engage in genuine shared thinking – and sometimes, in my experience, children's suggestions which appeared improbable have been endorsed by academics. (The shells which children thought were money were indeed used as currency!)

Sequencing sources

Historians sequence sources in order to trace the causes and effects of changes over time; to understand how and why past times were different from and similar to today. Young children love to put their own photographs in order, to put them on a time-line, to explain the sequence to and compare their sequence with their friends. They can link the photographs to relevant artefacts which remain – baby clothes, old toys, birthday cards, books and family stories. Linked to adults' time-lines the process has endless extensions and interest. Or children might sequence pictures of, for example, clothes or houses, over a long or a short period, or sort into age categories. It is fascinating to listen to the children's often surprisingly complex reasoning about sequences or categories, and their responses to challenges.

Extending vocabulary

Discussion about changes over time extends time vocabulary, and the process of making reasoned guesses about sources develops syntax and the language of viewpoint, argument, hypothesis and probability: I think, if . . . then; because; perhaps. Discussing sources, whether artefacts (button hook, castle, oil lamp) or written or oral sources (stories written a long time ago, fairy and folk tales, old rhymes which describe activities familiar in the past), introduces words no longer in everyday use: Mrs Tiggy-Winkle the *washerwoman* was an excellent clear *starcher*. The miller is *grinding* the corn into flour . . . Jack took the cow to *market* . . . Wind the *bobbin* up . . . Concepts often change over time (market, queen) or have several meanings (ball, coach), so that children may have a different image of market from an adult, although they may both think they are sharing meaning. Children often accept the unfamiliar without question (Donaldson 1978). Therefore it is important for adults to discuss meanings with children, to use words in a variety of contexts, to provide visual illustrations, to give children opportunities to use new words themselves in their own contexts.

Learning new vocabulary is an active process

If we see several pictures of different types of castle, or windmill or carriage, we can work out what their shared characteristics are: what their essential meaning is. This involves trial and error, risking using new words in retelling stories and in play, seeing which fit.

Comparing accounts of the past

There is no single 'correct' account of the past. Historians select from, piece together and interpret sources which remain. The accounts they write depend on their own interests. Are they interested in kings and queens or the lives of ordinary people; in the distant or recent past, in powerful women or helplessness; in clothes or how things work, in explaining good and evil, fairness and injustice; in the history of their own country or of others. As new evidence comes to light, and with experience, accounts of the past change. Accounts vary too depending on the time in which they were made.

Young children's exploration of the past can reflect each of these dimensions. They can look for similarities and differences in different versions of folk tales, myths and legends, explore the aspects which are different and suggest why. *The Magic Lands of Britain and Ireland* (Crossley-Holland 2001) is a collection of lesser known versions of folk tales, while *Fairy Tales* (Doherty 1999) goes back to early versions of the tales so that even Cinderella and Sleeping Beauty have surprising elements. *The Barefoot Book of Fairy Tales* (Doyle 2006) also contains a selection of stories from around the world. Three is often seen as a magic number in folk tales; how many stories can children remember where things happen in threes?

The stories children reconstruct through retelling or act out in play may appear fanciful, with imagination only loosely linked to what is known, but it is the process of understanding why versions may differ and change which matters fundamentally. Only in closed societies is there one true story of a country's past and this is politically contrived, open to manipulation and denies individual identity.

Interpretations and illustrations

Young children can compare artists' illustrations of stories set in the past. They may differ because of the times in which they were made – a Kate Greenaway illustration (1991) and a contemporary one, for example. Or they may both be contemporary but differ because the styles of the artists express different ideas and feelings; children can discuss how they do this through colour, line and shape, which they prefer and why.

Or the story in the text may tell a different story from the pictures. Thomas (1993) found that nursery children were able to recognise and suggest reasons for this and Hoodless (1998) found that three-year-olds could explain the difference between a story of a child's experiences in imaginary time and a parallel story of the parents' experiences told in real time.

Fairy Catalogue (Gardner 2000) works on the premise that children can make up their own versions of fairy stories by choosing the ingredients and categories from a selection of pumpkins, spinning wheels and wicked witches.

Interpretations and story

There are many versions of traditional fairy stories, often across cultures. Of course white mice do not turn into coachmen or wolves dress up as grandmas. However, it was argued above that these stories are rooted in the oral tradition. They therefore introduce the idea of past times and of continuity and provide contexts for discussing motives, causes and effects, values. Since there are so many versions they also help children to identify the common features and to discuss reasons for differences: why gender roles are inverted in modern versions (e.g. Little Red Riding Hood, Wilson 1998; *The Paper Bag Princess*, Munsch 1988) or why the story is told from the perspective of the villain, or set in a contemporary context. And there is evidence that by discussing such interpretations children learn to differentiate between fact and fiction.

Interpretations and 'living history' reconstructions

Very young children may need help in understanding the concept of a 'living history' reconstruction. One group of nursery children found the Beamish Open Air Museum fascinating but needed the concept of 'in role' explained; they thought what they saw was 'real'. Older children need to be encouraged to ask questions such as 'How did they know?', 'Are there others?', 'What might it have felt like when …?'. They can engage with the notion of how a reconstruction is made and that some may be more accurate than others.

Interpretations and oral history

Talking to more than one adult about the same aspect of the past (their schools, games they played, food they ate, celebrations) provides rich opportunities for considering how and why adults' accounts may be different. Is it because they lived in different parts of the country, or of the world? Did they do different jobs, are they different ages, in spite of having children or grandchildren the same age?

Reconstructing stories through play provides an ideal opportunity to engage with and make sense of the past. Imaginative play frees children from the constraints of the immediate environment and allows them to form new aspirations in role as a fictitious person. In play children behave beyond their age. Play begins with situations close to the real one but gradually children consciously realise the purpose of play and creating imaginary situations as a means of developing abstract thought (Vygotsky 1978). Tough (1976: 79) believes that imaginative play enables children to think in an historical way, to consider alternative possibilities about how the past may have been, to consider 'what if?' and 'as if' scenarios. An interesting starting point could be to support a traditional fantasy play area about pirates, then to challenge this by introducing the true story of Grace O'Malley, a real pirate – and a woman (Kirkland and Wykes 2003). In a different approach, Barnsdale-Paddock and Harnett (2002) give detailed ideas for developing a museum as a focus for play.

Meadows and Cashdan (1988: 39), Vygotsky (1978) and Bruner (1987) all consider that social interaction with adults can enhance the quality of play, although most teachers would agree that it is important to enable children to have a sense of ownership and to explore and make choices and take risks in their play.

Planning for play

Play needs to be planned for in terms of groupings and learning objectives, and time (for adults to observe, interact and assess learning), while remaining open-ended and integrated with the curriculum. Bennett (Bennett et al. 1997) describes how one teacher used a 'plan, do, review' model to discuss planned play, encouraged children to make links and connections, to experiment, initiate and follow up ideas, which fed into the teacher's curriculum plans. Shefatya (1990: 153) has shown that many children also need to learn how to play: how to say what their role is, how to use objects as symbols, how to create elaborate situations and co-operate.

Planning and assessment

Suggestions for long-term planning from Foundation Stage to Key Stage 1 are given in H. Cooper (2002: 142–3). This grid shows how Early Learning Goals (QCA 2000) link to statements in the Programme of Study for History at Key Stage 1 (DfEE/QCA 1999) and how the various strands of historical thinking are developed through case studies described throughout the book. Issues related to progression from nursery to Key Stage 1 are considered by Cooper (2000: 39–44, 48–9).

Examples of medium-term planning for Years 1 and 2 and related discussions are given in Cooper (2000: 54–60) and again in H. Cooper (2002: 129–73), supported by case studies and examples of children's work. Christine Cooper (2002: 152–67) and Farmer, Seward and Robson (in Cooper 2004) provide more examples of long/medium-term planning and resulting work from nursery to Year 2.

The progression in learning objectives for each of these case studies is based on the footsteps towards the Early Learning Goals (QCA 2000), exemplified in the *Foundation Stage Profile* (QCA 2003) and on the attainment targets for history at Key Stage 1 in the National Curriculum. However, these documents can only be used as rough guidelines because there are so many variables involved in tracking progression in history (a folk tale or a pictorial source can exist, for example, at many levels of complexity). Interpreting the thinking behind young children's often surprisingly thoughtful responses is equally complex.

Practitioners, then, need to be aware of the interweaving strands of historical enquiry and of the capabilities of the children they teach and to apply their teaching and creative skills to devise exciting activities which they and the children will enjoy: a shared ownership of engagement with and reflection on learning.

Continuing professional development

The workshops outlined below aim to raise practitioners' awareness of ways in which they can implicitly help children explore the past, to encourage them to experience some of the processes of historical enquiry at their own levels, to devise related activities which reflect their experience at appropriate levels for the children they teach, and so to develop collaborative action research approaches, which are dynamic and in which practitioners take the initiatives. Prior to the staff development sessions, read this chapter!

Aim: to share ways in which we already teach about time, and why

1 In pairs, write on cards all the contexts in which concepts of time have arisen in your teaching in the past three (?) weeks.

2 Whole group collate on flip-chart.

3 Group into aspects of historical enquiry: measuring time, sequencing, changes over time, continuity/change, similarity/ difference.

4 Discuss why these activities occurred; why they were important.

5 Consider how you might develop them to integrate the processes of historical enquiry more fully; what the benefits to children's development might be.

Source: photographs

Bring a collection of photographs of you taken over time

1 In pairs, try to sequence each other's photographs. How do you work out the sequence? Is it correct? If not, why not? Is it easier with more/fewer photos, longer time intervals? Is there evidence of changes over time (in clothes, people, and activities)? – rapid or slow?

2 Tell the other person's story from the photograph evidence. How true is it? What do you not know? Why?

3 How valid is the story? (E.g. are photos posed or snaps? What sorts of occasions do they depict? How typical (e.g. are people dressed up, always smiling?)) Would others in the photos tell the same story? Why not? Can you find out? Does the age of the photo (e.g. black and white) influence inferences?

Source: artefacts

1   Each person brings an interesting 'old thing' important to them. No one discusses their artefact. Artefacts are displayed as in a museum. In pairs, write explanatory labels saying: what it is, how was it made? why? how old? how used? how did it impact on the lives of those who used it? Differentiate between what you know, what you can 'guess' and what you do not know.

2   In turn, correct the label on your artefact. Reasons why incorrect? Could you find out more? How?

Reconstructions from oral history (for extroverts!)

1   Two people (or more) read different versions of a fairy story or folk tale.

2   Whole group lists similarities, differences, reasons on flip-chart.

3   In small groups re-enact the main theme of the story, with imaginative modifications: modify its meaning in the context of your personal experience, reverse gender stereotypes, set it in a different time or cultural context.

4   Perform some interpretations to whole group.

5   List ways in which they differ from original and why.

Planning for continuity

1   Try out, initially, one of the workshop ideas, in a simplified form suitable for children. Carry out the activity across different age groups of children. Keep records on (some) individual children's responses in each age group.

2   Collate for each age group in sequence. Is there progression? In what ways? If not, why not? Were there any surprises about some children's level of response?

And in conclusion, one of my favourite quotations.

If one respects the ways of thought of the growing child, if one is courteous enough to translate material into its logical forms, and challenging enough to tempt him to advance, then it is possible to introduce, at an early age, ideas and styles that, in later life will make him an educated man.

(Bruner 1966)

This is already an historical text! What about an educated woman?!

References

Anholt, C. (1988) *When I Was a Baby*. London: Heinemann.

Bage, G. (2003) 'In my view revolting subjects?', *Primary History*, **33**, 5–6.

Barkham, J. (2002) 'History book for the literacy hour: A Street Through Time', *Primary History*, **30**, 16–17.

Barnsdale-Paddock, L. and Harnett, P. (2002) 'Promoting play in the classroom: children as curators in a classroom museum', *Primary History* **30**, 19–21.

Bennett, N., Wood, E. and Rogers, S. (1997) *Teaching Through Play: teachers' thinking and classroom practice.* Buckingham: Open University Press.

Bracey, P. (2003) 'In my view: enjoying a good story', *Primary History*, **34**, 6–8.

Bruce, T. (1991) *Time To Play in Early Childhood Education.* Sevenoaks: Hodder and Stoughton.

Bruner, J.S. (1966) *Towards a Theory of Instruction*, 7th edn (1975). Cambridge, Mass.: Harvard University Press.

Bruner, J.S. (1987) *Making Sense: the child's construction of the world.* London: Methuen.

Burningham, J. (1984) *Grandpa.* London: Jonathan Cape.

Cooper, C. (2002) 'History: finding out about the past and the language of time', in H. Cooper and C. Sixsmith (eds) *Teaching Across the Ages 3–7: curriculum coherence and continuity.* London: Routledge, Falmer.

Cooper, H. (2000) *The Teaching of History in Primary Schools: implementing the revised National Curriculum*, 3rd edn. London: David Fulton Publishers.

Cooper, H. (2002) *History in the Early Years*, 2nd edn. London: Routledge, Falmer.

Cooper, H. (2004) (ed.) *Exploring Time and Place Through Play.* London: David Fulton Publishers.

Crossley-Holland, K. (2001) *The Magic Lands of Britain and Ireland.* London: Orion.

Department for Education and Employment/Qualifications and Curriculum Authority (1999) *The National Curriculum Handbook for Teachers in England.* London: QCA:

Doherty, B. (1999) *Fairy Tales.* London: Walker Books.

Donaldson, M. (1978) *Children's Minds.* London: Fontana.

Doyle, M. (2006) *The Barefoot Book of Fairy Tales.* Bath: Barefoot Books.

Erikson, E.H. (1965) *Childhood and Society.* London: Penguin.

Franklin, I.L. (1992) *The Old, Old Man and the Very Little Boy.* New York: Simon and Schuster.

Gardner, S. (2000) *Fairy Catalogue.* London: Orion.

Garvey, C. (1977) *Play, The Developing Child Series.* London: Collins Fontana.

Greenaway, K. (1991) *Nursery Rhymes Classic.* London: Cresset Press.

Hoodless, P. (1998) 'Children's awareness of time on story and historical fiction', in P. Hoodless (ed.) *History and English in the Primary School: exploring the links.* London: Routledge.

Kingsbury, B. (1998) 'Picture books for teaching history', *Primary History*, **20**, 17–18.

Kirkland, S. and Wykes, M. (2003) 'Grace O'Malley, alias Granaile, pirate and politician, c. 1530–1603', *Primary History*, **34**, 34–5.

Langley Hamel, K. (2002) 'Traditional stories and rhymes: Goldilocks, don't do owt', in H. Cooper and C. Sixsmith (eds) *Teaching Across the Years 3–7: curriculum coherence and continuity.* London: Routledge, Falmer.

Meadows, S. (1993) *The Child as Thinker: the development and acquisition of cognition in childhood.* London: Routledge.

Meadows, S. and Cashdan. A. (1983) *Teaching Styles in Nursery Education: Final Report to SSRC.* Sheffield: Sheffield City Polytechnic.

Munsch, R. (1988) *The Paper Bag Princess.* London: Hippo Scholastic.

Okri, B. (1996) *Birds of Heaven.* London: Phoenix.

Qualifications and Curriculum Authority (QCA) (2000) *Curriculum Guidance for the Foundation Stage.* London: QCA

Qualifications and Curriculum Authority (2003) *Foundation Stage Profile.* London: QCA.

Rogers, P. (1995) '"Silver linings": using the elderly as a resource', *Primary History*, **10**, 14–15.

Salter, K. (1996) 'Grace Darling and Reception children', *Primary History*, **14**, 18–19.

Scott, W. (2005) 'When we were very young: emerging historical awareness in the earliest years', *Primary History*, **39**, 14–17.

Shefatya, L. (1990) 'Socio-economic status and ethnic differences in socio dramatic play: theoretical and practical implications', in E. Klugman and S. Smilansky (eds) *Children's Play and Learning: perspectives and policy implications*. New York: Teachers College Press.

Siraj-Blatchford, I., Sylva, K., Muttock, S., Gilden, R. and Bell, D. (2002) *Researching Effective Pedagogy in the Early Years*, Research Report 356. Annesley: DfES.

Thomas, E. (1993) 'Irony Age Infants', *Times Educational Supplement*, 23 April.

Tough, J. (1976) *Listening to Children Talking*. London: Ward Lock.

Vygotsky, L.S. (1978) *Mind in Society: the development of higher psychological processes*. Cambridge, Mass.: Harvard University Press.

Wilson, H. (1998) *There's a Wolf in My Pudding*. London: Pan Macmillan.

Witherington, A. and Neate, B. (2003) 'Book for the literacy hour: what babies used to wear', *Primary History*, **34**, 30–1.

Woodhouse, J. (2001a) 'Teaching history through nursery rhymes at the Foundation Stage', *Primary History*, **27**, 17–18.

Woodhouse, J. (2001b) 'History in the Foundation Stage', *Primary History*, **27**, 8.

Woodhouse, J. (2002) 'History coordinators' dilemmas', *Primary History*, **31**, 8–9.

Woodhouse, J. and Lomas, T. (2002) 'History coordinators' dilemmas', *Primary History*, **32**, 9.

8

Teaching about the past at Key Stage 1

'Me' Years 1 and 2 – Key Stage 1 levels 1–3

THIS TOPIC MAINLY REFLECTS the first of the three areas of study of the Key Stage 1 History Programme, changes in the everyday lives of the children and in the lives of familiar adults. The fourth focus, 'Stories', could be extended to include the other two areas, stories about famous men and women and famous events; this would allow opportunities to discuss why people did things and why events happened, the second of the key elements of enquiry. However, it is not necessary to include all aspects of the Programme of Study in one topic. A topic in the following year might focus on a period in the distant past, and involve stories about people and events through a theme such as 'castles'.

Years 1 and 2 worked on the theme 'Me' with a history focus. Year 1 concentrated on their own time-lines for six years, which recorded their own experiences of change over time. They brought in their own baby clothes, and toys they had had over the previous five years, sequenced socks and mittens to illustrate growth, sequenced their photographs, and recounted memories. They interviewed one of the parents about a new baby who was brought into school, weighed, measured and compared with them. They listed their achievements since they were babies: talking, throwing and catching balls, and so on. The children were also paired with Year 6 children as part of the Year 6 work on 'human development'. Each pair worked on a cross-curricular theme planned by the older child for a week, at their own level. One pair, for instance, studied an old oil lamp, wrote about it, painted it and found out about it, each in their own way, then they put the resulting work in a book and discussed similarities and differences of the five-year-old and ten-year-old approaches. Both the Year 1 and Year 6 children enjoyed this, and it enabled the younger children to predict what they may be like and able to do when they are 'twice as old as now'.

The Year 1 teacher and the head teacher also participated 'at their own level'. The Year 1 teacher made her own time-line illustrated with photographs of her family and key events in her life, concluding with her Graduation Day and her wedding.

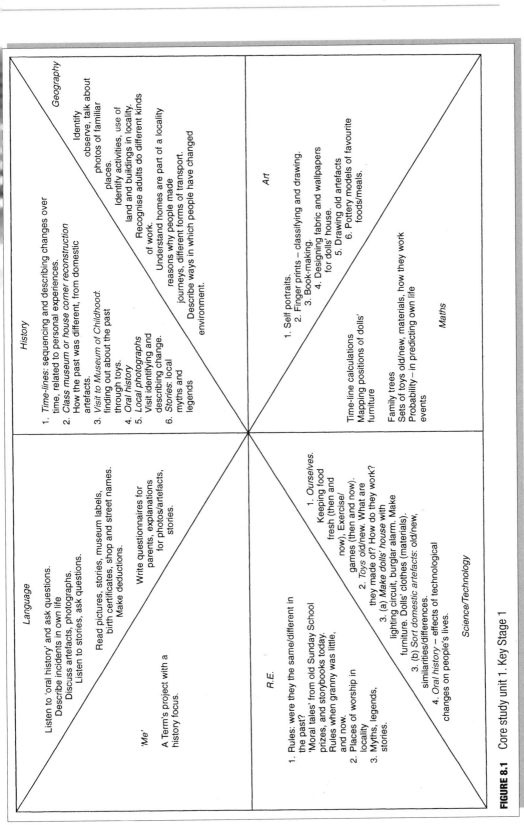

Language

Listen to 'oral history' and ask questions.
Describe incidents in own life
Discuss artefacts, photographs.
Listen to stories, ask questions.

Read pictures, stories, museum labels,
birth certificates, shop and street names.
Make deductions.

Write questionnaires for
parents, explanations
for photos/artefacts,
stories.

'Me'

A Term's project with a
history focus.

History

1. *Time-lines*: sequencing and describing changes over time, related to personal experiences.
2. *Class museum or house corner reconstruction*
   How the past was different, from domestic artefacts.
3. *Visit to Museum of Childhood*: finding out about the past through toys.
4. *Oral history*
5. *Local photographs*
   Visit identifying and describing change.
6. *Stories*: local myths and legends

Geography

Identify
observe, talk about
photos of familiar
places.
Identify activities, use of
land and buildings in locality.
Recognise adults do different kinds
of work.
Understand homes are part of a locality
reasons why people made
journeys, different forms of transport.
Describe ways in which people have changed
environment.

Art

1. Self portraits.
2. Finger prints – classifying and drawing.
   3. Book-making.
      4. Designing fabric and wallpapers
         for dolls' house.
            5. Drawing old artefacts
               6. Pottery models of favourite
                  foods/meals.

Maths

Time-line calculations
Mapping positions of dolls'
furniture

Family trees
Sets of toys old/new, materials, how they work
Probability – in predicting own life
events

Science/Technology

1. *Ourselves*.
   Keeping food
   fresh (then and
   now), Exercise/
   games (then and now).
2. *Toys old/new*. What are
   they made of? How do they work?
3. (a) *Make dolls' house* with
   lighting circuit, burglar alarm. Make
   furniture. Dolls' clothes (materials).
   3. (b) *Sort domestic artefacts*: old/new,
   similarities/differences.
4. *Oral history* – effects of technological
   changes on people's lives.

R.E.

1. Rules: were they the same/different in
   the past?
   'Moral tales' from old Sunday School
   prizes, and storybooks today.
   Rules when granny was little,
   and now.
2. Places of worship in
   locality
3. Myths, legends,
   stories.

FIGURE 8.1 Core study unit 1. Key Stage 1

What I want children to learn	What I want children to do	Assessment opportunities
To communicate awareness and understanding of history in the following ways: (i) sequencing objects and events in order to develop a sense of chronology	Time-lines Make own time-line 0–7 (i) place photographs of themselves in sequence on time-line (ii) compare with time-line for teacher; use words such as then, now	*Level 1* Can sequence photographs, events. Can recognise the distinction between past and present in their lives; in teacher's life: can use language such as now, then, next, before, after. Can use questionnaire to answer questions about their own lives
(ii) using words and phrases relating to the passing of time (iii) finding out about aspects of the past through learning to ask and answer questions which help to identify (a) differences between past and present (b) different ways in which the past is represented using artefacts	(i) bring in 'old things' for house corner role play/class museum Draw them; attach (by Velcro, which allows rearrangement) to a sequence line with categories (very old/old/new). (ii) Visit Museum of Childhood. Handling session – old toys What were they made of? What are they? How did they work?	*Level 1* Beginning to find out about the past from sources of information and to recognise a distinction between past and present *Level 2* Also beginning to identify some of the different ways in which the past is represented, and to answer questions about the past from sources of information through making books or presentation for grandparents, or tape or video recordings for 'Children's TV or radio' can:
Oral sources	(i) write questionnaire for granny, grandad, or older person about life when they were little, or tape-record interview at home	*Level 1* recognise distinction between past and present, in other people's lives

FIGURE 8.2 'Me' history grid

Photographs	(ii) invite several older people who were brought up in different parts of the world and in different circumstances to tell children about their early years, to show photographs of themselves in the past and of their treasured possessions. Collect and display selected old photographs of locality; take photographs of/visit same sites today	*Level 2* identify some of the different ways in which the past is represented *Level 1* ask and answer questions about photographs which recognise similarities and differences using concepts of time *Level 2* also demonstrate factual knowledge about events or people beyond living memory, related to photographs
Stories	(i) invite someone from a local history society to tell 'true stories' about locality which children can retell, draw, act out (ii) myths and legends from different cultures	*Level 1* can sequence events and use time vocabulary in retelling stories *Level 2* also can begin to explain why people acted as they did, demonstrate factual knowledge learned from 'true stories' and ask and answer questions about the past, based on the stories

FIGURE 8.2 cont'd

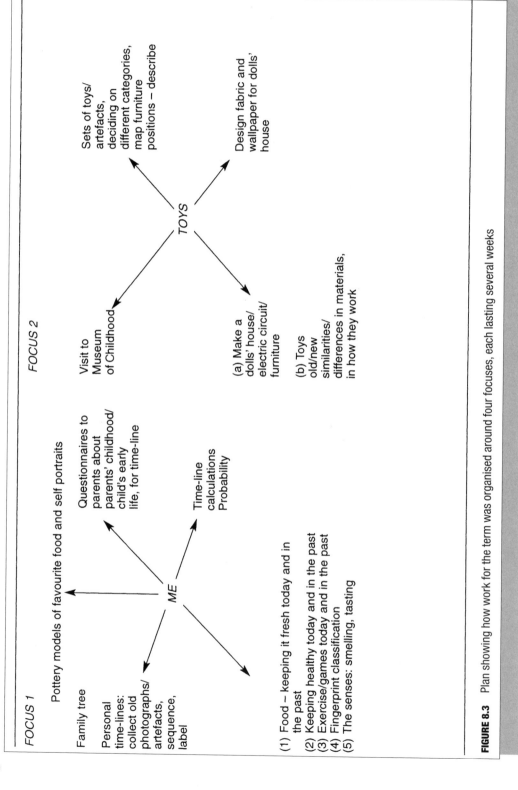

FOCUS 1

Pottery models of favourite food and self portraits

Family tree

Personal
time-lines:
collect old
photographs/
artefacts,
sequence,
label

Questionnaires to
parents about
parents' childhood/
child's early
life, for time-line

Time-line
calculations
Probability

ME

(1) Food – keeping it fresh today and in
    the past
(2) Keeping healthy today and in the past
(3) Exercise/games today and in the past
(4) Fingerprint classification
(5) The senses: smelling, tasting

FOCUS 2

Visit to
Museum
of Childhood

Sets of toys/
artefacts,
deciding on
different categories,
map furniture
positions – describe

Design fabric and
wallpaper for dolls'
house

TOYS

(a) Make a
dolls' house/
electric circuit/
furniture

(b) Toys
old/new
similarities/
differences in materials,
in how they work

FIGURE 8.3 Plan showing how work for the term was organised around four focuses, each lasting several weeks

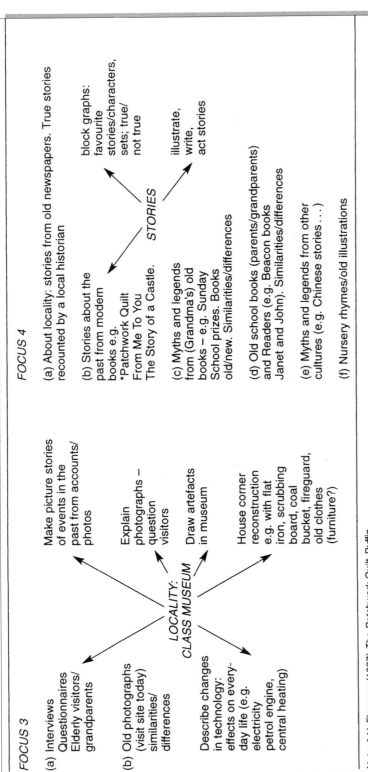

FOCUS 3

(a) Interviews
Questionnaires
Elderly visitors/
grandparents

(b) Old photographs
(visit site today)
similarities/
differences

Describe changes
in technology:
effects on every-
day life (e.g.
electricity
petrol engine,
central heating)

Make picture stories
of events in the
past from accounts/
photos

Explain
photographs –
question
visitors

Draw artefacts
in museum

House corner
reconstruction
e.g. with flat
iron, scrubbing
board, coal
bucket, fireguard,
old clothes
(furniture?)

LOCALITY:
CLASS MUSEUM

FOCUS 4

(a) About locality: stories from old newspapers. True stories
recounted by a local historian

(b) Stories about the
past from modern
books e.g.
*Patchwork Quilt
From Me To You
The Story of a Castle.

STORIES

block graphs:
favourite
stories/characters,
sets; true/
not true

illustrate,
write,
act stories

(c) Myths and legends
from (Grandma's) old
books – e.g. Sunday
School prizes. Books
old/new. Similarities/differences

(d) Old school books (parents/grandparents)
and Readers (e.g. Beacon books
Janet and John). Similarities/differences

(e) Myths and legends from other
cultures (e.g. Chinese stories . . .)

(f) Nursery rhymes/old illustrations

Note: * V. Flournoy (1987) The Patchwork Quilt. Puffin.
P. Rogers (1987) From Me To You. Orchard Books.
J. S. Goodall (1986) The Story of a Castle. Andre Deutsch.

FIGURE 8.3 cont'd

Since she was twenty-five, this was a very long time-line, and allowed the children to discuss their life span in relation to hers, and to compare different scales for recording time. The teacher displayed her own collection of books and toys, surrounding her wedding dress on a stand in the middle of the room and invited her own grandma to come to school! Gran, teacher, and children, all enjoyed exchanging memories. Meanwhile, in the foyer, the head teacher, who was new to the school, took the opportunity both to introduce herself and to support the history project, by making her time-line. This was very long indeed because she was nearly fifty years old. She was able to show us photographs of her father leaving home to go to war and other very personal records – a long swathe of her golden hair, cut when she was five, her fifty-year-old teddy, her first mitten. She told us in one assembly, a moving story of how she had found these things hidden in a secret box in her parents' home on their death. In other assemblies, she read to us moral tales from her parents' Sunday School prizes. This infant project developed excellent interpersonal under-standings and insights throughout the whole-school community, at far more than eight levels!

The Year 2 extension of the theme was originally going to be 'when granny was little', but since grannies ranged in age from mid-thirties to about sixty, this was not a very useful title, and certainly did not go back to pre-electricity and horse-drawn carts. So they stuck to an extended version of 'me'. This was not a multicultural school, but a Chinese boy had recently joined the class. He spoke little English and did not adjust easily. The class teacher seized this opportunity to develop his work on 'when Mummy was little' into a rich subtheme on what it was like to grow up in Shanghai, with the help of the boy's mother. The class went to the Chinese exhibi-tion, and went to see the Chinese New Year festivities in Soho. This led to work on old Chinese tales, with big collages and models of dragons and of the 'Willow Pattern Plate', work on Chinese paintings, experiments in writing with a Chinese brush in ink, and Chinese calendars and counting systems. The term concluded with a Chinese meal which Mrs Chan showed the children how to prepare, then they compared old China with what Mrs Chan told them about life in China today, and how life in Shanghai is different from and similar to life in Croydon! The Chinese work gave the project a far richer dimension and also led to greater personal understandings for all those involved.

Children's work

Some children's questionnaires for their parents ask about the arrival of cats, dogs, goldfish, brothers and sisters, about holidays, cuts and bruises, or moving home. This six-year-old, however, is already preoccupied with self-assessment and moni-toring her progress!

1 When did I first have our first tooth?
  I had my first tooth at five months old

2 When did I first Walk?
  I first walked at 9 months.

3 When did I first dress our selvs?
  I first dressed at 18 months

4 When did I First read a book?
  When I Was 4 years old

5 When did I first draw?
  When I Was 2 years old

6 When did I Start to write?
  I started to write When I Was 4 years

7 When did I have money?
  When I Was 3 years old

8 When did I Know my numbers?
  I knew my numbers When I was 4 years

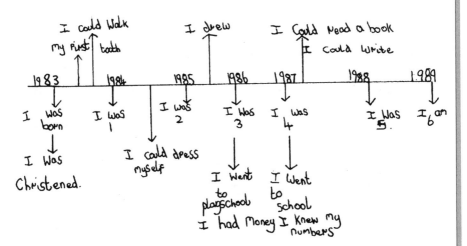

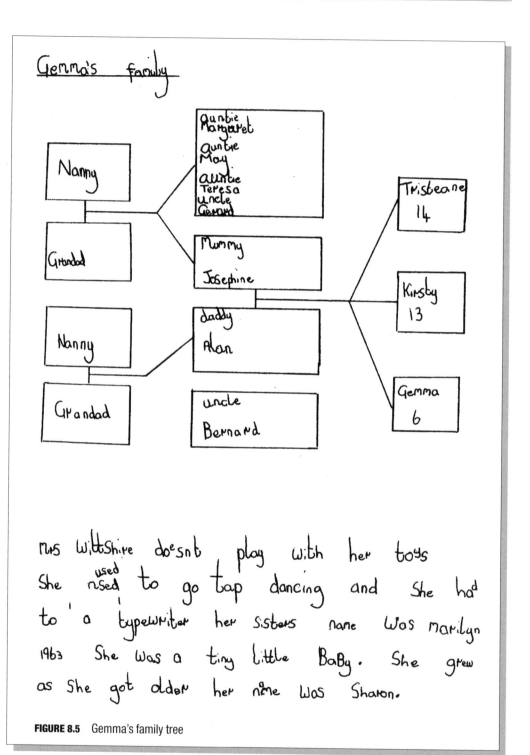

FIGURE 8.5 Gemma's family tree

OUR TRIP TO BETHNAL GREEN
TOY MUSEUM.

On Wednesday, 14th June, we went on the coach to the toy museum.
The coach driver took us to the wrong museum. We had to go on the underground
When we got to the toy museum James had a nosebleed.
In the museum we saw old toys:
Trains, cars, dolls, games, soldiers, puppets, doll's houses, boats, teddy bears, horses and theatres.
We found out that old toys were made from wood and our new toys are made from plastic.
WE found out that dolls were made out of wood, wax, china, clay, paper and plastic lots of old dolls had real hair.
We had a talk about old toys—it was very interesting.
We were tired when we got home.

A Story by Class 7.

Gemma

Toys

My grandprents would have played with hoops and ropes

FIGURE 8.6 Report on visit to a toy museum

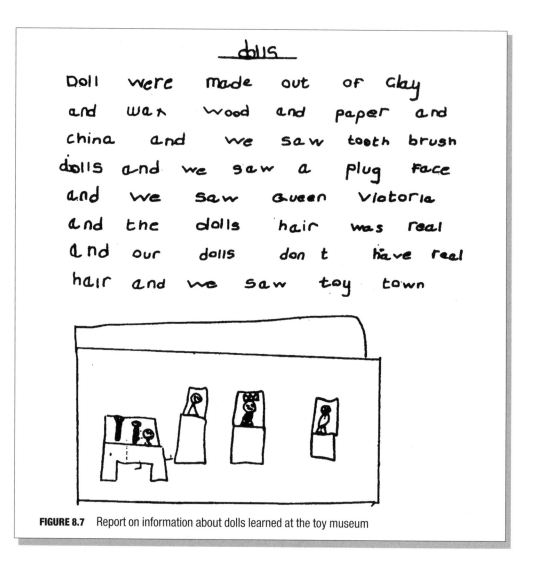

dolls

Doll were made out of clay and wax wood and paper and china and we saw tooth brush dolls and we saw a plug face and we saw Gueen Viotoria and the dolls hair was real and our dolls don t have reel hair and we saw toy town

FIGURE 8.7 Report on information about dolls learned at the toy museum

The information from the questionnaire was transferred to the time-line. There were great opportunities here for transactional writing and for parental involvement. Parental understanding and support is particularly important in family history which can be a sensitive area. The family tree was optional and done with help at home.

The children were very interested to use the information in their time-lines, photographs and collections of toys to make deductions about the past, and about changes over time. These were certainly 'interactive' displays.

The account of the visit to the Museum of Childhood is a piece of shared writing. It refers, in a very sanguine way, to the initial excitement of the day, when the coach driver deposited the children outside Burlington Arcade, telling the teacher, 'It's just up the road love' (assuming they were going to the Museum of Mankind!). Although she had made a preliminary visit, the teacher assumed that this was another entrance. The novelty of the tube journey from Piccadilly Circus to Bethnal Green was so exciting that James had a nosebleed before they were able to discuss such concepts as continuity and change, similarity and difference, during the 'handling session' led by the museum staff. Later, they wrote a book explaining how the toys in the past were sometimes different from theirs, and why.

Reconstruction of a ball at Belvoir Castle in 1814

In March 2005 I was asked to organise a workshop at Belvoir Castle for Key Stage 1 teachers, considering how the castle could be used as an historical source to plan a visit, and preparation and follow-up activities. The aim was to help them to respond to the *Excellence and Enjoyment* agenda, using blocks of time and cross-curricular activities. I was surprised at the challenge this would be for them, indicated by some initial remarks

> 'We have to download the QCA schemes in my school.'
>
> 'We are only allowed to do Florence Nightingale.'
>
> 'We have to fit into the timetable.'
>
> 'As a music co-ordinator, I should not want to mix music up with anything else.'
>
> Yet they all said they had come to 'get some creative ideas'.

Aims of the workshop

- To consider how to help Key Stage 1 children to 'reconstruct' an interpretation of a banquet at Belvoir in 1814, using primary and secondary sources.
- To link knowledge, skills and understanding of the National Curriculum for history, and other subjects when appropriate, to the objectives of the National Literacy Framework and other areas of the curriculum.
- To consider how a visit to Belvoir and preparatory and follow-up activities could be applied to other castles and stately homes.

The workshop

The tables below are some of the suggestions made, as the teachers moved through the rooms of the castle, about how children could select, carefully observe and record aspects of the castle for a purpose – to imagine and act out what a ball might have been like at Belvoir Castle at a particular date in the past, 1814. This involved all aspects of historical enquiry. (Of course this case study could be modified to apply to a large house or stately home near you.)

The enquiry would have a purpose, for children and teachers: to select, discuss and record sources (the building, the paintings, furniture, kitchen equipment, written evidence of who lived in the castle in 1814), in order to create and communicate their account (given the children's immaturity) of what the ball may have been like.

However, I think that teachers also need to see an enquiry as valid and interesting and worthwhile at their own level, if they are to generate enthusiasm in children. I modelled my own research so far, before visiting the castle. I read an extract from *War and Peace*, describing the ball at the Rostovs', typical of balls across Europe at the time. I played Regency ball music and read to the group about a day in the life of Careme, the great chef of the period who travelled around great houses catering for grand balls. I had found this and the music resources, and also information about dance steps, and wonderful Regency fashion plates on the internet. The sites are given below. Yes, this took some time, but I became genuinely interested and hoped that I could communicate this to the group. (Not sure that I was successful in every case.)

A ball was agreed to be a good idea, because of children's familiarity with parties in their own lives, and with castles and balls in folk and fairy stories, and their enjoyment in dressing up, in order to try to 'get into the skin' of other people, living in different times.

Resource notes

I include the resources I researched in detail, partly because you may wish to plan the visit to a 'great house' and use some of them, but also to illustrate the extent to which I became interested in the project at my own level and wanted to share this with the workshop participants, in this case, and with children, if I were their teacher. To me equal child/adult involvement and research is essential to good teaching. It enables us then to engage in what is called in the REPEY study (Siraj-Blatchford *et al.* 2002) 'sustained, shared dialogue'. The adult may know a little more than the children but they are both involved in the process of finding out together. Without this approach I should find teaching very boring! So the results of my researches are given in some detail at the end of this chapter.

The research informed the planning for the preparation to the visit (Figure 8.8), the visit (Figures 8.9–8.12) and the follow-up of the visit (Figure 8.13).

Activity	History NC	NLF
What do you know about castles? Make a 'concept map'; draw and label a picture of your idea of a castle and tell us about it. Look at pictures of different kinds of castles: How are they the same? Different? What is 'a castle'? (Could be modified as 'a great house')	1b a long time ago; now/then 2b identify differences between now and then	1.1.4 write captions 1.2.22 labels for drawings and diagrams 1.3.21 explain and describe
Who has been to a party? Why? What did you do? Introduce idea of balls and banquets, a long time ago. For example, read/retell (different versions of) Cinderella. Anyone got other stories and pictures of balls? Explain there used to be grand balls at Belvoir Castle a long time ago. Shall we pretend to have a grand ball? Shall we go to Belvoir to find out what it might have been like? What shall we need to find out? General discussion; group questions around key points. • How would they dress? • What would the rooms/ furniture be like? • What dances? • What would they eat? • How might it be cooked? • How would it be cooked?	3 identify different ways in which the past is represented 4b ask and answer questions about the past	1.1.1; 1.2.4; 1.3.5 read and retell familiar stories 2.1.4 understand time and sequence in stories 2.2.5 discuss story settings

FIGURE 8.8   Reconstruction of a ball at Belvoir Castle in 1814: before the visit

Activity	History NC	NLF	Other NC subjects
Take slides of room and of details, as before. How many words can we think of to describe the room? (Tape-record or list.) How is it different from the room where you eat? Why?	2b identify differences between life at different times	English speaking and listening 1b use words with precision	ICT 1a gather and retrieve info from variety of sources

FIGURE 8.9   During the visit to Belvoir: the state dining room

Activity	History NC	NLF	Other NC subjects
• Between ballroom and Elizabeth saloon, in the Chinese dressing room, look at family picture of children of the fifth Duke. Who are they? How old? What are they wearing? Draw/write notes about one of them.	4a find out about past from sources (e.g. historic buildings, pictures) 4b ask and answer questions abut past	1.1.4 captions, notes 1.1.5 describe story settings and relate them to their own experience and that of others	ICT 2a use images to develop their ideas
• Take slides. These can be projected in school to recreate ballroom during role play or details of furniture, fireplaces can be recorded to use later in making 'props'.	As above	1.1.14 write captions 1.1.15 lists for planning and reminding 1.1.6 write and draw simple instructions and labels, e.g. for use in role play	Art and design 1a record from first-hand observation
• Draw statue of the Duchess. What is she wearing? How is it made? What sort of material do you think? Why do you think that? Make notes on/draw her hairstyle • Look at portraits of the fifth Duke and Duchess and their children. Does the Duchess in the painting look different from the statue? How? Why? Do the children look different from the portrait in the Chinese room? Describe each of them: their clothes, what do you think they were like? Why? Who are they? • What sort of dances would they have done? Guess. Why do you think that? Do we know? How can we find out for our pretend ball?	3 identify different ways in which the past is represented 4a, b		4c work of artists and crafts people (e.g. sculptors

FIGURE 8.10 During the visit to Belvoir: the ball room

Activity	History NC	NLF	Other NC subjects
• Find the two ranges. What were they for? How long would it take to get them hot? How do you think the cradle spit worked? How could you boil water, vegetables, puddings? What was the hood for? What did the big tray collect? Why were the walls painted brown? • In groups find three kitchen utensils. Draw, label; what were they for? • In groups find a chopping board, pestle and mortar, fish kettles, water boilers, bench with revolving top; draw and label. • Can you see anything made of: iron? copper? brass? wood? Differences? Why? • Imagine the kitchen preparing for a banquet. What sounds would you hear? What smells? What might they be cooking? How can we find out more?	1b use words relating to time 2a recognise why people did things 2b identify differences between life at different times 4a find out about the past from artefacts and historic buildings. 4b ask and answer questions about the past	1.1.16 write and draw simple labels 1.2.23 extended captions 1.2 25 assemble info from their own experience 1.2.22 and labels or pictures	Science 1a use senses to recognise similarities between materials 1b sort into groups on basis of material properties 1c recognise and name common materials 1d Find out uses of materials and why they are chosen for different uses Art 1a record from observation

FIGURE 8.11 During the visit to Belvoir: the old kitchen

Dances at the ball

Video of ball scenes in Jane Austen's *Pride and Prejudice* (*Pride and Prejudice* DVD BBC) give the flavour. In spite of the *War and Peace* extract, dances were often walked, in a stately fashion, in time to the music. There are so many versions of a dance that it would be quite appropriate for children to make up their own dances to the music, using traditional country dance figures based on some traditional country dance patterns:

- to 'lead' – partners move up and down the set with joined hands;

- to 'cast off' – turn outwards and proceed around the other line of dancers;

- to 'cast one' – adjacent couples change positions at the end of a movement;

- to 'cross hands' – right/left hands of partners joined – or both hands crossed behind backs;

Activity	History NC	NLF	Other NC subjects
• Can you remember the children who lived here in 1814? I wonder what they were like? How might they have spent their time? • What games might they have played with? Are they different from yours? • What lessons do you think they had? • Do you think they might have made up stories like you do? What about? Why do you think that?	4 find out about the past from artefacts; ask and answer questions about the past 2b find out about differences in life at different times	2.3.14 describe character descriptions 1.1.5 describe story settings and incidents and relate them to own experience, and that of others 1.2.10 identify and compare basic story elements 2.1.5 identify and discuss reasons for events in stories	Physical education 7c play simple games. Music 1b, 2b sing songs, play tunes and untuned instruments

FIGURE 8.12 During the visit to Belvoir: the nursery/schoolroom (a stimulus for writing/telling stories set in a different place and time and for follow-up, e.g. simple games, old songs and rhymes)

- 'hands across' – opposite couples join right hands and move clockwise in circle;
- 'bows and curtseys'.

If you are interested, at your own level, there is a great deal of information on the internet:

- www.cam.ac.uk/societies/round/dances
- www.earthlydelights.com.au/english3.htm

Contemporary ball music, the Pride and Prejudice Collection, The Pemberley Players, is available from Fain Music www.fleming-williams.co.uk.

For clothes: very good, large images can be found on www.pemberley.com/janeinfo/ppbrokil.html.

The banquet

Famous French chefs were hired whenever possible (see *Cooking for Kings: A day in the life of Antonin Careme, the first celebrity chef* (Kelly 2004) for some of his recipes).

Activity	History NC	NLF	Other NC subjects
• Write invitations to the banquet, (modelled on party invitation).	5	1.2.13 substitute and extend patterns from reading through language play	ICT 3a make invitation cards
• Find out more about banquets and balls from non-fiction text and story illustrations (e.g. what to wear, food).	4 find out about past from range of sources 2b identify similarities and differences between life at different times 1a, b time vocabulary; place objects in order	1.2.18 1.3.17 2.1.14 2.3.14–18 non-fiction reading 1.3.22 2.3.19 read and record info	ICT 1b enter and store information
• Create the 'ballroom' and the 'dining room'. Project slides of parts on wall; discuss shapes, materials, colours. Paint on lining paper. Add 3D stucco, gold paint, velvet scraps, brocade, etc.	2b similarity/ difference 4a, 5 find out about past from sources and communicate 3 different ways in which the past is represented		Art and design 1a record from experience and imagination 1c collect visual and other info to help develop ideas, combine visual and tactile, and match to purpose of work 4 visual and tactile – colour, pattern, texture 4c roles and purposes of crafts people in different times
• Make models from drawings/ photos, slides, of selected detail (e.g. gilded chair back, clock, dining plates)	as above		
• Design dress or aspect of dress, e.g. brooch, necklace, necktie, tie pin, noted during visit or in book research or download illustrations from internet, e.g. http://hal.edu.~cathy/re/rd.html or http://locutus.ucr.edu/cathy/ reg3.html. Make an eighteenth-century fashion book.	as above		D&T 1–4 D&T 1–4

FIGURE 8.13 After the visit: planning a pretend ball at Belvoir Castle (NC History 5 organisation and communication: pupils should be taught to select from their knowledge of history and communicate it in a variety of ways (for example, talking, writing, drawing); NC History 3 identify different ways in which the past is represented)

• Listen to music for ball (see resources). Make up and practise dances suitable for the ball. Draw and label diagrams to record dance patterns.	2b similarity/ difference 4a ask and answer questions about the past 5 communicate findings	Read and record info (as above) 1.1.16 write simple instructions and labels 1.2.22 1.3.21 record in labels and drawings 2.1.17 use diagram as part of instructions 2.2.21 to explain a process	Music explore and express feelings about music using movement, dance and expressive and musical language 5c, d work in groups, as class; a range of recorded music from different times. PE 6a use move-ment imaginatively responding to dance music 6d create and perform dances using simple movement patterns including from different times
• Plan banquet. Use sources of information to design menu. (See resources; see also http://homepages.ihug.co.nz/ ~awoodley/Regency.html# recipes.)	2b (sim/diff) 4a, b ask questions about sources 5 communicate findings	simple lists 1.1.15 organise lists 1.2.25 read and record 1.3.22	D&T passim
• Make models of/draw and cut out, selected items for role play.	2b, 4a, b, 5	Use models (e.g. of food for each course) to organise sequentially, make simple notes from non-fiction texts	
• Write schedule for work in the kitchen to prepare banquet. (See resources; see also Woodhouse, M. (1992) Scrub-a-dub Nellie, The National Trust, for picture story of a day in the life of a kitchen maid.)	1b time vocab 4a use range of sources 5 communicate in variety of ways	1.1.15 make simple lists 2.1.16 use models from reading to organise points in order (see resources)	D&T passim
• Write recipe and cook small dish for banquet (see resources).		1.1.13, 16, 2.1.15 read and follow simple instructions	

FIGURE 8.13   cont'd

• Pretend you are in the school room. Which one of the children are you? Rewrite a traditional story, pretending it happened at Belvoir. Describe things you saw at Belvoir and put them into the story. Draw them in your illustrations. ...And now you can go to the ball...		1.1.10 use patterned stories as models using basic conventions 1.2.14 represent outlines of story plots 1.2.14 write stories based on reading 2.1.11 use the language of time 2.3.10 use the language of story	

FIGURE 8.13   cont'd

A day in the life of Antonin Careme

The evening menu consisted of seven services, rather than courses, offering eighteen choices of dish. Nearly all the food was presented on the table at the start of the meal with only the soups and entrees 'making an entrance hot'.

- 6 a.m. Stoves stoked and sauces set on hobs. Oranges hollowed. Cochineal added to orange jelly to fill half shells; blancmange into half shells. During day alternate layers built up.

- 7 a.m. Careme explained the menu to the staff: pastry chefs, underchefs, kitchen hands, table deckers and footmen.

> *Soups*
>
> *Fish: bass and cod*
>
> *Lamb garnished with quails*
>
> *Entrees: filets of beef; chicken; rabbit*
>
> *Roasts*
>
> *Chicken; pigeon*
>
> *Nectarine ice cream; oranges with marbled jellies*
>
> *Centrepiece: the castle made in sugar*

- 11 a.m. Quails, rabbits, pigeons, partridges, chicken in rows on table. Lamb boiled.

- Midday Work begun on making spun sugar for centrepiece – made in two copper pans and poured into mould.

- Mid-afternoon Make fish soup, garnished with oysters, crayfish, truffles.

- 4 p.m. Roasts on spit and cauldrons for boiling meat and fish (fowl, game, 45-pound beef, 35-pound veal).

- 6 p.m. Table deckers in dining room covered table with cloth. Each place had flat tablespoon, facing down. Napkins folded like water lilies. Centrepiece put in place.

- 6.15 Oranges cut in quarters to reveal layers of jelly and blancmange and arranged with laurel leaves in two pyramids.

- 6.45 Guests enter dining room. Footmen enter with two silver tureens. Roasts already on table. Host carves roasts. Beef fillets and rabbits brought in on silver salvers.

(Taken from Kelly 2004)

Similar reconstructions

In Cooper (2002), *History in the Early Years*, a variety of role-play interpretations in Foundation Stage and Key Stage 1 classes are described (pp. 24–32, 79–94). The rationale for learning about the past through play is explored in *Exploring Time and Place Through Play* (Cooper 2004: 5–11, 16–23, exemplified in case studies, 24–6).

People probably living in Belvoir Castle in 1814

These included John Manners (35), the fifth Duke of Rutland; his wife, Elizabeth Manners (34); his children, Elizabeth Manners (12), Emmeline (8), Katherine (6), Adeliza (3) and Charles, Marquess of Granby (baby).

Staff close to the family were Susanna Gooding, governess; Mary Hanby, lady's maid to Elizabeth and Emmeline; Mrs Griffiths, nurse to Katherine and Adeliza; Maria Holland and Elizabeth Howard, nurses to Charles; Anne Keeling, house keeper; Molly (13), tweeny; and Mary Brewin, housemaid.

Visitors to the castle included the Duke of Wellington, the Prince of Wales, Sir John Thornton, vicar.

Resources

- Dance, dress, music: DVD video BBC *Pride and Prejudice* (Jane Austen)
- Ball music: CD *The Pride and Prejudice Collection, A Selection of Dances Popular in the 18th and 19th Centuries, the Pemberley Players*, available from Fain Music, 8 Pensall Drive, Heswall, Wirral CH61 6XP (www.fleming-williams.co.uk).

A word of thanks

Finally I should like to thank Rhi Clarke, the education officer at Belvoir Castle, for her help, in particular for her information about the inhabitants of the castle in 1814 and about the use of the kitchen. Of course, a ball could be recreated at a different level by Key Stage 2 children. Nonsuch History and Dance Company think that Year 6 children are the perfect age for their Tudor dance workshops (www.nonsuch-history-and-dance.org.uk). This is an excellent opportunity for linking the dance and history curriculum.

References

Cooper, H. (2002) *History in the Early Years*, 2nd edn. London: Routledge, Falmer.

Cooper, H. (2004) (ed.) *Exploring Time and Place Through Play*. London: David Fulton Publishers.

Kelly, I. (2004) *Cooking for Kings: a day in the life of Antonin Careme, the first celebrity chef*. London: Walker & Press.

Siraj-Blatchford, I., Sylva, K., Muttock, S., Gilden, R. and Bell, D. (2002) *Researching Effective Pedagogy in the Early Years*, Research Report 356. Annesley: Department for Education and Skills.

9

Teaching about the past at Key Stage 2

Life in Tudor times, study unit 2, Years 5 and 6

THE UNIT ON LIFE in Tudor Times began with an initial overview of the period; Henry VIII and the break with Rome, followed by rivalry with Spain over religion and trade in the 'New World' which led to the Armada of 1588. Key events were located on a class time-line. Two focuses were selected within this topic, one on 'Houses' and one on 'Ships'. These focuses were chosen because they allowed children to explore aspects of Tudor history which represent complex underlying changes, in ways which they could understand. 'Houses' included both a visit to Hampton Court, the showpiece of Henry VIII's new style of government and also to a nearby timber-frame Elizabethan house representing the increasing wealth of the new 'gentry'. 'Ships' began with a visit to the *Mary Rose*, which represented the beginnings of British sea power under Henry VIII, created as a defence after the break from Catholic Europe, and which led, in Elizabethan times, to exploration, an increase in trade and the emergence of a new class of merchants and 'gentry'. Rivalry with Spain in the 'New World' over trade resulted in the Armada of 1588, an event about which loyal British Roman Catholics felt ambivalent and which reflected conflicting loyalties and rivalries throughout Europe.

This unit allows children many opportunities to consider non-Eurocentric and non-Anglocentric perspectives. Firstly, the competition between Britain and Spain to find new routes to India and the East Indies, and the ensuing conflict in Central America and the West Indies allows children to use sources which reflect both cross-cultural influences and cultural conflict. A Schools Council booklet *Akbar and Elizabeth* (1983) shows teachers how they can help children to discover from Indian miniatures (in the Victoria and Albert Museum) the rich cultural influences of India on Elizabethan England by comparing clothes, buildings and garden design.

Often, sources which challenge Eurocentric perspectives can be selected from books for older children. In Roberts (1992: 22–5) there are excellent Mughal pictures of the rejoicing at the birth of Jahangir, son of Akbar the Great in 1569. The relief at the birth of an heir and also the idealistic representation of this event suggests

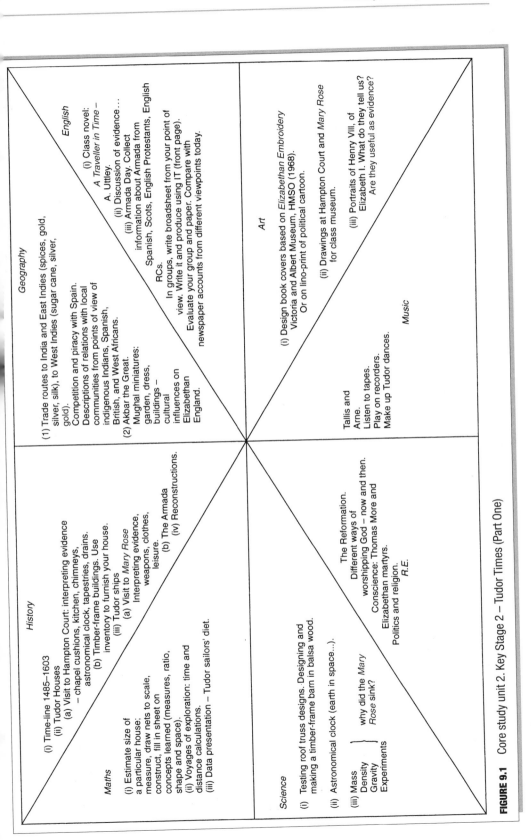

History

(i) Time-line 1485–1603
(ii) Tudor Houses
    (a) Visit to Hampton Court: interpreting evidence
      – chapel cushions, kitchen, chimneys,
      astronomical clock, tapestries, drains.
    (b) Timber-frame buildings. Use
      inventory to furnish your house.
(iii) Tudor ships
    (a) Visit to *Mary Rose*
      Interpreting evidence,
      weapons, clothes,
      leisure.
    (b) The Armada
    (iv) Reconstructions.

Maths

(i) Estimate size of
a particular house:
measure, draw nets to scale,
construct, fill in sheet on
concepts learned (measures, ratio,
shape and space).
(ii) Voyages of exploration: time and
distance calculations.
(iii) Data presentation – Tudor sailors' diet.

Science

(i) Testing roof truss designs. Designing and
making a timber-frame barn in balsa wood.

(ii) Astronomical clock (earth in space...).

(iii) Mass   } why did the *Mary*
Density   } *Rose* sink?
Gravity
Experiments

Geography

(1) Trade routes to India and East Indies (spices, gold,
silver, silk), to West Indies (sugar cane, silver,
gold).
Competition and piracy with Spain.
Descriptions of relations with local
communities from points of view of
indigenous Indians, Spanish,
British, and West Africans.
(2) Akbar the Great.
Mughal miniatures:
garden, dress,
buildings –
cultural
influences on
Elizabethan
England.

English

        (i) Class novel:
          A Traveller in Time –
          A. Uttley.
     (ii) Discussion of evidence....
(iii) Armada Day. Collect
information about Armada from
Spanish, Scots, English Protestants, English
RCs.
In groups, write broadsheet from your point of
view. Write it and produce using IT (front page).
Evaluate your group and paper. Compare with
newspaper accounts from different viewpoints today.

Art

(i) Design book covers based on *Elizabethan Embroidery*
Victoria and Albert Museum, HMSO (1968).
Or on lino-print of political cartoon.

(ii) Drawings at Hampton Court and *Mary Rose*
for class museum.

        (iii) Portraits of Henry VIII, of
        Elizabeth I. What do they tell us?
        Are they useful as evidence?

Music

Tallis and
Arne.
Listen to tapes.
Play on recorders.
Make up Tudor dances.

The Reformation.
Different ways of
worshipping God – now and then.
Conscience: Thomas More and
Elizabethan martyrs.
Politics and religion.

R.E.

FIGURE 9.1   Core study unit 2. Key Stage 2 – Tudor Times (Part One)

What I want children to learn: key elements	What I want children to do	Assessment opportunities
• To place events, people, changes within a chronological framework • To use dates and terms relating to the passing of time (e.g. century, decade, Tudor, Elizabethan, court, monarch, civilisations, trade) To explain to others: Reasons for and results of events, situations, changes and to make links between events and situations	(i) Make a class time-line 1485–1603, put on key events learned through class lessons and reference work (e.g. related to Reformation, voyages of exploration, Armada, Monarchs)	Level 3 Give a presentation to an audience, explaining the time-line with some explanation of causes and effect of events shown (e.g. of Reformation or of Drake's voyages to central America, or of Armada) Level 4 Can use more factual information and more detailed explanations to play a 'chaining game' which involves (orally or through devising clue cards) thinking of all possible effects of an event
• To select, organise and communicate historical information • To identify characteristic features of the Tudor period: buildings, clothes, music, drama	(ii) In groups, use variety of resource materials to collect pictures and other information and make a book (or display) on one of the following, in Tudor times: homes of different kinds; work; leisure (including theatres and music); health; trade	Level 5 Can devise a game involving selecting 'cause' or 'consequence' cards for a situation and explain what links there are between them (scoring based on number of reasonable causes/consequences identified) Level 4 Can explain overarching and characteristic features of one of the group books
• Have some understanding of diversity of political and religious ideas, beliefs and attitudes of men and women in Tudor times • Describe and identify reasons for and results of Armada	Collect information about the Armada ('press releases' can be pre-selected by teacher) In groups (English Protestants, English Catholics, Dutch, Scottish, Spanish, French) write a broadsheet account from one of these perspectives	Level 3 Can show a restricted perspective in broadsheet article Level 4 Can try to explain a given perspective in a broadsheet article

FIGURE 9.2 Study unit 2: Life in Tudor Times

•Give reasons for different ways in which the past is represented and interpreted	Look at postcards of portraits from National Gallery of (a) Henry VIII (b) Elizabeth I	*Level 5* Can suggest reasons why events and personalities in broadsheets are portrayed differently
•Have some understanding of the reasons for the symbolism of and attitudes and values represented in portraits of Henry VIII and of Elizabeth I	(i) Discuss to what extent they tell what the person was really like, and what else (symbolism) they represent (ii) Compare with written sources describing Henry VIII and Elizabeth I (given on p.??)	*Level 3* Can explain why the portraits are idealised images *Level 4* Can describe differences between written sources and portrait *Level 5* Can explain why portraits and written sources tell different story
1. Ask questions and make deductions and inferences about life in Tudor Times from a variety of sources (a) at Hampton Court: e.g. tennis court (leisure) chapel (beliefs) furniture, kitchens, cellars (food, daily life) paintings, images of Henry VIII; the Field of the Cloth of Gold astronomical clock (understanding of time and space) (b) in Mary Rose Museum: e.g. the ship and its contents (clothes, tools, leisure, weapons, medicine) 2. Organise findings, record and communicate to audience	1. Visit Hampton Court. Drawings and photographs used in school as clues to find out what they may tell us about Henry VIII and his court 2. Visit *Mary Rose* and Museum, Portsmouth. Use drawings and photographs as clues to find out about life on board a Tudor ship Present information in poster or book or as a video or audio tape for an audience	*Level 3* Can make inferences from selected sources; and write explanatory label *Level 4* Can combine inferences from several sources to write a poster, possibly using one piece of evidence to answer a question raised by another, e.g. how was the gun (on *Mary Rose*) fired?; use dates and special vocabulary where appropriate (e.g. court, monarch) *Level 5* Can select and evaluate sources using them in a structured way to make a book or a video investigating an historical question (e.g. who were the people on board the *Mary Rose*? Why did the *Mary Rose* sink?)

FIGURE 9.2 cont'd

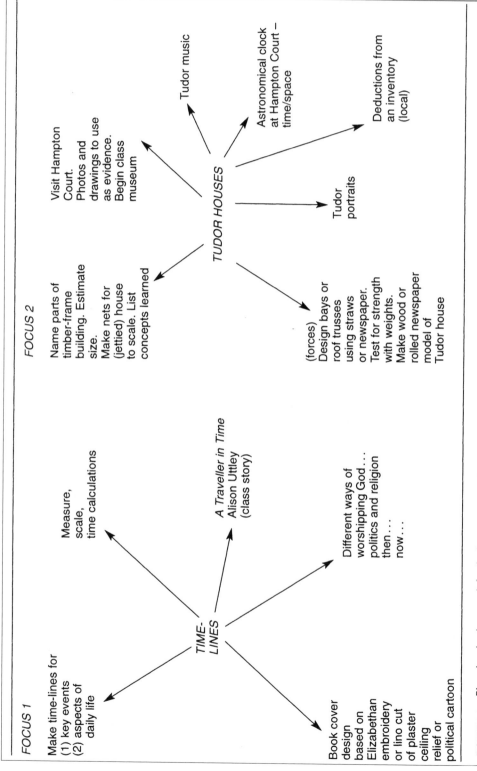

FIGURE 9.3 Plan showing how work for the term was organised around three focuses

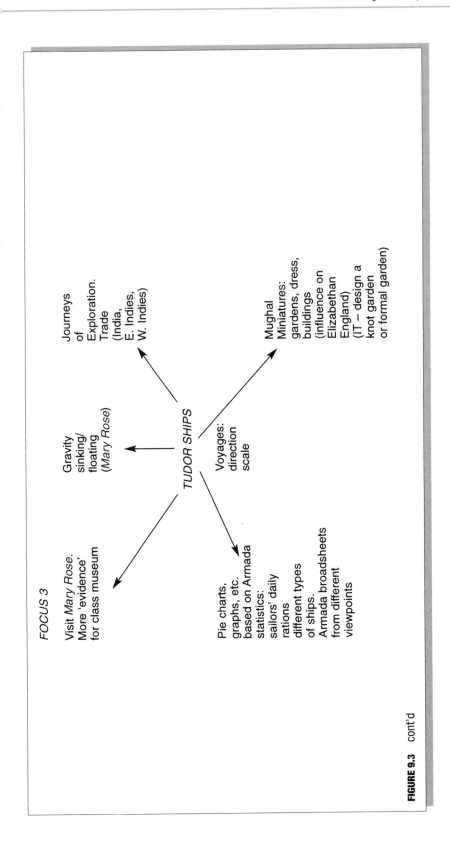

FIGURE 9.3 cont'd

similarities both between portraits of Elizabeth and her succession problems. It is interesting too that when Sir James Ross arrived at the Court of Jahangir, the Emperor thought most of the gifts from Europe were poor but he did like an English miniature portrait of a lady (a result of Indian influence on European art), and a map of India which he was given. However, Jahangir was not really interested in foreign rulers as he saw them as subordinates.

The Benin Empire was also at its peak at the same time as the Tudors were ruling England, which is when the British first arrived there. Sources about the Benin Kingdom can be found in the Museum of Mankind and the British Museum. They invite comparisons and contrasts with Tudor England; the mother of an Oba, or ruler, was of great importance, for example, and had her own palace and political power. Benin contained craft guilds of leather workers, weavers and blacksmiths. Written sources record its richly decorated palaces and houses. Extensive trade with Europe from the end of the fifteenth century included slaves. Smith (1992: 9) shows the crest of Sir John Hawkins, a successful English slave-trader of the sixteenth century, which he designed for himself and which depicts a defiant, captured African.

Similarly Green (1992) offers a picture of what life was like for the native peoples of the Americas, when Europeans first arrived and of how they perceived each other. For example, George Best who sailed with Martin Frobisher to North America wrote a detailed diary which is quoted, and there is also a contemporary painting of Frobisher's fight with an Inuit in 1577. From knowledge of such sources, children can develop a less Eurocentric and a more questioning attitude to life in Tudor times and view it from a range of perspectives.

As part of the focus on ships, both Year 5 and Year 6 spent two weeks finding out about the Armada. The competition between Britain and Spain to find new routes to India and the East Indies, and the ensuing conflict in central America and the West Indies, underlined by religious differences, was explained in class lessons. The viewpoints of different groups were discussed. How would the English Protestants feel, the English Catholics, the French, the Dutch, the Spanish? Why might the Scots be ambivalent? Children then worked in groups or individually to find out all they could about the daily progress of the Armada, making charts, maps and diaries. They made a display of daily rations for a Spanish and an English sailor, pie charts of the estimated food needed on a ship, and graphs showing ships of different kinds. Finally, each class worked in six groups together with the advisory teachers for ICT; by the end of a day, each group succeeded in producing a 'broadsheet' giving news of the Armada from the standpoint of a particular group. The French produced 'La Grenouille', the Spanish 'L'Escorial', the English Protestants 'The Golden Hind', the English Catholics 'The Priesthole', the Scots 'The Record' and the Dutch 'The Orange'.

Later, they evaluated the extent to which they had reflected different attitudes. These examples show that children are considering the reasons for behaviour and events.

LA GRENOUILLE

6f

10/7/1588

STAY OR DIE

The Duke of Madina Sidonia commented that if any Spanish Captain fails to maintain his position the penalty would be death, by hanging.

Soon the English are expected to run out of ammunition and surrender to the Spanish and the noble king Philip II is once more going to demonstrate his enormous power. We are all behind hm in the forthcoming final few battles at the sea.

THE PRIESTHOLE

1d

11th August 1588

SAIL AWAY, SAIL AWAY, SAIL AWAY

9 July 1588 6.0pm Captain Fleming of the Golden Hind has signalled the sighting of the Spanish fleet off the Lizard.

The tide will not allow the English fleet at Plymouth under Admiral Lord Howard of Effingham to put to sea till 9.0pm.

4 vessels of the English fleet managed to use their boats and anchors to warp out of Plymouth harbour before 9.0pm.

July 30 3.0pm Armada sighted by the English fleet to the south of Eddystone Lighthouse.

Beacons are reported to have been lit from Cornwall to London, local militia being organised to defend the English coastline.

July 31st the English pinnace Disdain opened fire off Plymouth at the rata encoranda.

At 9.0am this morning the Spanish flagship raised her national flag to signal the beginning.

After a four hour battle the Armada continues eastwood with the English in pursuit. Medina Sadonya gives the order for the fleet to form a cresent with the more heavily armed ships positioned at the horns. Drake reported to have left fleet during the night to investigate sails to the south.

FIGURE 9.4 Extracts from the French and English Catholic newspapers describing the Armada

The extracts from broadsheets representing different points of view were written on 'Armada Day'. They are based on 'press releases' and information in simulated teletext using 'Simtex', prepared by the Croydon Humanities advisor, Don Garman.

Models of Tudor timber-frame houses, based on particular examples, involved a range of mathematical concepts: measure, scale, properties of solid shapes. Figure 9.5 shows part of a child's self-evaluation sheet, made when he had finished his model, to explain the mathematics he thought he had learned in making it.

Mathematics
I Learned Making
Tudor House Models.

length estimate measure	metres centimetres	I estimated the height of my house as 4m.
Scale	1:100	The lenght of my house in real life would be 12m and on my model it is 12cm
Convert from one unit to another.	metres to cm, cm to mm (to nearest mm)	The width of my house is 6m which on my model would be 6cm it could also be 6mm. 6m = 600cm = 6000mm
area rectangle triangle	cm² m²	the area of my first rectangle is 72cm². The area of my roof is 16cm²
volume of cuboid	cm³ m³	The volume of my 2nd cuboid is 252cm³.
Properties of solid shapes Cuboid	faces edges angles	On a cuboid there is 6 faces 12 edges 24 angles
△ based prism	faces edges angles	5 faces 9 edges 12 angles
measuring angles right angle		the right angle on my roof is 90°. the rightangle on the side of my roof is 90°
acute angle		there are 4 acute angle on my house. the acute angles are 45°
obtuse angle		there are 0 obtuse angles on my house.

FIGURE 9.5 Child's self-evaluation of mathematical concepts learned in making a model of a Tudor house

L'ESCORIAL
2D

— JULY 1588 —

HE MUCKED UP OUR — INVASION PLAN

He Duke of Palma mucked up our invasion plan because he was not ready in Dunkruk to sail.

Philip II was very angry when he found out. On the other hand Philip was pleased with The Duke of Medina Sidenia because he had reached Calais but losing too many ships and not having a sea battle with Englande.

After this achievement, How did the Duke of Palma dare to say that his 17,000 men, 1000 cavalry, 170 ships would not be ready to 2 weeks.

THE GOLDEN HIND
lgr

— 1st August 1588 —

ARMADA SIGHTED

It was two weeks ago at south of Eddy-stone Lighthouse that the Armada was spotted by the English Fleet. 1 week ago the English Fleet positioned themselves behind the Spanish Fleet and had the advantage of being windward. A couple of days ago the prize ship. "San Salvardor" arrived at Weymouth badly damaged. We think that there was an explosion below decks. There were quite a few smoke blackened corpses on board.

Fight for Elizabeth
—She is our Queen—

FIRE SHIPS

A plan to send out some fire ships to Calais harbour in France is still to be decided on for Queen Elizabeth is not sure whether it is a good idea.

FIGURE 9.6 Extracts from the Spanish and English newspapers describing the Armada

THE ORANGE
AUG 1589

THE DUTCH LURE

We have been looking at our reports and they say that England ae going to win. We do hope so, when we went to interview Lord Effingham he said they have a good chance of winning. Spains ships are sinking by the hour and about 150 men have been killed. We will continue this story next week.

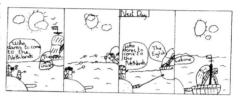

THE RECORD
AUGUST 14

4D

THE ARMADA

PHILIP OR ELIZABETH There has been months of conflict between England and Spain. Does it really matter to us Scots ? Our contacts inform us that defences have been set up in England, because rumours of the invasion, beacons have been set up in selected areas.

Rumours of Philips invasion plan have leeked out of Spain, he plans to make Elizabeth 1 pay for the invasion 2 stop helping the Dutch 3 stop killing catholics.

FIGURE 9.7 Extracts from the Dutch and Scottish newspapers describing the Armada

Britain and the wider world in Tudor times

The revised title of the study unit on life in Tudor times reflects recent scholarship which has done much to change perceptions of Elizabethan England. The study of the Armada from various perspectives could now include an Islamic perspective. For Matar (1999) has shown how the English were so afraid of 'popery' and of the Spanish that they became close allies with the forces of Islam. Indeed there was a permanent Muslim community in London and large numbers of Englishmen could be found in the Middle East and North Africa. The English were close military allies of the Moroccans and the Ottoman Turks: for example there was a joint Anglo-Moroccan attack on Cadiz in 1596.

In 1603 Ahmad al-Manser, the King of Morocco, proposed to Elizabeth I that England should help the Moors to expel their hated Spanish enemies from America and keep the land under joint dominion for ever. He suggested the colonists should be mainly Moroccan, 'in respect of the great heat of the clymat'. Such a proposal, which although finally rejected by Her Majesty, raised few eyebrows at the time, and would have completely changed the history of the modern world.

Interpretations of Queen Elizabeth I

In *The Teaching of History* the Year 5/6 case study on Life in Tudor Times did not explore children's understanding of why the past is represented in different ways, in subsequent periods. Yet this is central to understanding and participating in the process of historical enquiry which underpins this book. The reasons why accounts, reconstructions of the past, vary were discussed in Chapter 3. Historians' accounts may be different but be equally valid. But accounts of the past are constructed by people other than academic historians, for a variety of reasons. If young children compare and contrast accounts which are markedly different and consider why, they are learning, in an embryonic way, that accounts of the past are constantly reinterpreted for different reasons.

I visited a school where the Year 3/4 class were studying a unit on the Tudors. Their teacher allowed me to plan and teach an afternoon session with them. I decided to see, firstly, how they thought people who write books about history find out about the past, then to what extent they could identify ways in which three video clips of Elizabeth I were different and why, and finally, to let them make brief video recordings in three groups to reveal how their own interpretations of an event would also be different. While each group made their video in another room, the rest of the class wrote 'advertisements' for the video clips they had seen, showing in another way how and why they differed.

The lesson

How do we find out about the past?

One child said, when asked how people could find out about Queen Elizabeth I, 'there may not be sufficient evidence'. An encouraging start. Some things we cannot know. Others suggested looking at paintings. I showed them the Ditchingham portrait and asked them if that gave us some idea of what Elizabeth I looked like. There were interesting responses: 'You can't paint every tiny detail', 'Different people paint people in different ways', 'She can't have had a waist THAT small. It is trying to make her look beautiful and powerful.' I explained that Elizabeth had censored pictures of her and the reasons why, then went on to talk about the symbolism of Elizabeth standing on a map of England, dispelling the storm clouds and ushering in the sunshine. 'Was that after she won the Armada?' someone wondered. Someone else suggested that things get left behind or buried which give us clues about the past. Another child had a clear understanding of oral history: 'Someone tells their children and they tell their children and it goes on and on.' 'That is like the Bible,' someone else explained. 'Certainly these children understand something about "historical enquiry",' I thought. The lesson plan is shown in Figure 9.8.

Date	Duration	Year Group	Class size
27.02.06	1.00 p.m.–3.00 p.m.	Y3/4	

Activity	
Understanding why Queen Elizabeth I is represented in different ways; identifying differences in way she is represented and reasons for different interpretations.	National Curriculum Programme(s) of Study: History KS2, ksu 3, historical interpretation

Learning Objectives

Children will have some understanding of why the past is represented in different ways (incomplete evidence; sources often made for a particular purpose); accounts made by 'filling in the gaps'; accounts are made for different purposes.

Assessment

- Discussion of how accurate a representation of Elizabeth I is in Ditchingham portrait; reasons it was painted.
- Children's adjectives describing Elizabeth I in 3 different video clips (product).
- Children's explanations of different reasons why videos made (questioning + product – write TV advert flagging each programme).
- Children make own videos of Queen Elizabeth and Walter Raleigh in groups then compare similarities and differences.

Times	Introduction, activities, conclusion
1.00–1.15	• Whole-class discussion of Ditchingham portrait 1. Who is it? 2. Explain official, censored image; explain symbols (map, cloud, etc.). 3. How much does it tell us of what she was really like? 4. What do people do when they want to make a film about e.g. Elizabeth I and they don't know everything about her?
1.15–1.30	1. Explain going to watch a clip of one interpretation of Elizabeth I: *Blackadder*. 2. Ask children to remember how Elizabeth looks; behaves. 3. Show clip. 4. Children asked in groups of 4 to discuss and write words describing how she looked, behaved on red cards (6 cards per table); list cards on board using Blu-tack.
1.30–1.45	Repeat above activity, using clip of *Gloriana*, recording adjectives on blue cards and making separate list on board.
1.45–2.00	Repeat activity using *The Virgin Queen* clip and green cards. Form third list on board.
2.00–2.10	1. Whole class compare lists; identify similarities and differences. 2. Why is Elizabeth different in each video (audience, purpose, validity)?
2.10–2.25	Read story of Sir Walter Raleigh putting his cloak on ground for Elizabeth to walk on from *Our Island Story*. Explain this is old book written for children. Discuss illustration; interpretation; purpose.
2.25–3.00	Three groups. Each group, with adult support, writes flier to advertise one of the videos as a TV programme. Each group taken out in turn to make a video of the Walter Raleigh story (10 minutes each group) in separate room. Next lesson watch and compare videos, recapping on what children learned about why interpretations are different.

Resources: video recorder, Hi8 and video tape, Ditchingham portrait
Cards in 3 colours and felt tips, H.E. Marshall (1905) *Our Island Story*
Blu-tack, clips put onto CD for showing on interactive whiteboard

FIGURE 9.8 Lesson plan: comparing interpretations of Elizabeth I

Three video clips

The three five-minute clips I selected were from *Blackadder II* (carefully avoiding innuendo which might have upset parents!), *The Virgin Queen* (BBC) and Benjamin Britten's *Gloriana* (ambitious!). The children's adjectives describing the Queen in each clip are collated in Figure 9.9. They clearly describe the differences in the three portrayals of her personality. They also identify certain similarities: When asked why *Blackadder* was made, one child immediately said, 'To make money and to make you laugh!' *The Virgin Queen* was probably made 'to help history teachers with their lessons'. *Gloriana* was 'a musical, like *Joseph and his Amazing Technicolour Dream Coat* – which we are doing for our concert'.

The children's three interpretations

I read from *Our Island Story* (Marshall 1905) about Sir Walter Raleigh throwing down his cloak for the Queen to step on to avoid a puddle, and, since we were examining interpretations, showed the accompanying illustration. The children were noticeably unimpressed by the quality of the picture – and I had forgotten how bland and patronising the prose is!

They enjoyed making the videos, in which everyone took part as courtiers, cheering crowds or the hooves of the approaching horses. We had a 'quiet, calm, gracious Queen', a 'funny Queen', and a silent movie from the group too overawed to speak. The 'funny Queen' included some interesting jokes. For example, when the Queen was considering turning back, to the disappointment of the roaring crowd, a courtier suggested she might cross on a great big bird, 'since aeroplanes haven't been invented yet'. Next week I shall show the class the videos and discuss with them why they made the interpretations they did.

Television previews

The previews, written to advertise television showings of each of the video clips the children had seen, reinforced their previous understanding that the different interpretations were made for different audiences.

Blackadder	The Virgin Queen	Gloriana
excitable	unhappy	excited
very giddy	grumpy	big voice
sneaky	thoughtful	powerful
very noisy	nervous	serious
greedy (wanted to go to the	powerful	important
feast)	sad (at end of last clip)	old
very girly	cross	in charge
happy	extremely cross	theatrical
bossy	rude	strict
laughs a lot	annoyed	sad
bold	like she wanted to run away	bossy
joyful	angry	
funny	worried	
mean (she tricked them in the	furious	
game)	moody	
strict	selfish (she wanted to marry	
crazy	who she wanted)	
good fun	scared	
	a bit bossy	
	powerful	
	upset	
	posh	
	making a fuss	
	moody	
	bossy	
	not pleased	
	nervous of all the powerful	
	people	
	bad tempered	
	ratty	
	not nice to the old Spanish	
	king	
	silly (cos if the Spanish King is	
	old he may be wise)	
	arguing	
	gloomy	
	in a paddy	
	cool	
	bored	
	in a bad mood	
	tired	
	happy (because she got a	
	ruby)	
	sad (because she couldn't	
	marry Essex)	
	frustrated	
	hot	
	frowny	
	ungrateful	
	unconvincing	
	rude (at end of last clip)	
	powerful	
	very loud	
	horrible	
	weird and strange as well	
	insane	

FIGURE 9.9 Adjectives used by Year 3/4 children to describe Queen Elizabeth I

Blackadder

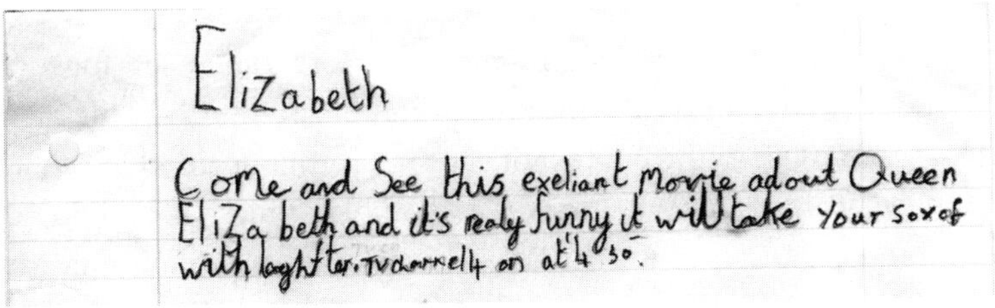

> Elizabeth
>
> Come and See this exeliant movie adout Queen Eliza beth and it's realy funny it will take Your sox of with laghter. tv darrell 4 on at 4'30.

FIGURE 9.10 Television preview of *Blackadder II*

The Virgin Queen

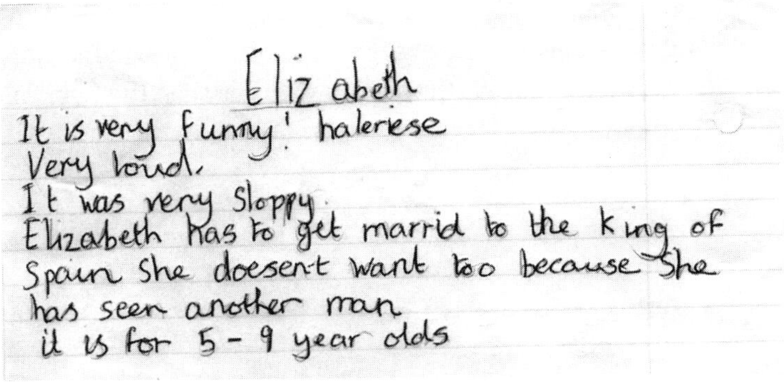

> Elizabeth
>
> It is very funny! haleriese Very loud.
> It was very sloppy.
> Elizabeth has to get marrid to the king of Spain She doesent want too because She has seen another man
> it is for 5 - 9 year olds

FIGURE 9.11 Television preview of *The Virgin Queen* (BBC)

Gloriana

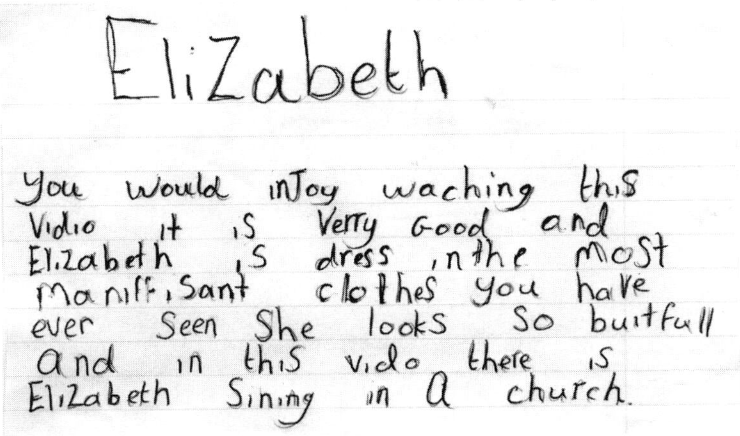

> Elizabeth
>
> You would inJoy waching this Vidio it is Verry Good and Elizabeth is dress in the most maniff, sant clothes you have ever Seen She looks So buitfull and in this vido there is Elizabeth Sining in a church.

FIGURE 9.12 Television preview of Benjamin Britten's opera *Gloriana*

A good history lesson?

Much later, I was looking through my lesson observation guide for tutors in school and college, which was designed by history tutors to be used for formative assessment of students' lessons. (The checklist is an interpretation of the Standards for the Award of QTS (2005) in the context of each subject.) I decided to see how my lesson reflected the checklist for 'what makes a good history lesson?' I had not used this before and had certainly not used it as a checklist for my planning. My completed checklist is shown in Figure 9.13. What I found interesting was the extent to which, however well a lesson may be planned, the checklist requires responses to an ongoing interactive situation: 'goes beyond the objectives'; 'accommodates the varied experiences of the pupils'; 'uses personal knowledge to challenge and inspire'; 'picks up on misconceptions'; 'conveys a sense of drama and emotion'; 'uses analogy; utilises pupils' personal and family experiences'; 'adjusts and modifies tasks'. We expect student teachers to have good subject knowledge and good knowledge of the individual pupils and to weave a web between the two. And they generally do! Good for them.

Checklist	Notes
Planning	
• Is confident in constructing imaginative schemes of work.	Imaginative lesson ✓
• Takes into account the varied requirements of the National Curriculum.	NC links ✓
• Has clear objectives for lessons but may also seize opportunities to go beyond these objectives.	e.g. utilised 'aeroplane fixation' of child with Asperger's syndrome to develop anachronistic joke ✓
• Is able to accommodate the varied experiences of all pupils.	Drew on children's experiences of 'musicals' and of TV to discuss reasons for interpretations.
Development of skills	
• Has high expectations based on pupils' previous learning.	Drew out what children already understood of 'how we find out about past'.
• Uses personal knowledge to inspire and challenge pupils.	Included relevant 'stories', e.g. Elizabeth and Essex; Elizabeth's quarrel with Ditchingham.
• Utilises a range of interactive strategies designed to promote pupils' historical skills and conceptual understanding.	Discuss: how 'true' is Ditchingham portrait? Videos: list adjectives through group discussion. Write advertisement. Video-record role play.
• Bases these strategies, where possible, on evidence-based tasks.	Use of primary and secondary sources.
• Is able to pick up on pupils' misconceptions to develop understanding.	Addressed misunderstanding that Elizabeth in *Gloriana* actually was Queen Elizabeth!
• Uses historical language fluently and appropriately.	Sources, interpretations, bias, symbol; courtiers; Elizabethan.
• Conveys a sense of the drama and emotion inherent in the subject.	In 'love story' – Elizabeth could not marry for love – engaged everyone's point of view; in narration of Sir Walter Raleigh story.
• Is able to use analogy to relate the present to the past.	Comparison of Elizabeth I and Elizabeth II.
• Is able to utilise pupils' own person/family experiences to develop their historical understanding.	??

FIGURE 9.13 Checklist to support observations: what makes a good history lesson?

Assessment and Evaluation	
• Is able to adjust and modify tasks to ensure all children are challenged.	Advert – extended prose or picture and captions. Level of narrator's input in role play varied. ✓
• Identifies tasks appropriate for assessment purposes.	Evidence in video!
• Encourages children by providing constructive and positive responses.	Periods of time: drew on previous knowledge of 'Tudors'.
• Demonstrates knowledge of level descriptors and can apply appropriately.	Identify different ways past represented.

FIGURE 9.13   cont'd

References

Curtis, R. and Elton, B. (1999) *Blackadder: The Whole Damn Dynasty*. Harmondsworth: Penguin.

Gerrard, R. (1998) *Sir Francis Drake, his Daring Deeds*. Harmondsworth: Puffin.

Green, J. (1992) *Native Peoples of the Americas*. Oxford: Oxford University Press.

Marshall, H. E. (1905, reprinted 2005) *Our Island Story*. Cranbrook: Galore Park.

Matar, N. (1999) *Turks, Moors and Englishmen in the Age of Discovery*. Columbia: Columbia University Press.

Roberts, F. (1992) *India 1526–1800*. London: Hodder and Stoughton.

Schools Council (1983) *Akbar and Elizabeth*. London: Schools Council Publications.

Smith, N. (1992) *Black Peoples of the Americas*. Oxford: Oxford University Press.

Principles, theory and practice

10

Creativity, innovation and research-based practice

PART 1 OF THIS BOOK began with small-scale research studies exploring interesting ways of teaching the three strands of historical enquiry which underpin the National Curriculum. Interestingly they were not all undertaken by English history educators. They included studies from Portugal, Turkey, Malta and Brazil, influenced by previous English research. Meanwhile history in English primary schools became marginalised. Yet many teachers have continued to develop innovative practice, as is evident from the articles quoted in this book which they have contributed to *Primary History* and the *Times Educational Supplement*. Classroom-based research, which explores new approaches, analyses, evaluates and reflects on them, comes from freedom for teachers to take professional responsibility for the timetable and curriculum and freedom from fear of taking risks.

Doing classroom-based research

Deciding on a question

This need not take extra time. The 'data' is collected as part of normal teaching and its analysis will inform future practice (both yours and, if you publish it, that of others) in a more precise and useful way than unfocused reflection. Identify a small aspect of your teaching or children's learning which you want to explore. This will probably have arisen from something which puzzled you. It may be just one child's misconception. Why did they think that? How did you or could you intervene to take their thinking further? It could be a careful consideration of the evidence you collect from different children for summative level assessments; does this raise any questions? It could be keeping notes on how you make your own subject knowledge more secure; what is least time-consuming and most effective: internet information about content, reference books, doing research at your own level by, as a starting point perhaps, visiting a site before you take your class there, or watching a film on an historical subject made for adults and deciding you would like to find out more? It could be working with a practitioner to inform your subject knowledge as a leisure activity! One of my colleagues decided to join an archaeological dig at Hadrian's

Wall before teaching a unit on the Romans in Britain. It may be tracking the process of finding out how children and their parents work together: who finds out what; from where? (The dialogue between a child and a parent can be fascinating.) Or what did children learn from a living history reconstruction? All these opportunities arise through normal practice. Jotting down ongoing notes can turn into a fascinating process of discovery.

Keep it small scale

Your 'data' may simply be a discussion with or observation of one child, or even with one parent. You are more likely to get interesting and manageable data from this than from talking to a class or even a group. Often this gives you insights far beyond the focus child and raises further questions. It is not necessary to involve everybody.

Collecting the 'data'

'Data' can be collected by note taking, tick lists, using writing frames, tape recording or video recording. You may choose to ask 'semi-structured' questions – an open question followed by two or three key questions, but which allow open responses. You may observe children, identifying specific things to focus on: how they work together on a particular task, their roles, how they support, extend, correct each other. Video recordings take time to watch later but often reveal things which you did not notice at the time – and children and parents enjoy both making and watching them.

Analysing the 'findings'

Remember what the question was that you were investigating. Perhaps it was the focuses of an observation, the sections on a writing frame. The question, and how you went about collecting the data, will have provided categories of information. Take each category in turn. There are almost certainly significant similarities, differences, or points which spring out. So now you can jot the information for each category under new subheadings. Gradually a picture begins to emerge which is multi-layered, meaningful, useful and interesting.

Don't keep it to yourself!

Send your 'study' to *Primary History*, or the *Times Educational Supplement*. I speak from experience. Light years ago I was 'sent' on an afternoon computing course to learn how to make a database, using the cumbersome technology of the time. I felt my performance was so feeble that I decided to 'show them'. My class and I made databases of stone circles, Iron Age huts and Roman villas, using plans in an archaeology book, and decided on common fields to record and investigate. Next week I amazed everyone! I wrote about this and sent the article to *Junior*

Education – who published it. I also sent a synopsis of my dissertation on a diploma course to *Teaching History*. 'It may not be wise to leap into print so soon,' my tutor warned. But it was!

This chapter gives the flavour of research which I undertook as a Year 4 class teacher. It was an attempt to apply constructivist learning theories to thinking skills in history, through cross-curricular activities, site visits and class lessons teaching children to ask questions about sources, in order to build up the 'big picture'. This turned out to be quite a large study (Cooper 1991). Since one focus of the National Curriculum Programme of Study, Invaders and Settlers, is on the Saxons I shall begin with some of these Year 4 children's deductions, inferences and questions about Saxon sources they had not previously seen, then in Chapter 11 go on to describe other aspects of the study which could stimulate ideas for further classroom research.

Discussion of Saxon sources

The outline of the lesson plans on the Anglo Saxon unit and examples of children's inferences about the Sutton Hoo sceptre are given in Chapter 2. Since 'the Saxons' is one of the National Curriculum units of study, some examples of children's discussion of Anglo Saxon sources are included in this edition.

Visual source: illuminated manuscript of harvest

This was a British Museum manuscript, F 21985, made into a slide. It shows one man apparently in charge of three bowed peasants, two carrying grain and one a sickle, and three others loading a two-wheeled cart. Children related details in it to abstract concepts learned in previous units: agriculture, community, communication, trade, crops, transport.

Agriculture

In their 'archaeological reports', children talked about crops, farming methods and the cycle of the farming year.

'The people seem to be cutting logs and transporting them – maybe to trade them – if they live near a forest.'

'They had flour, so they had bread.'

'They could be putting animals and crops in barns. It's cold. It's wintertime.'

'They had carts and sickles; they could shape wood and metal. They could move things around.'

> 'There is only a small hole in the cart to pull with. It might have been pulled by a person not a horse.'
>
> 'They carry loads on their back – which must be sore.'
>
> 'Where did they store things?'
>
> 'The cart could also be used to take a body and grave goods to the burial ground.'

Social organisation

Children referred to the jobs people are doing and the relationship between them. They recognised that the man on the left appears to be in charge and discuss what he is doing.

> 'We can guess the man on the rock is the leader. He looks as if he's telling them what to do. Therefore they had important people. The men carrying things are slaves – or they might be the king's servants.'
>
> 'I think they had money, but not like ours. They learned to trade money for something like food.'
>
> 'They are working in groups; they have got the jobs sorted out.'
>
> 'There are two men on the cart. One is higher up and one is carrying a weight – perhaps a sheep. They are working together.'
>
> 'Only men are working. Is the work too hard for the women?'

Communication

There are various suggestions about the meaning of the writing.

> 'Is it Latin? If so was it learned from the Romans?'
>
> 'I guess it was learned through monks. I guess the monks wrote it. Therefore it would be Latin. Monks were taught to read and write in neat writing.'
>
> 'Therefore they could write calendars and they could tell the months of the year and they kept in touch with the date.'
>
> 'I think the picture goes with the writing to give the reader a clearer picture in his mind. It shows they had imagination.'
>
> 'Yes but since it was done in Saxon times it is probably true.'
>
> 'They could draw and write. Therefore they had literature.'

Plan: the Saxon church at Cirencester (Wilson 1976)

The building

The children had previously learned that St Augustine brought Roman-style Christianity from Rome to Canterbury.

> 'The church apse design is Roman. Therefore St Augustine had preached and made that part Christian.'
>
> 'They could build proper buildings. Therfore they probably picked up ideas from the Romans.'
>
> 'The apse shows they could curve the end of a church.'
>
> 'Did the Romans live here before because I think I have heard of a Roman villa in Cirencester?'
>
> 'If St Augustine came here – because of the Roman bit – have all the churches round here got a semi-circle bit?'

The people

> 'It's big. It could hold a lot of people. Therefore the population must have been high.'
>
> 'I guess it had more adjuncts that haven't been excavated.'
>
> 'It might have had more adjuncts because more and more Christians came to Cirencester. Maybe more Saxons were becoming Christians.'
>
> 'In some churches there is an echo. If it was crowded it might be very noisy.'
>
> 'Who paid for it?'
>
> 'We can guess a lord built it. Therefore he must be powerful. So they had powerful lords.'
>
> 'It must have taken time to build. I wonder what they used in the meantime?'
>
> 'They needed a church and they worked hard for something they really wanted.'
>
> 'Did it have more to it because I would like to see it being excavated. Did it have a graveyard?'
>
> 'Was it used for more than one purpose? The little rooms might be for discussing things.'
>
> 'They could share things and be part of a group.'
>
> 'Some of the rooms might be for storing bread and fuel.'
>
> 'I wonder if they had bells.'
>
> And finally, 'I wonder if the monks enjoyed their life reading and writing because I get tired of it.'

Map: Croydon in Saxon times

This simple map shows the meanings of Saxon place name endings (e.g. don/den, valley; stead, farmstead; ing, the people of). It shows chalk downs, the rivers and modern settlements along the spring-line a little way up the sides of the downs where the clay in the valley meets the chalk downs or on the top of the downs. The children had discussed the significance of the geology on settlements on a visit to the downs with the field studies advisor, that the settlements were along the spring-line between the clay and the chalk, and dated some of the hedges to eight hundred years. (Pace one hundred yards; every new species represents one hundred years.)

In discussing the map children used their knowledge from maps discussed in a lesson, that the Saxons sailed down the tributaries of the Thames, and that settlement depends on suitable soil for crops and on a water supply.

'We know where they settled from the place names . . .'

'Croydon is on a river and a spring. Therefore they might have a bigger community.'

'How many springs do you get to one settlement?'

'Are there any deserted settlements?'

'They needed plenty of water because in them days they had to plough the fields and it was hard.'

'I wonder why they moved to another place and if they sent someone on ahead to find a good place.'

'We know that, unlike the Stone Age and the Iron Age they farmed on clay. Therefore they had more sophisticated ploughs.'

'I guess there would be a track running between the settlements. Maybe they sort of banded together to protect each other.'

Written source: *Beowulf* (lines 824–38)

The children had read other extracts from *Beowulf* previously and discussed the idea that it is a folk tale idealising courage of earlier warrior bands in which Grendel personifies danger.

Attempts to understand individual words

'"Made good his boast" means he boasts for a reason – to be popular and get support for his next encounter.'

'"He had come from afar" means it took a long time to get there.'

'Why did they call it a "gable roof"?'

Applying learned concepts

The children did not necessarily use the abstract concepts they had learned but used a range of subordinate concepts from their own vocabulary. Many of them described Beowulf as 'a hero', or as 'good, strong, clever, famous'.

Significance of writing in Saxon times

'It is a Saxon poem. Therefore they had different forms of writing. Beowulf was made up. Therefore it would have been a folk tale or a legend. There may have been this famous warrior.'

'Was it a lesson to people?'

'We know the Saxons could write. They probably had people who could write for the rich people. Stories meant a lot to them.'

'They may have made things up to make the story good to hear. They put the monster in the story. Therefore it is made up.'

Attempt to make a distinction between truth and fiction

'It was probably a famous warrior. Therefore it would be partly true. It could have been set in a real place. Therefore they would know about it.'

'Where is Heorot, because I'd like to know if it was a real place.'

'It came from Denmark. Therefore a Saxon who knew it off by heart introduced it to the Saxons in England. Therefore it was passed around countries and settlements. Tales like Beowulf passed around countries.'

'The bit about the monster is not true because no monster ever lived. Anyone who saw him whole was eaten!'

'I would like to know how many times it had been changed because it would be interesting to know how it started off.'

'Why make it up? Because it sounds good!'

Understanding feelings, attitudes and values of another society

'Grendel can't be true. Therefore it's a folk tale. Therefore in some ways we know the Saxons' beliefs.'

'Some people might have thought Grendel was going to come at night . . . Therefore they might have been scared.'

'Beowulf was very brave. I guess they liked brave, strong people.'

> 'I know for certain it is a <u>symbol</u> of fighting. It must have been through lots of places. Therefore they wanted us to know they had <u>courage</u>.'
>
> 'I guess it was a symbol for fighting and <u>braveness</u>.'
>
> 'I guess they wanted more land for their <u>crops</u> so they had to fight before they <u>settled</u>. Was Grendel a monster or just an <u>enemy</u>?'
>
> 'I guess Beowulf was under God's power and he might have God's <u>power</u> and feelings in him.'
>
> 'Why did Beowulf like <u>vengeance</u>? Because he liked fighting?'
>
> 'This is a story of vengeance. Therefore Beowulf was a <u>hero</u>. They must have been glad they'd got Beowulf.'

The concepts underlined certainly identify characteristics of people arriving and settling in a new land.

History/literacy links

At Key Stage 2 the National Curriculum for English speaks of reading 'myths and legends', 'poetry from oral and literary traditions' and 'texts from other cultures and traditions which represent different voices and forms'. *Beowulf* satisfies these conditions and is a springboard for a wider understanding of heroes and heroines: the crucial journey, task or sacrifice. This can lead on to current heroes. Who are they? As part of the Key Stage 2 unit on Invaders and Settlers, *Beowulf* identifies the values central to Anglo Saxon culture in the same way as the Norse myths do for the Vikings: family kinship, friendship, moral and physical courage, ritual, material pleasures and love of life. Alexander (1973) provides a version of *Beowulf* suitable for children.

Construct your own Saxon village

Sue Bingham (2004) describes a project in which her school built an Anglo Saxon house in the school grounds. They contacted 'real archaeologists' through the East Sussex Museum. They helped them to make shingles, and wattle walls, to dye, spin and weave wool, to make pots, to use a pole lathe to make furniture, to create a fire and make Anglo Saxon meals, even cooking bread in a clay oven. She says that she felt the project improved the children's questioning and problem-solving skills, their communication and mathematical skills, developed their imagination, their team-making skills and their ICT, through recording, researching and communicating with the experts by email. Children were able to follow the learning paths which interested them.

A re-enactment

If you are in Viking territory, Kim Seddorn may be the man you should contact (Starkey 2004). As he and his companion in arms, equipped with specially made and authentic mail shirt, sword and helmet, shields and spears, advance towards them, children have been known to flee in terror! Kim Seddorn works in the Bristol area (kimseddorn@blueyonder.co.uk). Regia Anglorum is a nationwide company and will despatch the nearest Viking (or Saxon) to your school (www.regia.org). An alternative perspective is provided by Louisa Gidney (aka Sister Wisberger) (www.rentapeasant.co.uk). Her 'Rent a Peasant' workshop aims to put across the two fundamental aspects of life in the past: finding food and clothing. Children grind pulses and grain, are yoked as oxen, handle fleeces. Or children could create the role play themselves. They may wish to join the Young Archaeologists' Club (www.britarch.ac.uk). Chapter 11 describes the investigation, Young Children's Thinking in History, of which the Anglo Saxon data is a part.

References

Alexander, M. (1973) *Beowulf*. London: Penguin Classics.

Bingham, S. (2004) 'Exploring Anglo-Saxon times', *Times Educational Supplement*, 19 November.

Cooper, H. (1991) Young Children's Thinking in History, unpub. PhD. London University Institute of Education.

Starkey, D. (2004) 'Back to the Viking invasion', *Times Educational Supplement*, 23 April.

Wilson, D. (1976) *The Anglo-Saxons*. London: Pelican Penguin.

11

Young children's thinking in history

The research design

TWO 'EXPERIMENTAL' CLASSES OF Year 4 children were taught during consecutive years using carefully defined and documented teaching strategies and compared with a control group in another school taught by an experienced teacher using his own methods. The three groups were initially compared for ability by analyses of variance and covariance using NFER Non-Verbal Reasoning Test BD as covariate. All three groups were taught the same four units of history – the Stone Age, the Iron Age, the Romans and the Saxons – each unit lasting half a term. Each unit was taught within an integrated curriculum with an historical focus. About two hours each week were spent specifically on history.

The teaching strategies for the experimental groups involved discussion of key evidence, differentiating between what you could know 'for certain', what reasonable 'guesses' you could make, and what you 'would like to know' about the evidence. The discussion involved selected key concepts of different levels of abstraction (e.g. arrow, weapon, defence). Each unit of study involved one visit to a local area where there was evidence of settlement at each period and one 'further afield' visit to extend beyond the locality. For example, the Stone Age 'further afield' visit was to Grimes Graves, and the Roman one was to Lullingstone Roman Villa.

At the end of each unit, all three groups took five written 'evidence tests' which each lasted about half-an-hour on consecutive days. In each unit these consisted of five different types of evidence about which children had to make inferences: an artefact (or slide of one), a picture, a diagram, a map and written evidence. The aim was to investigate whether they found 'concrete' evidence more difficult to interpret than more abstract maps and written evidence. A list of evidence used is given in Table 11.1.

The experimental groups were also given an oral 'evidence test'. The children made a tape recording of a discussion of each piece of evidence in small groups. During the first year the discussions were led by the teacher, and during the following year, no adult was present.

TABLE 11.1 Evidence used in written and oral evidence tests

Unit	Test 1 Artefact	Test 2 Picture	Test 3 Diagram	Test 4 Map	Test 5 Writing
1	Slide. Palaeolithic flint hand axes c. 200,000 BC Museum of London. Slide OL91	Slide. Font de Gaume Lascaux. Ray Delvert S. Lot.	Stone circle. The Druids Circle. Caernarvon. Stone circles of the British Isles. A. Burle	Map showing site of neolithic artefacts on North Downs	Petroglyphics from 'How Writing Began', Macdonald
2	Bronze helmet (1 BC) Slide BM	Uffington Horse photos	Little Woodbury. Iron Age house plan Wilts. In Cunliffe, R.K. 1974	Lynchets of Iron Age Fields Butser Hill, Hants.	Strabo 1.4.2. Description of British exports
3	Shield boss found in River Tyne. Slide BM.	Detail from frieze of great dish, Mildenhall Slide BM PRB 47	Villa plan Chedworth, Gloucs.	Roman roads across South Downs	Tacitus Annales XII 31–40 Boudicca Revolt
4	Replica of Sceptre. Sutton Hoo ship burial. BM Slide MZ 18	Illuminated manuscript of Harvest made by BM F21985	Plan Saxon church Cirencester	Saxon settlements in Surrey	Beowulf slays Grendel Penguin 1973 trans 824–38

In addition, the second experimental group was given a story-writing test. They were given a piece of evidence related to the topic which was concerned with religion, beliefs, myth and ritual, so that it invited the children to piece together their knowledge into a coherent picture of the past and to attempt to consider and explain the beliefs and ideas of the period.

An assessment scheme on a ten-point scale was devised for the evidence tests. This was constructed from patterns in the development of deductive reasoning defined in cognitive psychology and in previous research relating this to history. It is not possible to quote it in detail, but it ranges from:

level 1 – illogical;

level 2 – incipient logic not clearly expressed;

level 3 – restatement of information given;

levels 4 and 5 – one or two statements going beyond the information given;

level 6 – an attempted sequential statement inadequately expressed;

levels 7 and 8 – one or two logical sequential statements, where the second statement is based on the first, connected by 'therefore' or 'because';

levels 9 and 10 – a synopsis of previous points, using an abstract concept.

For example, given a map of an area of the North Downs where Stone Age implements have been found, a typical level 3 answer is 'There are clay areas, and chalk areas and steep slopes' (which are given on the map). A level 4 statement is 'They had rivers to get water from.' An example of a level 8 statement is 'Chalky ground is not wet, therefore the tools are found there because Stone Age people could live there. And they were near a river, so they could get water to drink.' An example of a level 10 statement refers to a diagram of an Iron Age hut: 'They had huts. Therefore they could build huts. They had vegetation. Therefore they had materials to make huts. They had houses, shelter and stores.'

A system was devised for analysing group discussions and recording points made using this scale by dividing a page horizontally into ten sections, recording synopses of points under levels and mapping the children's development of each other's arguments (Figure 11.2). This analysis could then be transferred to a variety of other diagrammatic forms (Figures 11.3 and 11.8).

The story-writing test was assessed using a scale based on Ashby and Lee (1987) and Piaget (1932). This ranged from no awareness of ideas, beliefs and values and so no attempt to explain them, through intermediate levels when children mention symbolic artefacts in passing, but do not reflect on the ideas they may represent, and finally to an attempt to suggest the significance of symbols.

The findings

The relationship between interpreting evidence and the development of historical imagination and empathy – implications for story-writing

In analysing the written 'evidence tests' unit 1, The Stone Age, it became apparent that the deductive reasoning scale reflected levels of reasoning, but did not reflect a difference in the quality of the inferences of the control and experimental groups. The experimental groups' answers were more varied and more closely derived from the evidence, while the control group often simply repeated given information which was not rooted in the evidence. The control group displayed more anachronisms and stereotypes, and the assumption that people in the past were simple. Given a plan of a stone circle, for example, the experimental children suggested a variety of possible purposes (KM 'reconed it was for war dances, trading flint, praying'), and they suggested how it may have been made. The control group's answers were dominated by repeating received information about 'magic oak trees', 'Druids in white cloaks', and 'scarey magic'.

This difference in quality was examined further in unit 2. Answers were grouped under Collingwood's (1939) three categories of historical enquiry: How was it made? How was it used? What did it mean to people at the time? The following analysis of the experimental groups' responses to the 'Waterloo Helmet' evidence (British Museum slide) shows how they considered each of these questions (although they had not been explicitly asked to do so). They had been asked 'what do you know for certain? What reasonable guesses can you make, and what would you like to know?' Their answers suggest that it is through asking questions of evidence that children gradually learn to consider and attempt to explain the viewpoints of people who lived in other times. It also seems likely that the experimental groups were better able to do this because they had been taught through discursive teaching strategies which encouraged them to make a range of valid suppositions about evidence.

Experimental groups

Written test

I How was it made?
HC Exp 1. Qu 1 NVR 97
'They had metals . . . they could make things.'

JG Exp 2. Qu 1 NVR 120
'They could smelt iron and bronze . . . they had a furnace for getting iron out of rock.'

Discussion tapes

I How was it made?
JH Exp 2. NVR 100
'They made it carefully with the right kind of metals. Certainly they used a mould and little rivets.'

MF Exp 2. NVR 129
'They had the right tools to shape the metal.'

IW Exp 1. Qu I NVR 123
'They had charcoal to separate metal from ore.'

ML Exp 1. Qu 3 NVR 102
'I would like to know if the horns were hollow, because if they are it would be lighter.'

RL Exp 1. Qu I NVR 107
'They must have had good minds to remember things . . . They knew how to get to learn.'

NH Exp 1. NVR 105
'They could print patterns on it. They had a habit of putting circles on their working.'

GP Exp 1. NVR 133
'They had weapons – shields and swords too. At the British Museum, I copied a sword with a bronze hilt.'

II   *What was it used for?*
(a) *For protection in battle*
HG Exp 1. Qu 2 NVR 129
'They wore it to protect their heads . . . they had fights. They made it . . . they made weapons. They had wars.'

MF Exp 2. Qu 3 NVR 129
'I would like to know how they got the idea of armour, and why did they fight?'

II   *What was it used for?*
(a) *For protection in battle*
NH Exp 1. NVR 105
'They invented things. They knew how to smelt metal.'
Exp 1.
'It's got horns. It looks fierce – like an ox that could kill. Like a Stone Age hunter's deer antlers – to hide in the bushes. The pattern could show what side you were on so you didn't kill your own men.'
'They fought for food. If there was a bad winter and cattle died . . . to steal another tribe's cattle, or to cut another tribe's corn if they didn't have enough.'

(b) *As a ceremonial symbol or trophy*
KC Exp 2. Qu 2 NVR 111
'It might be made for a chief . . . he would wear it at ceremonies to look special.'

NH Exp 1. Qu 2 NVR 105
'They might have used it at chariot races . . . they might have had it as a medal. They might have liked beautiful things and had it as an ornament.'

(b) *As a ceremonial symbol or trophy*
NH Exp 1. NVR 105
'Maybe the more metal you had it showed how high up you were. They'd start with a bracelet 'til they were all covered in metal then they'd be a chief.'
Exp 2.
'It may have been awarded for extreme bravery in battle. Or in a contest for new warriors. Maybe they had races and contests, and the armour was awarded for use in a battle.'

SH Exp 1. Qu 2 NVR 104
    'It might have been for a
    goddess.'

Exp 1.
'If they found other things in the River
Thames, they may be offerings to a
water goddess, to thank her for water to
drink.'

(c) *A commodity to trade*

ES Exp 1. Qu 3 NVR 129
    'How did the archaeologists
    come to find it, because it
    would tell me if it was made
    there, or if they traded them.'

RL Exp 1. Qu 3 NVR 107
    'And was there one people in
    the place who made them? . . .
    if he did he would be rich.'

(c) *A commodity to trade*

Exp 2.
'They could have traded it for helmets
made in another land. Or maybe for
metal to make more weapons. Maybe,
as we learned in a lesson,
Julius Caesar wrote they used rods of
equal weight, or coins, to trade. They
could have traded it for bronze or
iron – probably for metal of some kind.'

III *What did it mean to the people*
    who wore it?

PC Exp 2. Qu 1 NVR 114
    'They were not afraid of going
    into battle . . . they looked fierce
    . . . they put fierce patterns
    on them.'

III *What did it mean to the people who*
    wore it?

Exp 2.
'The patterns make it look sort of
mysterious – they look like flowers
. . . it might mean something like "long
live our tribe" or "our tribe is the horse
tribe". Or special orders from their God.
Or a magic helmet to help them in
battle. Or the wearer's name. Or to
describe the wearer – how good he was
at hunting or fighting.'

ML Exp 1. Qu 2 NVR 102
    'I guess it had a kind of strap.'

KL Exp 1. Qu 3 NVR 107
    'Did they make different shapes
    and sizes, because it would
    have to fit . . .?

DS Exp 1. Qu 3 NVR 88
    'I would like to know what
    it felt like to put it on. It must
    have been heavy to handle.'

Exp 2.
'The strips at the side probably had
vines or strings attached to hold it on
to the wearer . . . they must have put
something on it to make it
shine . . . maybe it was measure for the
wearer's head.'

Exp 1.
'It's so heavy they probably took it with
them and put it on when they got there.'

When the study was planned, it had seemed that making deductions from evidence and historical imagination were different and discrete aspects of historical thinking, and for this reason, separate evidence and story-writing tests were devised. However, analysis of the evidence tests suggested that historical imagination develops through making valid suppositions about how things were made and used in the past and so considering what they may have meant to people at the time, and that this is the vehicle through which historical empathy may develop. Since historical imagination and historical empathy are defined in innumerable ways, their relationship as defined in this study is given in Figure 11.1.

Assessing levels of argument

The written evidence tests

In the written evidence tests, the children were given an answer paper which they were told to fill in, pretending they were archaeologists reporting on the evidence (the example shows how Andrew filled in his 'archaeologist's' report on the petroglyphics at the end of the Stone Age unit). Answer papers were laid out to encourage the highest levels of response, based on the ten-point scale described on page 190.

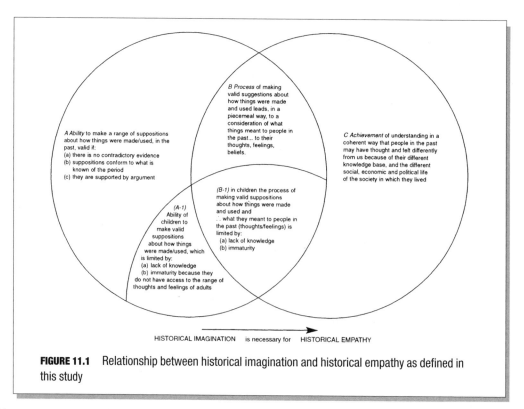

FIGURE 11.1 Relationship between historical imagination and historical empathy as defined in this study

Experimental Group 1

NAME: Andrew

DATE: 6.12.85

UNIT ONE: THE STONE AGES

EVIDENCE: writing

What do you know FOR CERTAIN from this evidence? Level 9		
they communicated	**Therefore** they made signs for communicating	**Conclusion** they needed other people
they draw	**Therefore** They had thing to draw with	

What reasonable GUESSES can you make about it? Level 8		
they may of had spcshells thing to do writing with	**Therefore**	**Conclusion** they might of had spcshell hunting signs
I think it had a meaning	**Therefore** It migh of taken them a long time to get the writing	

What would you LIKE TO KNOW about it? Level 6		
What it ment	**Because** then we could make little word	**Conclusion**
had they got to know what the signs ment	**Because** then we could do stone age writing	

They made a distinction between 'knowing', 'guessing', and 'not knowing', and encouraged children to make two statements for each of these categories, to follow each with a sequential argument and to write a 'conclusion'.

However, it was frequently necessary to look for the underlying logic of the thinking processes behind an answer in order to assess the level of thinking. Often this was obscured by poor spelling or handwriting. An answer may span several levels and would then be scored on the basis of the highest scoring statements within the answer and lower levels ignored. The logic of the answer does not always correspond to the divisions on the paper, so that the statements need to be carefully considered.

The oral evidence tests

Figure 11.2 shows how the oral evidence tests were also analysed on the ten-point scale. These synopses refer to the written evidence used in the Iron Age unit (Strabo 1.4.2).

> Most of the island is level and well-wooded, but there are many hilly districts. It produces corn, cattle, gold, silver and iron. They are all exported, together with leather, slaves and good hunting dogs. The Gauls use these dogs, and their own, for war as well.

Figure 11.3 shows how the levels were then mapped, so that they could be transferred to tables to compare levels of argument achieved in individual written answers and in group discussion over the four periods of study.

Making a distinction between 'knowing' and 'supposing'

In the written evidence tests, the children were asked three questions about each piece of evidence: question one, what do you know for certain? Question two, what reasonable 'guesses' can you make? Question three, what would you like to know? It is interesting that they were able to make these distinctions. Analysis of the unled discussion tapes – where they were not specifically asked to differentiate between knowing, guessing and not knowing – nevertheless show the discussions dominated by probability words (could be, maybe, unlikely, I wonder, what you think?). The children occasionally make certainty statements. 'They [the axe-heads] were all chipped and smoothed' and sometimes these are challenged by other children: 'It's got two heads' (cave painting). 'That could be a tail.' 'Bit thick for a tail.'

The unled groups also sometimes mention things that they would like to know. 'It must have been for some reason?' 'How do you think they made the banks?'

It is interesting that in the written evidence tests the children were able to make 'certainty' statements, and reasonable guesses (questions one and two) with almost equal ease. The graph (Figure 11.4) based on analysis of variance tests to compare groups, questions and types of evidence in each unit, shows a significant difference between the types of question, with question three (what would you like to know?)

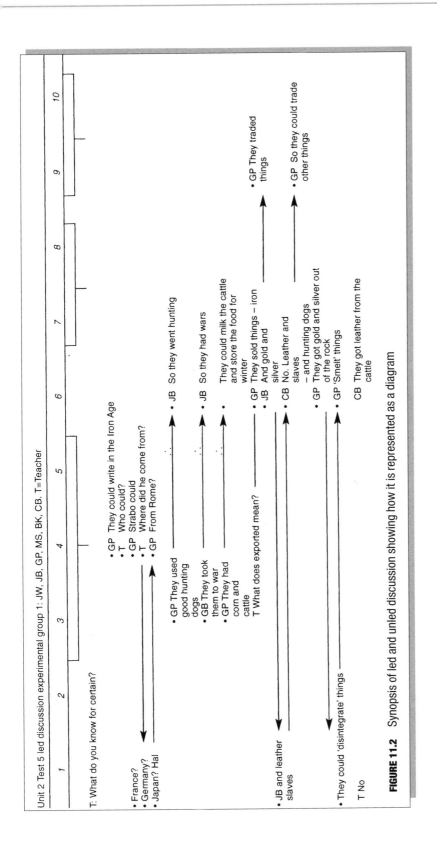

Unit 2 Test 5 led discussion experimental group 1: JW, JB, GP, MS, BK, CB. T=Teacher

1	2	3	4	5	6	7	8	9	10

T: What do you know for certain?

• GP They could write in the Iron Age
• T   Who could?
• GP Strabo could
• France?
• Germany?
• Japan? Hal
• T   Where did he come from?
• GP From Rome?

• GP They used good hunting dogs
• GB They took them to war
• GP They had corn and cattle
• JB So they went hunting

• JB So they had wars

• They could milk the cattle and store the food for winter

T What does exported mean?

• GP They sold things – iron
• JB And gold and silver

JB and leather slaves

• CB No. Leather and slaves – and hunting dogs
• GP They got gold and silver out of the rock

• GP 'Smelt' things

• They could 'disintegrate' things

T No

CB They got leather from the cattle

• GP They traded things

• GP So they could trade other things

FIGURE 11.2 Synopsis of led and unled discussion showing how it is represented as a diagram

197

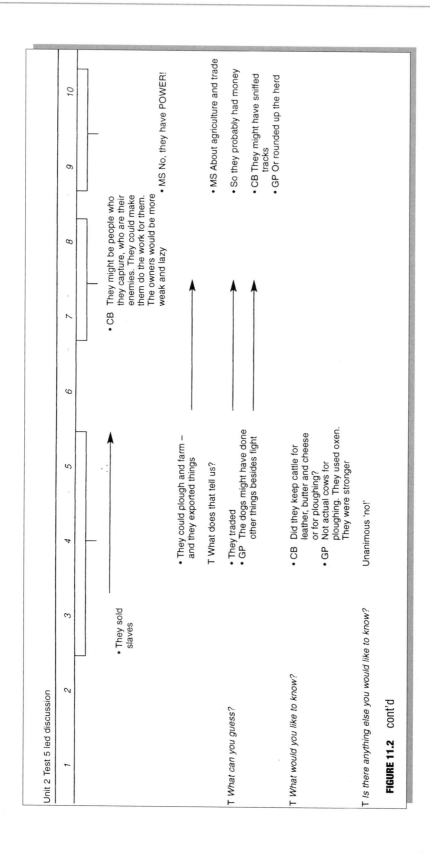

Unit 2 Test 5 led discussion

1   2   3   4   5   6   7   8   9   10

• They sold
slaves

• CB They might be people who
they capture, who are their
enemies. They could make
them do the work for them.
The owners would be more
weak and lazy

• MS No, they have POWER!

• They could plough and farm –
and they exported things

T What does that tell us?

• MS About agriculture and trade

• So they probably had money

T What can you guess?

• They traded
• GP The dogs might have done
other things besides fight

• CB They might have sniffed
tracks
• GP Or rounded up the herd

T What would you like to know?

• CB Did they keep cattle for
leather, butter and cheese
or for ploughing?
• GP Not actual cows for
ploughing. They used oxen.
They were stronger

T Is there anything else you would like to know?

Unanimous 'no!'

FIGURE 11.2 cont'd

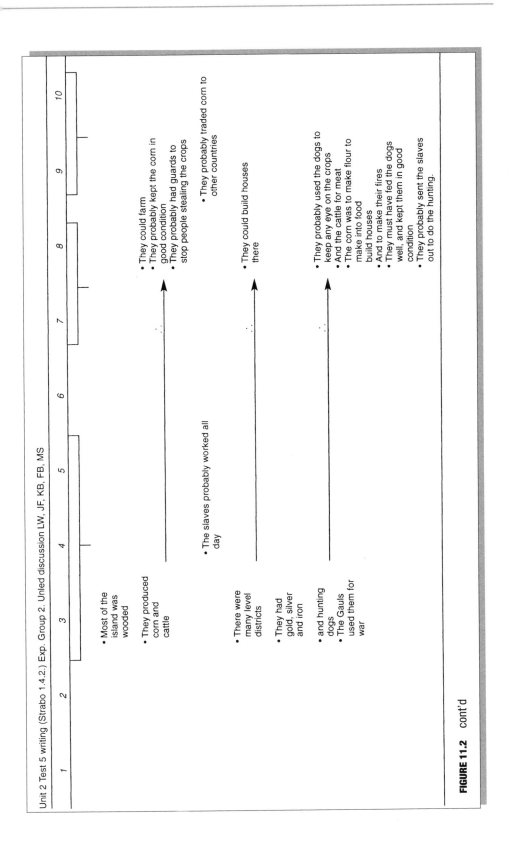

Unit 2 Test 5 writing (Strabo 1.4.2.) Exp. Group 2. Unled discussion LW, JF, KB, FB, MS

1	2	3	4	5	6	7	8	9	10

• Most of the island was wooded

• They produced corn and cattle

• There were many level districts

• They had gold, silver and iron

• and hunting dogs
• The Gauls used them for war

• The slaves probably worked all day

• They could farm
• They probably kept the corn in good condition
• They probably had guards to stop people stealing the crops
    • They probably traded corn to other countries

• They could build houses there

• They probably used the dogs to keep any eye on the crops
• And the cattle for meat
• The corn was to make flour to make into food build houses
• And to make their fires
• They must have fed the dogs well, and kept them in good condition
• They probably sent the slaves out to do the hunting.

FIGURE 11.2 cont'd

Points made at each level in led and unled discussions

Led Discussion

level 1/2	5 points
level 3/4/5	13 points
level 7/8	8 points
level 9/10	5 points
Total:	31 points

Unled Discussion

level 1/2	4 points
level 3/4/5	3 points
level 7/8	11 points
level 9/10	1 point
Total:	19 points

FIGURE 11.3   Led and unled discussions, unit 2, test 5, writing. Strabo 1.4.2

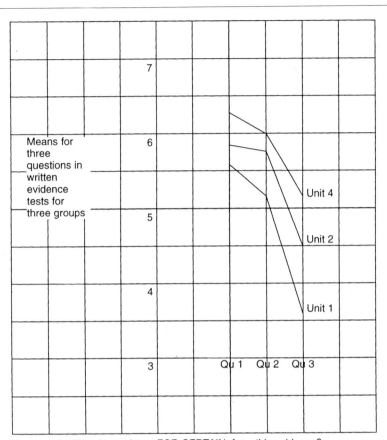

Question 1 What do you know FOR CERTAIN, from this evidence?
Question 2 What REASONABLE GUESSES can you make from this evidence?
Question 3 What WOULD YOU LIKE TO KNOW about this evidence?

FIGURE 11.4 Graph showing means of scores for questions 1, 2 and 3 for units 1, 2 and 4. (Unit 3 was taught and tested but the results were not analysed due to shortage of time)

by far the most difficult. The Sheffe test of multiple comparison shows the difference between the first two questions and question three to be significant. These children then are able to make a distinction between knowing and valid suppositions, and they find both types of inference equally easy, but they find it far harder to say what they 'would like to know' about evidence.

Although these results were statistically significant, there were exceptions to the main effects. There were significant interactions between the questions and types of evidence. In unit 1, for example, there was little difference in difficulty between knowing and guessing about the cave painting, the plan of the stone circle, or the map. This is not surprising because not much is known about how these things were made or used or what they meant to Stone Age people, even by archaeologists, so there are fertile opportunities for reasonable guesses. On the other hand, it was easier to make certainty statements about axe-heads because these are central to a study of the Stone Age. The experimental groups had three lessons on tools and weapons and had seen them made at Grimes Graves. This is important because it shows how statistically significant main effects are blurred by other variables, by a particular example of a type of evidence, by interest and by motivation.

There do however, seem to be implications for teachers in the general finding that children are equally able to say what they know, and to make reasonable suggestions, but find it difficult to say what they 'would like to know'. It suggests that children of this age do not need to be restricted to repeating 'facts' and that they are able to become actively involved in historical problem-solving. They can learn to control their own thinking, and become increasingly aware of what constitutes a valid supposition. This is an important staging post on the way to true historical understanding. However, 'what would you like to know?' is a question with an unknown starting point, and is too open. It does not encourage children to control their own investigation. This is significant because children are frequently told to 'find out about . . .', particularly at the ends of chapters in history books, assuming this encourages motivation and independent learning. These tests suggest that such a question is too unstructured.

Different types of evidence

The study set out to investigate whether children find it easier to make deductions about artefacts and pictures than about more abstract evidence, diagrams, maps and written sources. The relationship between groups, questions and evidence in each unit was statistically analysed using analyses of variance. The findings are shown in Figure 11.5.

Although in unit 1 there was a significant difference between the levels of response to the five types of evidence, and the children found the diagram and the map the most difficult, it is interesting that by unit 2, and again in unit 4, there was no significant difference in their ability to interpret 'concrete' and 'abstract' evidence. This is not to suggest that it is not very important for children to be introduced to artefacts and pictures (which are, at the very least, stimulating sources), but rather that if they are given more abstract evidence as well, as part of a continuum, and have learned to discuss evidence, they can interpret abstract sources equally well. This seems to be because, having learned how to discuss evidence and the kinds of responses required, they can relate abstract evidence to 'concrete' evidence – maybe through visits to sites or museums. The experimental groups had visited Grimes Graves, the British Museum and local sites, and related these to maps, geology, vegetation and relief. They could therefore draw on these experiences in interpreting, for example, the Stone Age axe-heads, the Waterloo Helmet, the plans of the stone circle, the Iron Age hut, and the maps.

Their level of response depends, not on the level of abstraction of the evidence, but on language, on concepts and on argument, because remains of the past are only

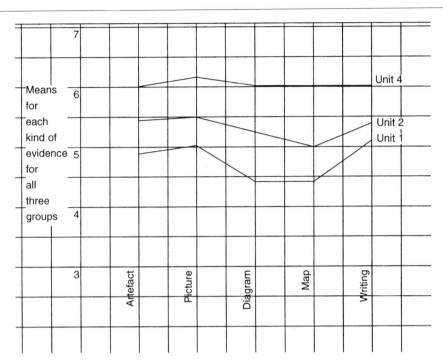

FIGURE 11.5 Graph showing means of scores for questions 1, 2 and 3 for units 1, 2 and 4. (Unit 3 was taught and tested but the results were not analysed due to shortage of time.) The marking scale is outlined on page 190

evidence to the extent that they can tell us about the people who made and used them. Children need to experience physical evidence, and to learn to discuss it, if it is to have meaning for them. They are then able to transfer this process to new evidence, and to more abstract evidence.

There are implications here for older students. It has often been assumed that artefacts and pictures are more appropriate for younger children who cannot read and write easily. However, if tangible sources are not easier to interpret, this strengthens the case for using a range of sources at any level of study.

Again, it is important to bear in mind that while the main effects shown in Figure 11.5 are statistically significant, there were variations in this pattern, influenced by particular examples of evidence, and by teaching strategies. In unit 4, the level main effect across the five kinds of evidence resulted from opposite trends across the experimental and control groups, although the span was only across one mark. It is likely that the control group found the Beowulf extract easier to interpret than the other evidence because they had more experience of 'comprehension exercises', but they had not learned how to interpret historical evidence.

Using learned concepts

The concepts which children had been taught in each unit as 'spellings' and which they had learned to use in discussing key evidence during class lessons the following week were used spontaneously by at least some of the children both in the written tests and the taped discussions. It was also encouraging that in unit 4, they were using vocabulary which they had learned in connection with previous units, transferring it to a new period and new material. Not surprisingly, the children in the control group who had not learned specific concepts only used those which were labelled in the evidence, and these were rarely abstract concepts. Figure 11.6 and Figure 11.7 show how children used concepts they had learned in previous units in both written and oral evidence tests.

Although no claim is made that the children totally understood the abstract concepts they used (e.g. vegetation, belief, power, agriculture, transport, society, religion), it seems that these concepts are becoming part of their own vocabulary.

It may be that the experimental groups were able to make a far greater range of valid suppositions about the evidence because they had a conceptual framework of both concrete and abstract concepts to which they could relate new pieces of evidence, even if the concepts themselves were not mentioned in their answers. Freedman and Loftus (1971) concluded that concepts play an important part in organising semantic memory. For example, in interpreting the written evidence in the Iron Age unit (see page 196) many children make deductions concerned with trade, agriculture, metal production and social structure.

IW 'We know that Grece people traded with us . . . they must have had something to trade with.'

FF 'We know that gold, silver and iron are all exported across the sea.'

NH 'They had corn and cattle . . . they could farm and so they had learned to live in one place.'

MF guessed that 'since they had gold, silver and iron, they had miners' and he wondered how they mined and transported it because he had seen neither mining tools nor Iron Age boats in pictures.

Similarly, in interpreting the illuminated Saxon manuscript showing harvest, children in the experimental groups focused on ideas connected with agriculture, community, and communication. They discussed crops, farming methods and the cycle of the farming year.

RD 'The people seem to be cutting logs and transporting them maybe to trade them – if they lived near a forest.'

They refer to the jobs people are doing and the relationship between them, and make various suggestions about the meaning of the writing.

1 cm represents the use of the concept in one evidence test on one or more occasions

■ represents led discussion groups (Exp 1)
▨ represents unled discussion groups (Exp 2)

	Led (Exp 1)	*Unled* (Exp 2)	
Concrete	11	Concrete	9
Abstract	9	Abstract	8
Superordinate	10	Superordinate	1

This bar chart shows how both the led and unled groups used their taught vocabulary in unit 2 discussions and, when appropriate, used concepts learned in unit 1. The led groups, however, used more superordinates than the unled groups

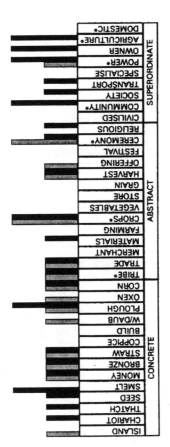

Note: * concepts learned in unit 1.

FIGURE 11.6   The taught concepts in unit 2 used in discussion tapes

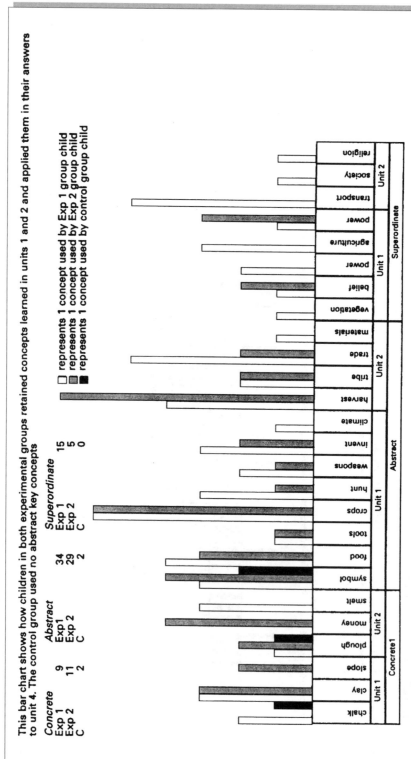

FIGURE 11.7 Concepts taught in unit 1 or unit 2 which were used in written evidence tests in unit 4 by Exp 1, Exp 2 and control group children

It seems then that not only do children enjoy learning to use and spell 'hard words', but that learning key concepts gives them a reference point, or framework, to apply to new material, and that this helps to generate a range of new ideas about it.

Led and unled group discussion

The content of the discussion was similar in both the led and unled groups. It was concerned with how the evidence may have been used and what it may have meant to those who created it, although the children had not been asked at any point to consider these aspects. However, the groups differed in the way they expressed their ideas. The led groups tended to make general statements and seemed to assume that the teacher knew where the discussion was leading, whereas the unled groups paid more attention to physical description, and sometimes explained their ideas through valid stories and images, about brave warriors for example, who may be commemorated by a stone circle, or who may have hidden their treasure there and defended it. However, in both the led and unled groups, there was genuine argument. They both made some illogical points. In the unled groups, they were either ignored or corrected, with respect, by another child. In the led groups, it was usually the teacher who queried them. In both groups, the children developed each other's points and the quality of the discussion improved over the four units. There was an increase in the numbers of points made and in the number of sequential arguments, and a decrease in the number of illogical points. The structure of the discussions differed slightly in the led and unled groups. The led groups tended to explore all the possibilities suggested by one point, then move on to the next point whereas the unled groups usually followed up a point with one further argument, then made a fresh point. Sometimes, they backtracked, and ideas were less systematically explored.

It seems then that both led and unled discussions have a place in helping children to interpret evidence. If children have learned the thinking patterns required, discussion in small groups without the teacher may sometimes be more valuable than teacher-led discussion; children are more able to explain their ideas in their own way, to defend them and so to make them their own. This has implications for classroom organisation and for the value of group work not directly led by the teacher (Figure 11.8).

Teaching strategies

Visits

The children were able to transfer information learned on visiting a site to new evidence. For example, on the visit to Farthing Down, they had been asked how, if they had lived there in Neolithic times, they could have made a dry, warm, comfortable shelter, what they could have eaten, where they might have found water, how

Led Discussion   Unled Discussion

Test 1. Artefact. The Sutton Hoo Sceptre

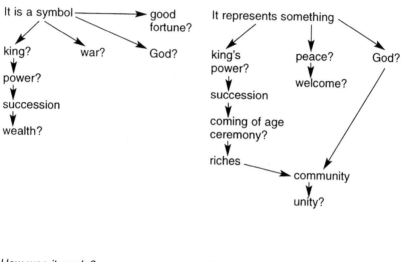

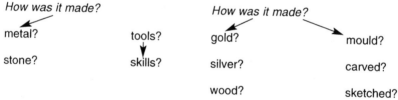

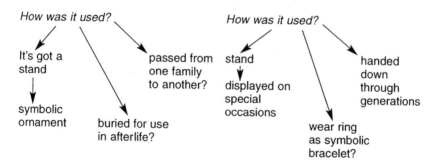

FIGURE 11.8 A comparison of the content of the led and unled discussions about previously unseen evidence. Unit 4: The Saxons

Led Discussion   Unled Discussion

Test 2. Illuminated picture of harvest from Saxon calendar

How was it used?
↓
show time to do things?
↓
to communicate?

How was it used?
↓
to remember something to do
with Harvest?
↓
list of jobs to do on the land?

How was it made?
↓
some people could write/read
↓
they could help others

How was it made?

*What did it mean to people
at the time?*

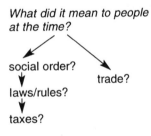

social order?
↓   trade?
laws/rules?
↓
taxes?

*What did it mean to people
at the time?*

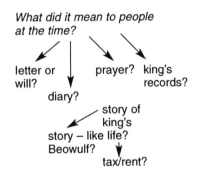

letter or   prayer? king's
will?   records?
            diary?
                        story of
                        king's
            story – like life?
            Beowulf?   ↓
                    tax/rent?

Test 3. Diagram. Plan of Saxon church at Cirencester

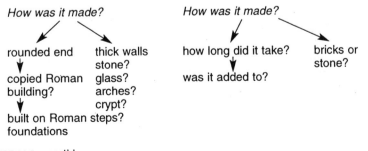

How was it made?

rounded end   thick walls
↓   stone?
copied Roman   glass?
building?   arches?
↓   crypt?
built on Roman steps?
foundations

How was it made?

how long did it take?   bricks or
↓   stone?
was it added to?

FIGURE 11.8   cont'd

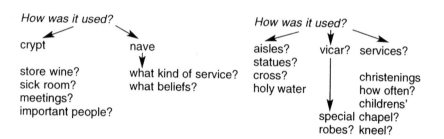

Led Discussion   Unled Discussion

How was it used?   How was it used?

crypt   nave   aisles?   vicar? services?
                                  statues?
store wine?   what kind of service?   cross?   christenings
sick room?   what beliefs?   holy water   how often?
meetings?   childrens'
important people?   special chapel?
                                           robes? kneel?

Test 4. Map of the Croydon area in Saxon times

Physical Character   Physical Character

Springs rivers slopes valleys   hills valleys flat tops
woods clay chalk

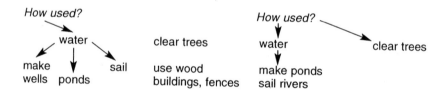

How used?   How used?

     water   clear trees   water   clear trees
make   sail use wood   make ponds
wells ponds   buildings, fences sail rivers

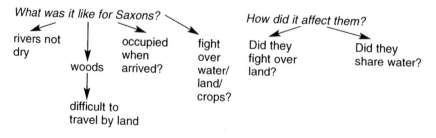

What was it like for Saxons?   How did it affect them?

rivers not   occupied   fight   Did they   Did they
dry   when   over   fight over   share water?
        woods arrived?   water/ land?
                          land/
        difficult to   crops?
        travel by land

FIGURE 11.8   cont'd

they might have made tools, weapons and pots. When given a map of another similar area of the North Downs they were able to apply these points to the new map and make a range of deductions and suggestions in their written answers. Table 11.2 shows the information children had discussed on their visit to Farthing Down on the left. This visit stimulated their deductions about the map of a similar but unknown area which are given on the right.

TABLE 11.2 Examples of written answers, showing how visit to Farthing Down helped children to interpret the map

Evidence discussed on visit to Farthing Down	Children's use of this evidence applied to the map (Exp Group 1) Written Evidence
Geology: Top of Down is chalk with flints. Sparse vegetation and well-drained.	CL Qu 1. They had a lot of chalk. They could build huts on it because it's flat. They would not build a hut at the bottom of the hill because the water would not run away. (Score level 8) AM Qu 2. They would have camped on the slopes because when it rained the rain would run down the slope, their camp would not be flooded and their huts would not get destroyed. (Score level 7) CL Qu 3. I would like to know what flint implements were used for because they already had hand tools for killing animals. (Score level 6)
Clay soil – sticky – heavy	HC It has got a lot of clay on the surfis . . . it must of been soggy. It must of been wet. (Score level 7) IW Qu 2. I can guess that they made things . . . they would use clay to built pots. We can also guess that there is chalk . . . there is flint. (Score level 8) HC Qu 2. There might have been a lot of wetness . . . it could of been cold. There might of been Stone Age people living there . . . they might of been living on the chalk bits.
In valley bottom there is marsh and a stream	ML Qu 2. They might have routes to the rivers . . . they would have an easy way to go. They used pots to get water . . . they can get water in time. (Score level 8)
Hachures show slopes	KM Qu 1. We know that Hachures mean steep slopes . . . the hachures on the map mean there are shallow and steep slopes. (Score level 7)
Vegetation (+Geology) grass on top yew and oak on clay slopes	JW Qu 2. I can guess what kind of trees grew there . . . I think oak and fir trees grew there. There were big chalk and clay areas where they could make pots. They could of lived near the clay area so they wouldn't have to walk far. (Score level 8) CL Qu 2. We can guess which plants they used for medicine . . . some people knew which plants cure illnesses. We can also guess which plants and leaves they used for a bed . . . they would choose the best things to make it. So they would select things to use. (Score level 7)
Animals	ES Qu 3. I would like to know if animals lived there when Stone Age lived because I want to see if they ate small animals.

(cont'd)

TABLE 11.2 cont'd

Evidence discussed on visit to Farthing Down	Children's use of this evidence applied to the map (Exp Group 1) Written Evidence
Examples. Experimental Group 2. Unit 1. Test 4. Showing use of visit in interpreting map	
Geology: chalk/flint, clay, slope, wind, river	PC (level 8) Qu 1. They found that chalk sucks the water through it . . . we know it was dry. They lived in places like Farthing Down. DF (level 9) Qu 2. They lived near to chalk and clay areas . . . they didn't have to go far to get flints. They lived near slopes . . . they were in a place with not many trees. They knew exactly where to live. JG (level 8) Qu 2. I guess they could have shelter from the cliffs . . . they would be safe. They would have water . . . they could have land for farming on the chalk soil. FB (level 8) Qu 2. They probably went fishing in the river . . . they probably had quite a lot of fish. They probably had to wash in the river . . . they probably didn't wash much! JG (level 8) Qu 1. Neolithic people must have been in the area . . . they had camps there. Trees might be in great numbers on the clay soil . . . they had shelter.
Vegetation	MF (level 7) Qu 3. Why they chose that place. What animals lived there, because I'd like to know what they ate. RF (level 7) Qu 2. I can guess there must have been a lot of woods . . . I can guess there must have been lots of animals nearby. I know there must have been a lot of food nearby.
Animals	

The scores were surprisingly high for such abstract evidence; this seems to be because the visit enabled the children to relate real experiences and images to the map. As AW wrote in his conclusion 'This is the best evidence game'!

Similarly, in the Iron Age unit, they had again visited Farthing Down to trace the lynchets, the soil banks formed by turning the plough, which indicate Iron Age field patterns. Figure 11.9 shows how they were able to transfer discussion of these to the Iron Age map fields at Butser, on the South Downs.

At the end of unit 2 the children were given a previously unseen map of Iron Age fields on Butser Hill in Hampshire. In their written answers, experimental group 2 developed between them many of the arguments inherent in this evidence which showed lynchets and trackways.

Table 11.3 analyses how children in the written answers related the new evidence about Butser to their visit to Farthing Down, and also to their class discussion on Iron Age farming, and finally to their own ideas. This shows how they were able to transfer the experience of the visit and following class discussion to new evidence, and, in so doing, also to form their own valid suggestions and questions.

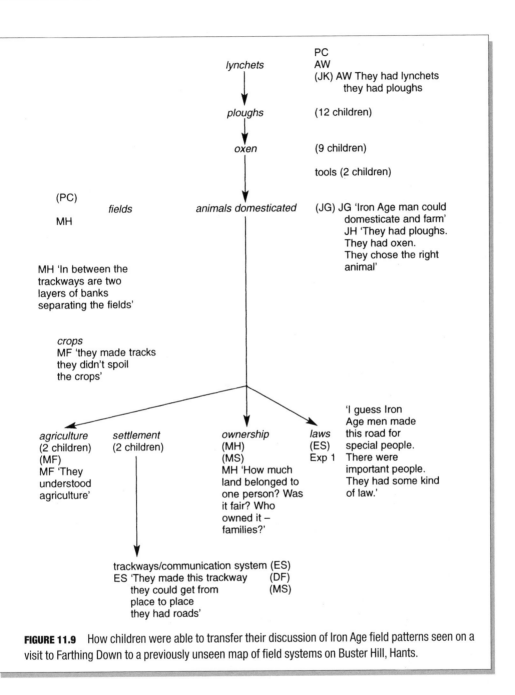

PC
AW
(JK) AW They had lynchets
they had ploughs

lynchets

(12 children)

ploughs

(9 children)

oxen

tools (2 children)

(PC)

MH

fields   *animals domesticated*   (JG) JG 'Iron Age man could
domesticate and farm'
JH 'They had ploughs.
They had oxen.
They chose the right
animal'

MH 'In between the
trackways are two
layers of banks
separating the fields'

crops
MF 'they made tracks
they didn't spoil
the crops'

'I guess Iron
Age men made
this road for
special people.

agriculture   *settlement*   *ownership*   *laws*   There were
(2 children)   (2 children)   (MH)   (ES)   important people.
(MF)   (MS)   Exp 1   They had some kind
MF 'They   MH 'How much   of law.'
understood   land belonged to
agriculture'   one person? Was
                                  it fair? Who
                                  owned it –
                                  families?'

trackways/communication system (ES)
ES 'They made this trackway   (DF)
they could get from   (MS)
place to place
they had roads'

FIGURE 11.9 How children were able to transfer their discussion of Iron Age field patterns seen on a visit to Farthing Down to a previously unseen map of field systems on Buster Hill, Hants.

The visits probably also helped them to discuss the plans of a stone circle, an Iron Age hut, and a Saxon church, although they had not visited similar sites, because they had considered geology, vegetation and relief, and the effects of these on a settlement in each period.

TABLE 11.3 How children, in written answers, related new evidence about Butser to their visit to Farthing Down and also to their class discussion about Iron Age farming and finally to their own ideas

Butser Map	Farthing Down Visit	Class Discussion	Own Ideas
PC There are bumps. We know where the fields were	They could use machinery like a plough They farmed They grew crops.	There was probably a settlement there. They probably grew vegetables (re: evidence of beans, vetch, crop rotation)	If they thought a horse was a god or something why did they not use it? (in farming)
JG They had ploughs	They understood how to grow crops. They could farm and domesticate	There might be tools or there might be bones of oxen still there. (re: evidence of bones found, and tools, at Glastonbury) (re: oxen bones similar to modern Dexter)	A cart could carry crops from the field. How long did it take to make (invent?) a cart? If there are bones there, archaeologists could make up an oxen like they make dinosaurs in Natural History Museum
RF I know for certain this map give us clues. I know some people can find these ditches (i.e. I know they exist and what they look like)	I guess they had patterns in soil and chalk (i.e. I know soil or chalk is thin – viz the Uffington Horse)	I guess they had lambs (re: sheep probably Soay, as at Butser) or as JK said 'sheep would give wool and meat and keep the grass down'	
MS They had fields. They must have had a plough	I guess the tracks were for taking the plough across	They might grow things like peas and beans (re: Butser evidence)	I guess the tracks were made of wood. There must have been timber to make them from. I would like to know what transport they had, and we would know what skills they had

(cont'd)

TABLE 11.3 cont'd

Butser Map	Farthing Down Visit	Class Discussion	Own Ideas
SK They had roads	They could take the oxen across to another field because if the plough went over the corn it would crush it up and it would not grow again	I think had a field of *herbs* (re: discussion of flavouring and preserving)	They could eat them and (use them to) make other foods
MH In between the two trackways are the two layers of banks separating the fields	They must transport the plough through gaps in the banks	The blank bits might be for *settlements* (re: post-hole evidence)	Maybe the owners might live there. Maybe ownership separated by trackways. I would like to know how much land belonged to one person; if they had the same amount and if they lived in families next to each other

The stimulus of the 'further afield' visit to Grimes Graves and the British Museum probably helped the experimental groups to make a greater range of suppositions than the control group about artefacts, about the Stone Age axe-heads, for example, and the Waterloo Helmet.

Language: discussion, concepts and language as an objective tool

Discussion

Class lessons were based on discussion of selected evidence, using learned concepts. Each unit consisted of four such lessons taught over consecutive weeks. One of the four lessons was based on the local visit to an area of settlement, and one focused on ideas and beliefs.

This study endorsed the importance of learning through open-ended discussion, in which children learn the thinking processes of history. They learn that many suggestions are possible, and remain uncertain, and that arguments must be supported and can be contested. This is how criteria for validity become understood. It seems likely that this is the most important factor in the difference between the control group and experimental groups' responses. Firstly, the experimental groups achieved both a higher level of inferential reasoning, and a wider range of valid suppositions. Secondly, the control and experimental groups used the factual information they had in different ways. They were not required to rehearse it in their answers but nevertheless, it underpinned their answers. The control group, however, tended to repeat information given, which was only loosely related to the evidence, and when they went beyond it, they often revealed misconceptions. The experimental groups were more likely to test given knowledge against the evidence. Their suggestions, for example, about the Anglo Saxon sceptre were dependent on their knowledge of Anglo Saxon kings and kingdoms, laws and succession.

It seems, then, that discussion is important in the development of historical understanding. However the discussion must be based on selected key evidence. Children need key factual information, but if they learn it through discussion, they do not simply repeat it, but they both retain the information and are able to transfer the pattern of discursive thinking to new evidence.

Concepts

The importance of teaching and using selected concepts of different levels of abstraction to interpret key evidence has already been discussed (page 204). It was seen that children were able to use abstract, learned concepts as an organising framework against which to test new evidence, even when they did not mention the concept itself. This helped them in discussing the Sutton Hoo sceptre to talk about the king, ceremonies, symbols and laws; Beowulf deductions involved power, vengeance, courage and beliefs. Learned concepts helped children to make a greater range of valid suggestions about evidence, to develop arguments, and so to make suggestions about different attitudes, behaviour and beliefs.

Language as an objective tool

The experimental groups had also discussed the nature of language as a tool for communication. They were able to talk about the relationship between the written and spoken word, the symbolism of language and to suppose how language originated and changed. A child could say of the Stone Age petroglyphics, for instance, 'They made signs for communicating; they had things to draw with; they needed people.' Or 'They wrote strange writing . . . they had different words from today. This writing is found in Italy . . . it could have been found in other places.' One child wrote, 'They had to teach each other how to speak . . . they had to cooperate in making writing.' Another guessed that 'in different countries they had different signs . . . if someone went to a different country, he would not understand. It took a long time to carve the signs . . . they would not move from place to place.'

In considering the Strabo excerpt in unit 2, JG wondered 'how long after the Romans the Iron Age wrote'. AW observed that 'they had different language over different times. They did not have the same language everywhere . . . I would like to know how they made their languages up.'

Acceleration

The study suggested that if children are taught consistently, applying the same teaching strategies to new material, they learn patterns of thinking that can be transferred, and the quality of their thinking improves. In unit 4, the experimental groups achieved higher levels of deductive argument than in previous units, and used more abstract concepts. It seems then that it is important for children to learn patterns of thinking, and for teachers to be clear what these should be. In unit 4, although the means for all three groups were higher than in the first two units, the means for the experimental groups were much higher than the control group mean (Figure 11.10).

The integrated curriculum

The study did not aim to prove the benefits of learning history through an integrated curriculum. However, the links between responses to the history tests and other areas of the curriculum can be traced. From the science components, the children seem to have learned both to question and respect the technology of other societies.

They discuss how things were made and used. For example, the discussion of the Waterloo Helmet reflects their knowledge of iron smelting learned in the Iron Age unit. Their experience of historical fiction (e.g. The Changeling, Sutcliffe 1974; and The Bronze Sword, Treece 1965) may well have helped children to recognise the difference between fact and imagination. There are many examples of children transferring their knowledge of geology, vegetation and relief to maps of other areas; geography

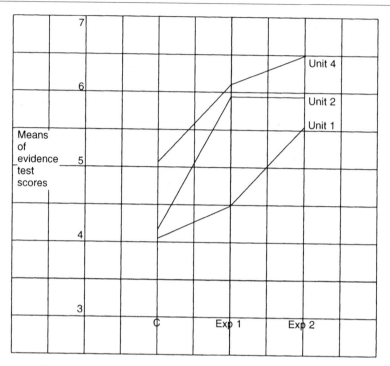

FIGURE 11.10   Graph showing means of evidence test scores for control and experimental groups for units 1, 2 and 4

probably also influenced their references to trade, transport, and migration of peoples. Art taught the experimental groups careful observation through drawing (slides of cave paintings, Iron Age artefacts in the British Museum, or Anglo Saxon pottery). It also seems to have taught them both an interest in the techniques and materials used in the past, and an understanding and respect for different interpretations. SH guesses that 'Stone Age people may have kept their oxides in pots and used their hands to paint'. The experimental groups suggest why the Uffington Horse may be unrealistic. DS NVR 88 (Exp 1. Qu 1(7)) owns a horse and brings her own keen interest to bear, in spite of difficulties with spelling!

> I kown that they had Horse Because it is a piter of one. They must of copid the Bones of the Horse And the shape of the Horse And it must of bein bukin because of its back legs and the sape of it . . .

MH NVR 135 (Exp 2. Qu 1(9))

> Two of the legs do not join up to the body. Therefore I think that is a special 3D effect. It has whiskers on a kind of chin. Therefore either they have not observed well, or their horse has whiskers.

The dimension of religious education involved the discussion of the symbolism of light and dark in cave painting and in other cultures, the needs and fears of Iron Age people, the nature of Roman gods, the teachings of early Celtic and Roman missionaries. It may be that this helped children to consider reasons for beliefs and rituals in their own and other societies. The mathematics component may have encouraged deductions involving estimates. ('It might take 1,000 people to fill the church. The population must have been big.') They consider shape. One child says of the circle, 'They had another shape in maths', and the Uffington Horse has a 'special 3D effect'. The Iron Age fields are 'square or rectangular'.

A degree of integration, with a clear history focus seems the most economical way, in a crowded curriculum, to allow children to become steeped in a period. It also demonstrates that history involves the history of thought in all disciplines and in all aspects of society, and can, in turn, give a purpose to experiment in science and to calculations in mathematics.

Ways in which teachers can evaluate and develop the National Curriculum in the light of experience and good practice

This research indicates some of the problems involved in assessing patterns in the development of children's thinking in history. However, the study was undertaken as an integral part of class teaching, and refined the thinking of the teacher and the quality of her teaching in the process, so that it suggests that action research by practising teachers is both possible and desirable, and should therefore be supported and encouraged.

It is not necessary for such detailed analysis to be carried out all the time, or by all teachers; the purpose of the study described was to indicate broad patterns of development, and the relationship between different aspects of historical thinking which could form a basis for planning and for ongoing assessment by teachers. It is essential that the broad brushstrokes with which the National Curriculum aims to paint a map of the past is also balanced by detailed and carefully focused discussion of key evidence. Young children cannot grasp a holistic view of complex social structures; they do not understand the workings of adult minds, and cannot address difficult political and religious issues. The need to list and memorise 'causes and effects' killed school history for many people and there is still a danger that teachers will overinterpret the content specified in the revised curriculum.

Experience suggests that children are interested in detail, and in problem-solving in which they can be validly and genuinely engaged: what did sailors on the Armada ships eat? What did the sailors on the *Mary Rose* do? Who lived in my home before I did?

Therefore, the curriculum must be taught in an economical way if it is not to be overloaded. Planning must be carefully focused to centre on real problem-solving in each curriculum area, and in a range of contexts. Planning, activities and evaluation must form a related sequence so that assessment is an integral part of all the work children do and of the constant interaction between teacher and child. Work planned in history must reflect the thinking processes of history, and allow for a range of differentiated outcomes. It should also involve learning history through the rich variety of activities on which good primary practice is based:

- information technology (simulations, word-processing and data-handling);

- art (drawing, printing, painting, embroidery, modelmaking);

- science and technology (cooking, spinning, weaving, grinding seeds, building and testing structures, using tools, moving loads, using a range of materials);

- language for different audiences (transactional and expressive writing, reading, discussion, role-play, making video and audio tapes).

In conclusion

There are many opportunities to interpret the curriculum for history in creative ways, planning activities which reflect an increased understanding of the nature of history, an articulate rationale for its importance, and the sharing of teachers' own enthusiasms. Nevertheless, the position of history in the curriculum is probably more precarious than before. The statutory requirement is minimal, with a recognition that some outline studies are inevitable; on the other hand, there is increasing emphasis on tests in 'basic skills' and on published league tables of the results. Yet

> The present is where we get lost
> If we forget our own past and have
> No vision of the future.

> (Ayi Kwei Amah in Fryer 1989)

Whether or not this is allowed to happen will depend on the enthusiasm, efforts and expertise of all those who care about primary history, working together with conviction.

Postscript – a Starkey contrast!

Of course you need not only to understand the process of historical enquiry but also to be able to articulate it with confidence to those who know nothing of history education, and certainly nothing of young children's thinking in history. The British Education Conference at the Institute of Historical Research in February 2005 brought together teachers, historians, film makers, television producers makers to discuss how history should be taught in the future and its British education safeguarded. Dr David Starkey spoke first on, 'What should we be teaching in the twentieth century?' I was invited to speak on, 'History in Primary Schools: identity, progression, dialogue'. All the papers can be found on www.history.ac.uk/education/conference.

Yes, there were other speakers – sixteen to be precise – and I did not follow on directly from Dr Starkey. I juxtapose here contrasting statements from each of our talks, in the form of the debate I should like to have had with him, if he had not escaped after giving his paper.

DS   We can justify history at the centre of the curriculum by memory. Societies have a collective memory. A society that loses its collective memory has nothing.

HC   But there is a problem with whose identity we are talking about. As Jerome Bruner (1996) has said, it is not easy, however multicultural your intentions, to help a ten-year-old create a story that includes him in a world beyond his family and neighbourhood, having just been transplanted from . . . wherever, so there are questions in looking at history in terms of identity. I should like to suggest that the way around this is to take a constructivist approach to history, to ensure that children are involved in the process of enquiry, from the very beginning . . . I am not saying that children create their own histories in their entirety. They should clearly work within what is known, a planned framework. It is the process that is important – there is no one story.

DS   It leads to a universal scepticism which, I think, is profoundly dangerous . . . Simon Schama, Niall Ferguson and I all gave the same answer at the Summer School organised by the Prince of Wales, who plays a very important role in this area. What matters is **content**; what matters is **narrative**. And what goes on in schools has been deliberately modelled on university teaching. We have become research led, in a way that I think is entirely unsuitable for a subject which, we are arguing here, is worthy of a place in the curriculum . . . The first job is to be **confident** in **content**.

HC   I would follow Collingwood's definition of the process of historical enquiry; making inferences and deductions about sources.

DS   I am profoundly sceptical about the use of documents at early stages in teaching.

HC   This process does not necessarily require documents. When you are three years old written sources might mean your birthday cards or hospital baby tag, artefacts or pictures. Children at Key Stage 2 can be introduced to the idea that sources are often incomplete and of differing status. And when children construct their own accounts of the past by selecting and combining sources, they gain an understanding, from the beginning, of why different accounts may be equally valid. Of key significance here is the role of dialogue. If you are talking about interpreting sources and recognising that very often, especially with ancient sources, there is no single correct answer, this involves listening to others, sharing ideas and possibly changing your mind as a result. I would argue that this is at the centre of learning history.

DS   A skills-based approach consumes endless time. It is profoundly wasteful of time ... The way we teach history is fundamentally wrong, or rather the dominant message of the way we teach history is catastrophic ... leading to an utterly vulgar notion of relativism ... In other words I get a bit worried about the emphasis on the critical ... I think we have overdone the critical element of history.

HC   Let me give you some examples of two four-year-olds reasoning about whether a story about dragons was true.

'I've seen pictures of dragons in books ... dragons might have existed, since dinosaurs did, and they've died out now.'

'It might be the Loch Ness monster. That lives in Scotland and Robert's going on holiday and he's going to look for it ...'

DS   It is silly ...

References

Ashby, R. and Lee, P.J. (1987) 'Children's Concepts of Empathy and Understanding in History', in C. Portal (ed.) *The History Curriculum for Teachers*. Lewes: Falmer Press.

Bruner, J. (1996) *The Culture of Education*. Cambridge, Mass.: Harvard University Press.

Collingwood, R. G. (1939) *An Autobiography*. London: Oxford University Press.

Cooper, H. (1991) Young Children's Thinking in History, unpub. PhD. University of London Institute of Education.

Freedman, J. L. and Loftus, E. F. (1971) 'Retrieval of Words from Long-Term Memory', *Journal of Verbal Learning and Verbal Behaviour*, **10**, 107–15.

Fryer, P. (1989) *Black People in the British Empire – An Introduction*. London: Pluto Press.

Piaget, J. (1932) *Moral Judgement and the Child*. London: Kegan Paul.

Sutcliffe, R. (1974) *The Changeling*. London: Hamish Hamilton.

Treece, H. (1965) *The Bronze Sword*. London: Hamish Hamilton.